TEXTS AND STUDIES

CONTRIBUTIONS TO

BIBLICAL AND PATRISTIC LITERATURE

EDITED BY

J. ARMITAGE ROBINSON B.D.

HON. PH.D. GÖTTINGEN HON. D.D. HALLE

NORRISIAN PROFESSOR OF DIVINITY

VOL. IV.

No. 1. THE ATHANASIAN CREED AND ITS EARLY COMMENTARIES

THE ATHANASIAN CREED

AND ITS EARLY COMMENTARIES

BY

A. E. BURN M.A.

TRINITY COLLEGE CAMBRIDGE

RECTOR OF KYNNERSLEY WELLINGTON SALOP

Wipf & Stock

PUBLISHERS

Eugene, Oregon

Wipf and Stock Publishers
199 W 8th Ave, Suite 3
Eugene, OR 97401

The Athanasian Creed and Its Early Commentaries
By Burn, A.E.
ISBN: 1-59244-869-0
Publication date 9/18/2004
Previously published by Cambridge, 1896

CONTENTS.

CHAPTER I.

§ 1. Introductory. Dr Waterland's view. Dr Swainson and his two-portion theory, supported by Dr Lumby and Prof. Harnack; the objections of Mr Ommanney and Dr Heurtley. Plan of the Essay. § 2. MSS. of the 8th and 9th centuries. Paris B. N. 13,159. Paris B. N. 1451. Paris B. N. 4858. Milan O. 212 *sup.* Utrecht Psalter. § 3. Testimonies of the 8th and 9th centuries: Hincmar, Riculfus, Ratramn, Aeneas, Theodulf, Benedict d'Aniane, Agobard, Florus the Deacon. Canons of unknown Synod: Anskar, Haito, Boniface, Libellus de Trinitate, Ps-Gennadius, *De Fide*, Synodus Orietana. § 4. External evidence alleged for the two-portion theory. (1) Vienna MS. 1261. (2) Profession of Denebert. (3) The Trèves fragment. § 5. The three assumptions underlying the two-portion theory: (i) the silence of Paulinus, Alcuin, Rabanus Maurus, (ii) the supposed authority of the document as from the hand of Athanasius, (iii) the assumption that the Quicunque would be a useful weapon against Adoptianism . pp. xiii—xliv

CHAPTER II.

Early Commentaries. An increased number now known. 1. The Bouhier Commentary. 2. The Orleans Commentary. 3. The Stavelot Commentary. 4. The Paris Commentary. 5. The Oratorian Commentary. 6. The Troyes Commentary. 7. The Fortunatus Commentary, found in two recensions. (1) History of the text. The MSS. (2) Internal evidence: (*a*) heresies named, (*b*) the 'sixth milliary.' The authorship attributed to (i) Venantius Fortunatus, (ii) Euphronius of Autun. (3) The form of text of the Quicunque embodied in the commentary. The omitted clauses . . pp. xlv—lxxi

Note on G, a lost MS. of the Fortunatus Commentary.

CHAPTER III.

Date and Authorship of the Creed. *Internal Evidence.* Augustinian and Gallican phrases. Apollinarianism the latest heresy implicitly condemned. Priscillianism. *External Evidence.* (1) The Canon of Autun. (2) The 4th Council of Toledo. (3) Caesarius of Arles. (4) Avitus of Vienne. (5) Vigilius of Thapsus. (6) The Brotherhood of Lerins. Faustus. Vincentius. Honoratus. The authorship to be traced to a member of their society. Summary . . . . pp. lxxii—xcix

TEXTS AND ADDITIONAL NOTES.

Page

I. The text of the *Quicunque uult* edited from early MSS. and Commentaries . . . . 1—6

II. Texts of Commentaries: (1) Orleans, (2) Stavelot, (3) Troyes, (4) Fortunatus . . . . 7—40

III. Additional Notes . . . . 41—65

A. List of 8th and 9th century testimonies.
B. Chart showing which clauses were quoted by 8th and 9th century authors and early Commentaries.
C. A list of Commentaries.
D. Victricius of Rouen.
E. Fulgentius of Ruspe.
F. The date of the Utrecht Psalter.
G. Table of parallels in Augustine, Vincentius, Faustus and others.
H. Chart of the Lerins Brotherhood.
I. The Fides Romanorum and the Creed of Damasus.
J. Ps.-Gennadius *De Fide.*

INDEX 67, 68

ADDENDA.

p. lxiv. Dom Morin has kindly sent me the following note: "Deux autres notes chronologiques écrites au VIIe siècle font finir le 'sextum miliarium' avec le huitième siècle (à la fin de l'an 800): 1° Cod. Bodl. e Mus. 113 (olim. 94), fol. 114^{v} et 115; 2° Cod. Wirceburg MP. th. f. 28, fol. 68."

p. 3. I owe to M. S. Berger's *Histoire de la Vulgate* the reference to a Psalter at Amiens, No. 18, of the 8th or early 9th century. The text of the Quicunque is cut short by a torn page at clause 22, the word *genitus*. The Librarian, M. Henri Michel, kindly informs me that the only variation from my text is the spelling *relegione*.

CHAPTER I.

§ 1. *Introductory.*

THE final Report of the Ritual Commission of 1867, while it gave rise to a prolonged controversy on the use of the Athanasian Creed in the English Church, led also to a fresh investigation of its early history. Up to that time the received theory among scholars was that of Dr Waterland, whose 'Critical History' of the Creed has remained a standard work for more than 160 years. The following is his own summary of his conclusions[1]:

"That Hilary, once Abbat of Lerins, and next Bishop of Arles, about the year 430, composed the Exposition of Faith, which now bears the name of the Athanasian Creed. It was drawn up for the use of the Gallican clergy, and especially for the diocese or province of Arles. It was esteemed by as many as were acquainted with it as a valuable summary of the Christian faith. It seems to have been in the hands of Vincentius, monk of Lerins, before 434, by what he has borrowed from it; and to have been cited in part by Avitus of Vienne, about the year 500, and by Caesarius of Arles, before the year 543. About the year 570 it became famous enough to be commented upon like the Lord's Prayer and Apostles' Creed, and together with them[2]. All this while, and perhaps for several years lower, it had not yet acquired the name of the Athanasian Faith, but was simply styled the Catholic Faith. But before 670 Athanasius's admired name came in to recommend and adorn it; being in itself also an excellent system of the Athanasian principles of the Trinity and Incarnation, in

[1] Waterland, *Critical History*, New Ed. Oxford, 1870. p. 171.

[2] W. refers to the Commentary which he assigned to Venantius Fortunatus.

opposition chiefly to Arians, Macedonians, and Apollinarians. The name of the Faith of Athanasius, in a while, occasioned the mistake of ascribing it to him as his composition. This gave it authority enough to be cited and appealed to as a standard in the disputes of the middle ages, between Greeks and Latins, about the Procession: and the same admired name, together with the intrinsic worth and value of the form itself, gave it credit enough to be received into the public service in the Western Churches: first in France, next in Spain, soon after in Germany, England, Italy, and at length in Rome itself."

A new turn was given to the discussion by the researches of Dr Swainson and the theory which he founded upon a fresh review of the whole of the facts. His *History of the Creeds*, published in 1875, contains much new material for their literary history, the fruit of extensive enquiries in English and Continental libraries. He was much influenced from the first by a suggestion of Bishop (then Professor) Westcott[1], that the so-called Trèves fragment contains an earlier version of the part relating to the Incarnation than is found in any other MS. He was thus led on to the conclusion that the Profession of Denebert, containing clauses 1, 3—6, 20—22, 23, and this Trèves fragment, containing cl. 28—40, represent the component parts of the Creed in a prehistoric solution; that in the 9th century they were brought together and moulded into their present form, which took final shape in the province of Rheims between the years 860 and 870.

The same case has been very succinctly stated by Dr Lumby as follows[2]: "(i) Before A.D. 809 there is no trustworthy notice of any confession called by the name of St Athanasius. (ii) Before that date two separate compositions existed which form the groundwork of the present Quicunque. (iii) That for some time after that date all quotations are made only from the former of these compositions. (iv) That the Quicunque was not known down to A.D. 813 to those who were most likely to have heard of it had it been in existence. (v) That it is found nearly as we use it in A.D. 870. (vi) A comparison of the various MSS. shews that, after the combination of the two parts, the text was for some time

[1] Sw. p. 263 ff.

[2] *Hist. of the Creeds*, Ed. 3. Deighton, 1887. p. 259 f.

in an unsettled or transition state. On every ground therefore both of internal and external evidence it seems to be a sound conclusion that somewhere between A.D. 813—850 the Creed was brought nearly into the form in which we use it."

On the same lines another English writer, the Rev. E. S. Ffoulkes, in pamphlets and in a short book[1], '*The Athanasian Creed,* by whom written and by whom published,' had suggested that Paulinus, Archbishop of Aquileia, c. 800, was the author, and that the Creed was fraudulently palmed off as the work of Athanasius by Charlemagne.

In Germany the two-portion theory has been supported in a slightly modified form by Prof. Harnack[2].

The fresh evidence, which was held to put out of court the whole array of arguments on which Dr Waterland had built up his conclusion, did not include many new MSS. It rather consisted in correction of dates and examination of the meanings of titles. Waterland knew the Profession of Denebert and the Colbert-Trèves fragment; but he did not foresee the use which would be made of these documents, and did not discuss the internal evidence of MSS. containing portions or the whole of the Creed, in connection with the theological controversies of the 8th and 9th centuries.

[1] Published by Hayes, c. 1873.

[2] *Dogmengeschichte*, II. p. 299: Das sogenannte Athanasianum ist in seiner ersten Hälfte höchst wahrscheinlich eine gallische Glaubensregel zu dem Symbol von Nicäa. Als solche ist sie seit dem 5. Jahrhundert mit den Mitteln der Theologie des Augustin und des Vincentius von Lerinum als Lehrordnung für den Klerus (die Mönche) zur gedächtnissmässigen Einprägung allmählich gebildet worden. Als regula fidei zur Erläuterung des Nicänums ist sie fides catholica oder fides Athanasii (auch andere Namen gibt es) genannt worden und hat schon vielleicht um 500 mit den Worten: „Quicunque uult saluus esse" begonnen. Wahrscheinlich im Laufe des 6. Jahrhunderts ist sie wesentlich in ihrer jetzigen kunstvollen Gestalt in Südgallien ausgeprägt worden, wo der Widerspruch gegen den westgothisch-spanischen Arianismus noch immer herausgefordert war. In der Mitte des 6. Jahrhunderts war sie, oder doch eine ihr sehr ähnliche Recension, bereits als massgebende Lehrordnung des Klerus in Südgallien verbreitet und wurde neben den Psalmen auswendig gelernt. Aus den Psalmbüchern und Brevieren der Mönche und Geistlichen ist sie in die Beschlüsse einzelner Synoden gedrungen, indem dieselben an einzelne Sätze dieser Glaubensordnung zu appelliren begannen. Von hier aus wurde sie allmählich zum Bekenntniss der fränkischen Kirche im 8. und 9. Jahrhundert. Jetzt erst trat die zweite christologische Hälfte hinzu, über deren Ursprung ein vollkommenes Dunkel herrscht; sie ist natürlich nicht erst im 9. Jahrhundert angefertigt.

In reply to the two-portion theory appeared two books by the Rev. G. D. W. Ommanney, *History of the Athanasian Creed*[1], and *Early History of the Athanasian Creed*[2], in which he traced it back to the 5th century and supported Antelmi's theory that Vincentius of Lerins was the author. He traversed many of Dr Swainson's statements as to the dates of important MSS., appealing to the authority of the learned palæographer, Dr Ceriani, of Milan, to uphold an 8th century date for the oldest MS. of the Creed, in the Ambrosian Library at Milan, O. 212 *sup.* One such MS., if its date can be securely assigned, is in itself sufficient to overthrow the two-portion theory. Mr Ommanney also collected much valuable information about other MSS., both of the Creed and of early commentaries, and printed four commentaries which were unknown to Waterland, three of them for the first time. He dated them as follows[3]: "the Paris commentary not later than the 9th century and not earlier than the 7th, the Bouhier in the 8th, the Oratorian at the beginning of the 8th, or quite the end of the 7th, and the Troyes between A.D. 648 and 680."

The present state of the discussion is unsatisfactory. Dr Lumby has replied to Mr Ommanney's arguments in a short appendix to the 3rd edition of his *History of the Creeds*[4]. He refuses to believe that the Paris, Bouhier, and Oratorian commentaries, which contain the whole Creed, can be earlier than the 9th century. The Troyes Commentary, like that of Fortunatus on which it is founded, appears to contain a shorter form and is no evidence for the existence of a complete Creed before 813.

On the other hand, Dr Heurtley, in his *History of the Earlier Formularies of Faith*[5], supports Mr Ommanney. Independent study had led him to the following conclusion: "I am not disposed to press the argument from internal considerations, though I am far from regarding it as of no account....For anything that appears to the contrary the Creed may have been written at some time in the fifth century; but all that I venture to assert is that it was in existence in the middle or the earlier part of the seventh."

[1] Rivingtons, 1875. [2] Ibid. 1880.
[3] Om. *E. H.* p. 273. [4] L. p. 260.
[5] Parker, Oxford, 1892. p. 128.

After this it is somewhat startling to read in Dr C. F. Arnold's recent monograph on Caesarius of Arles[1] (p. 212), that "the Creed appears to come from Africa and to have lain before Caesarius in a form already complete."

The whole subject requires a broader treatment than it can receive in the following essay. But at least I may offer to students a guide to the rich collections of materials—quite embarrassing in their riches—gathered by Dr Swainson and Mr Ommanney, together with the fruit of some independent research.

It will be convenient to state at once the general plan which I shall follow, and the main results which I hope to establish. My endeavour will be:

i. To recapitulate in a condensed form all the evidence of 8th and 9th century MSS.[2] which contain the Creed, and to show that it was known and used in the 8th century in its complete form, supporting my argument from the testimonies of authors of those centuries who have quoted it.

I have classified these testimonies geographically, showing that those which might be supposed to refer only to a portion of the text can be supported by the evidence of entire texts belonging to the same diocese. Further, I have examined the evidence of the three fragments on which the two-portion theory is built up, together with three assumptions by which it is supported, drawing the conclusion that the evidence is incomplete and the assumptions unjustifiable.

ii. To examine the evidence of forms of text embedded in early commentaries.

I have traced out the history of the seven earliest, four of which I have printed under the names of Stavelot, Orleans, Troyes, Fortunatus. The last-named offers the key to much that is difficult in the problem of the early history of the Quicunque. From it may be extracted the earliest form of text, showing the two parts on the Trinity and the Incarnation wedded together in an indissoluble bond. With the aid of new MSS. I have re-edited this

[1] Leipzig, 1894: a learned work, which has been favourably reviewed in the *Revue Benedictine*, May, 1895.

[2] As a rule I have not corrected the Latin of the MSS.

commentary, and on the authority of a S. Gall MS. (now unfortunately lost) I have attempted to identify as its author Euphronius, Bishop and earlier Priest of Autun, the friend of Faustus of Riez and other scholars of Lerins. I have shown that this hypothesis can be supported from the internal evidence of the commentary.

iii. To discuss the date and authorship of the Creed, beginning with the internal evidence which points, as the irresistible argument of Waterland showed, to "Apollinarian times."

I have tried to distinguish between Augustinian and Gallican elements; and to account for the special elaboration of doctrine in both portions, and the special form of the teaching on the Resurrection ("of all men with their bodies"), by the suggestion that it was designed to meet the heresy of Priscillian, which was spreading in Gaul at the beginning of the 5th century. Turning to the external evidence of quotations found in the Canons of Autun (c. 670), the Canons of Toledo (633), Caesarius of Arles, Avitus of Vienne, with the interesting series of parallels in the writings of early monks of Lerins (Faustus, Vincentius, Hilary), I have followed Waterland in tracing the Creed back to the Monastery of Lerins as its possible birth-place (c. 425—430).

§ 2. *MSS. of the 8th and 9th Centuries.*

The complete text of the Quicunque has been found in some nineteen MSS. of the 8th and 9th centuries. Of these, fourteen are Psalters and the rest collections of canons or theological writings. It is not necessary here to take later MSS. into account, because all critics are prepared to agree on the date 870 as a time from which onwards the Creed was admitted into Psalters in its present form. In the list prefixed to the text of the Creed I have given references to the works of Dr Swainson and Mr Ommanney in which the various MSS. are described: the five earliest, however, it is desirable to discuss in some detail.

In my *apparatus criticus* will be found the various readings of all of them, together with the readings of the most important commentaries and of the Trèves fragment.

8th Century MSS. 1. P_1. 795—800 A.D. This is a Gallican Psalter from the Abbey of S. Germain des Prés, now Paris B.N. 13,159[1]. Its date is fixed by the evidence of some Litanies in which prayers are offered for Pope Leo III., elected in the year 795, and for Charlemagne as *Rex Francorum et Longobardorum ac patricius Romanorum.* The MS. must have been written before his coronation as Emperor in 800. The Litanies contain invocations of S. Hilary of Poitiers and S. Martin of Tours. The last litany seems to have been drawn up for use in a school. The Responses are to be said by the scholars: *Exaudi Deus. RP Leoni papae vita. Exaudi Christe. RP Carolo regi vita.* This may have been the school founded by Charlemagne at Paris.

The text of the Quicunque presents the general features of the early text. The spelling agrees with that of Paris 1,451 (P_3).

To the same monastery, S. Germain des Prés, belonged formerly a MS. collated by Montfaucon, who assigned it to the middle of the 8th century. Mabillon called it Cod. Corbeiensis, as it had been taken from the library of the Abbey of Corbey in 1638. It is now lost, but there is some hope that it may be preserved at St Petersburg, whither other treasures of the library of S. Germain des Prés have been taken.

2. P_3. c. 796. Paris B.N. 1,451[2], is a collection of Canons which belonged formerly to the Abbey of S. Petrus Fossatensis (or Mauratensis), on the river Marne, some two leagues from Paris. Prof. Maassen called it the Collection of S. Maur. It contains some interesting indications of date. On f. 6 v. there is a list of popes ending on f. 7 with the 97th, Adrian I. (†795). Between this and the next line is inserted in another hand, 'XCVIII. Leo papa.' No mention is made of Leo's death (†816), and the insertion was probably made during his pontificate. There is also a reference to the 25th year of the reign of Charlemagne as king. According to the reckoning in his life by Poeta Saxo, this can be calculated from the year 771, when he became by his brother's death sole king, which would make the 25th year come in 796, thus tallying exactly with the reference to Leo. We may thus date the MS. with some confidence c. 796.

[1] Om. *E. H.* p. 181.
[2] Om. *E. H.*, pp. 174 ff.; Sw., p. 268.

The text of the Quicunque agrees with that given in Paris 13,159, and with the quotations in the profession of faith made by Denebert, Bishop-elect of Worcester in 798 (see p. xxxiv). One reading however is unique, the inversion of the order of clauses 8, 9, 10, which this MS. changes to 10, 8, 9. This, as Mr Ommanney has shown, derives some support from the order in 11 and 12, *aeternus increatus immensus*.

3. P_2. A fragment, now Paris B.N. 4,858[1], has been assigned to the 8th century both by Montfaucon and by the present Librarians. It contains only the Chronicon of Eusebius in a Latin translation, with clauses 1—11 (*tres aeterni*) of the Quicunque, the next page and the rest of the volume having been torn off.

4. B. The most important early MS. of the Creed is in the Ambrosian Library at Milan, O. 212 *sup.* It comes from the monastery of Bobbio, and according to Montfaucon is written in Lombardic characters. Dr Ceriani assigns it confidently to the 8th century, and thinks that it was written in Ireland or England[2]. It contains the 'Book of Ecclesiastical Dogmas,' which has been ascribed to Gennadius; 'the Faith of Bacchiarius[3],' followed by a short prayer; and the Quicunque without a title (a mark of early date); then a sermon on the Ascension, and 'the Faith of Jerome.'

Dr Lumby (p. 222) lays great stress on the point that "this MS. marks the transition stage of the Quicunque." He speaks (p. 224) of "the Ambrosian MS. with its unsettled text." He selects the following variations to support this position:

(1) cl. 5. The repetition of the word *persona* before *Filii* and *Spiritus Sancti*. This was, it is true, an addition made also by Hincmar[4], but is unimportant as the word is implied in any case.

(2) cl. 22, after *sed procedens* add *Patri et Filio coaeternus est.* Dr Lumby argues that the variation is "of such a character as to stamp this MS. with a date posterior to the great controversy on the Procession of the Holy Ghost. It is an expansion and affirma-

[1] Om. *E. H.* p. 171; Sw. p. 330.

[2] See J. W. Burgon in the *Guardian* of Feb. 3, 1873.

[3] See chap. III. *infra*, for the story of this monk.

[4] In a paraphrastic passage (*infra* p. xx). Cf. Alcuin, *de Trin.* III. 22.

tion of the preceding portion of the verse which could hardly be expected before that controversy had excited a considerable degree of attention, that is at the end of the eighth or beginning of the ninth century." But this argument loses much of its weight when it is pointed out that the words may have been taken from 'the Faith of Bacchiarius[1],' or Gennadius's 'Book of Dogma[2],' which the scribe had just been copying. Such an expression was common in the writings of S. Augustine and Fulgentius, and there is a similar phrase in the Fortunatus Commentary, l. 12, which is taken from the Second Creed of Damasus. No other MS. of the Quicunque has this addition, and no writers in the Procession Controversy of the 9th century add this to their quotations of cl. 22. On an isolated variation we cannot base a theory of a transitional form of text.

(3) In clauses 30 and 35 the reading *rationabilis* is found, in the former clause[3] in agreement with the Trèves fragment (A) and C D Q* Troyes Stav Fort (*p*), in the latter with Troyes, Paris. The reading *rationalis* has good support in both clauses from E and the S. Gall MSS., with the best MSS. of Fortunatus; so that it is not easy to decide which is the original reading.

(4) In cl. 33 *in carne...in deo* are plainly the older readings, being supported by A C D E F G_2 H L $P_{1,3,4}$ U V Fort (early MSS.) Troyes Or_1 Paris.

(5) In cl. 36 B omits *tertia die*. This is one of the cases in which the text of the Quicunque has been influenced by the text, or variations in the text, of the Apostles' Creed. Omit *tertia die* BCDF$G_{1,2,3}$$P_{1,2}$Q*S*UVY Fort Paris Stav Tol.: + *tertia die* EG_4HL Or Bou Orl: + *die tertia* A Troyes. So in this case also it is plain that B has the old reading of the clause. The words were naturally enough added in A, a sermon which quotes the Apostles' Creed.

(6) In cl. 38 the only variation is *in* for *cum* (*corporibus*). Photographs of the MS. show distinctly the words *resurgere habent in corporibus suis*, which Dr Lumby supposed to have been omitted. Therefore his argument that it took more than one step to alter *resurrecturi* into *resurgere habent* falls to the ground.

[1] W., p. 182. [2] Om. *E. H.* p. 192.

[3] L. by misprint 'latter,' but cl. 35 is omitted from A.

Dr Swainson[1] has argued that the words *ante saecula genitus* in cl. 29, which in this MS. are found in the margin, and in the Trèves fragment are found in a line which has been erased and rewritten, were not part of the original text. But the words *ante saecula* are found in the parallel passage in S. Augustine[2], and more probably were omitted from the text in B by an oversight. No MS. of the Quicunque omits them altogether, and it is scarcely possible that this MS. with its marginal addition was the archetype of all the rest.

One last argument against the theory that this or any other MS. shows "an unsettled or transitional state of text," is the following. Where would evidence of such a state be more likely to appear than at the junction of the two parts, viz. at clauses 25—27? But here we find nothing of the kind. The order of the words in cl. 25 *unitas in trinitate* &c. is reversed in about half the MSS., but the 8th century MSS. are divided here no less than the rest (C against BEP). As to cl. 26 and 27 the only variation is in 27, where P_1 omits *est*.

At the end of the Quicunque the scribe of B adds an apostrophe to the Blessed Virgin: 'Lacta mater eum qui fecit te quia talem fecit te ut ipse fieret in te. Lacta eum qui fructum foecunditatis tibi dedit conceptus et decus uirginitatis non abstulit natus.' I have found a much longer form of the same apostrophe following the last words of the Quicunque in a Munich MS. (*n*) of the Fortunatus Commentary (Cod. lat. 14,508, saec. X). Such rhetorical language is much older than the time of Alcuin, with which Dr Swainson[3] would connect it. A sermon on the Nativity ascribed to Faustus of Riez[4] has: 'Lacta, Maria, creatorem tuum, lacta panem coeli, lacta pretium mundi,' etc.

5. At this point I may also include the lost archetype of the Utrecht Psalter, which, while it cannot be reckoned as an existing MS., may be asserted to have existed in the 8th century.

The Utrecht Psalter is connected by Sir E. Maunde Thompson[5] with the north-east of France, and is assigned to the beginning of

[1] Sw. p. 321. [2] *Enchiridion*, c. 35.

[3] Sw. p. 321. [4] *Ed.* Engelbrecht, p. 231.

[5] Letter of Feb. 15, 1894. *Manual of Palæography*, Kegan Paul, 1893, p. 189. For the recent pamphlet of Count Durrieu see Add. Note J.

the 9th century. But it seems to be a copy of a more ancient original, for it is written in rustic capitals, a style which had gone out of use. Sir E. M. Thompson suggests that "in order to maintain the same relative arrangements of texts and drawings, the scribe found it the simplest course to copy the actual character of the letters, the text thus filling the same space as the original and leaving the proper intervals for the insertion of the drawings. And yet the text was not so exactly copied as to be quite consistent with ancient usage; for titles are introduced in uncial letters—an intrusion which would have been quite impossible in the earlier and purer period of rustic capital writing."

We may therefore assign the archetype to the 8th century or earlier, and we may argue that the Quicunque was contained in it because it is headed by one of the pictures which the scribe wished to copy so exactly.

The Utrecht Psalter contains the Apostles' Creed in our present form, which is already found in a sermon of Pirminius (†758), the founder of Reichenau. We may safely say that this form was in use at the beginning of the 8th century, so that it presents no argument against the date assigned to the archetype of the Psalter.

Thus on the authority of such eminent palæographers as Dr Ceriani, M. L. Delisle, and Sir E. Maunde Thompson, we may appeal to four MSS. at least which prove the existence of the entire Creed in the 8th century.

Among the important variations found in the text of these early MSS. may be mentioned the following: (1) the order of words in clause 25, *trinitas in unitate et unitas in trinitate*, is supported by BE$P_{1,3}$ Or $Bou_{1,3}$ Paris Den, as against C. (2) In clause 28 the reading *pariter* has strong support from ABCP_1* Fort Tr Or Paris, as against EP_3. (3) In clause 33 *carne...deo* are the readings in ABCE$P_{1,3}$ Fort Or_1 Paris.

Other variations show that the same changes were made in Quicunque as in the parallel clauses of the Apostles' Creed. In cl. 33 *ad inferna*, which is found in A Fort Or, became *ad infernum* Tr Paris, and *ad inferos* B (*-nos* C) E$P_{1,3}$ Tol. The interest of this reading belongs rather to the Apostles' Creed, but I may remark that *ad inferna* is found in Caesarius (Ps. Aug. *Serm.* 244),

Gallican Sacramentary (c. 650), and Pirminius (c. 750); Vigilius (*ad Eut.* II.), Fulgentius (*Serm. Fast.* XX.) and Venantius Fortunatus agree in the use of the phrase *ad infernum*; while the Bangor Antiphonary 680—691 has *ad inferos*, a change which only begins to be general in Creeds of the 9th century[1].

Similarly the addition of the words *dei* and *omnipotentis* in clause 37, which, though absent from A and the earlier commentaries Fort Tr Or Paris, are found in $EP_{1,3}$ Bou Orl, points to the 9th century. The addition of the words *tertia die* in cl. 36 has been already dealt with on p. xxi, in reference to the text of the Milan MS. O. 212 (B).

§ 3. *Testimonies of the 8th and 9th Centuries.*

In an Additional Note (A) I have gathered all the quotations of the Creed which can to my knowledge be gleaned from writings of the 8th and 9th centuries, grouping them as far as possible geographically. In this way the evidence of entire texts may be brought to the support of doubtful testimonies. Unless we can prove that such texts were extant in the districts in which the writers lived, we have no guarantee that they did not quote from a portion only of the Creed. And the wider the area over which early MSS. were dispersed, the less likely does it appear to be that the Creed was compiled by some court-theologian and that copies were distributed to order. The evidence does not point exclusively to the one province of Rheims, as some critics have suggested: and even for that province it is fuller and richer than has sometimes been supposed.

Province and Diocese of Rheims. The testimony of Hincmar, Archbishop of Rheims 845—882, is continuous throughout his episcopate, and includes the whole Creed as it is found in two MSS. (Q and D) which are connected with this province.

About the year 848, during the controversy on Predestination raised by the wandering monk Goteschalk, a hymn by that writer was brought under Hincmar's notice which contained the phrase 'trina deitas.' He at once condemned it as heretical, suggested 'summa deitas' as an emendation, and wrote a book *De una non*

[1] L., p. 177.

trina deitate in which he quoted in defence of his position clauses of the Quicunque as the work of Athanasius under the title 'Fides Catholica.' The words here italicized are his explanatory notes.

(cl. 3) Fides catholica haec est, ut unum Deum in trinitate *personarum* et trinitatem *personarum* in unitate *deitatis* ueneremur.

(cl. 4) neque confundentes personas, *sicut Sabellius ut tres non sint*, neque *ut Arius* substantiam separantes *ut trina sit.*

(cl. 5) *quia* alia *et non aliud* est persona Patris, alia *et non aliud est persona* Filii, alia *et non aliud est persona* Spiritus Sancti.

(cl. 6) sed Patris et Filii et Spiritus Sancti una est diuinitas, aequalis gloria, coaeterna maiestas.

(cl. 24) et in hac *sancta et inseparabili* trinitate nihil *est* prius aut posterius, nihil maius uel minus, sed totae tres personae *Pater et Filius et Spiritus Sanctus* coaeternae sibi sunt et aequales.

(cl. 25) ita ut per omnia sicut iam supradictum est, et trinitas *personarum* in unitate *deitatis* et unitas *deitatis* in trinitate *personarum* ueneranda sit[1].

In a previous passage he had quoted also:

(cl. 19) *quoniam* sicut singillatim unamquamque personam Deum et Dominum .... confiteri christiana ueritate compellimur, ita tres Deos uel Dominos dicere .... catholica religione prohibemur.

The title, 'F. C.,' and this reading of cl. 25 are found in Q, a Psalter which is connected by an added Litany with Archbishop Fulco, Hincmar's successor, though the Psalter itself is of an earlier date[2].

In 857 and 859 Hincmar wrote two treatises on Predestination[3]. In the second of these he quotes clause 38, with its unusual idiom 'resurgere habent,' as from 'the Catholic Faith': *De Praedest. Epilogus* c. 6, 'Ad cuius aduentum, *secundum fidem catholicam,* omnes homines resurgere habent cum corporibus suis.'

The quotation is the more noteworthy because in his 'Ex-

[1] Mg. cxxv., p. 616, cf. p. 603 ut Athanasius dicit.

[2] Sw. p. 357.

[3] The first of these has recently been discovered and printed by Dr Gundlach, *Zeitschrift für Kirchengeschichte*, x. 1889, from a MS. of the 10th century in the University Library at Leyden.

planatio in Ferculum Salomonis' he followed very closely the thought of the Quicunque in clauses 37, 38, 39, but used his own words, writing the synthetic futures 'resurgent' and 'reddent' for 'resurgere habent' and 'reddituri sunt.' He also added his own opinions on grace and free will, which he wished to read into the Creed. Surely if he had been its compiler he would have introduced into it some technical terms belonging to this controversy.

Hincmar took pains to spread the use of the Creed. Dr Gundlach[1] has found a Pastoral, written for Charles the Bald, in which he directed: 'ut sicut presbyteri psalmos et sermonem fidei catholicae, cuius inicium est: Quicunque uult saluus esse, et canonem missae ac cantum uel compotum, ita et consignationem infantum .... memoriter teneant.'

A synod held in his metropolitan city of Rheims in 852 commanded: 'Necnon et sermonem Athanasii de fide cuius initium est, Q. u. s. e., memoriae quisque commendet, sensum illius intelligat et uerbis communibus enuntiare queat.' This sentence in itself suggests that in Hincmar's time the language of the Creed was felt to be that of an earlier period and to stand in need of exposition. The title 'Sermo Athanasii de fide' corresponds to the title of the Creed in the Psalter of Charles the Bald (D), and to the title found in a profession of faith, addressed to Hincmar by one of his suffragans Adalbert, on his consecration as Bishop of Morinum (Térouanne) in 871.

Adalbert refers to both portions of the Creed, and shows that he has endeavoured to understand the meaning: 'In sermone b. Athanasii quem ecclesia catholica uenerando usu frequentare consueuit, qui ita incipit: Q. u. s. e., post documentum quo docemur quomodo trinitas personarum in unitate diuinitatis et unitas deitatis in trinitate personarum ueneranda sit, euidentissime continetur unam ex eadem sancta trinitate personam dominum et saluatorem nostrum Iesum Christum dei hominisque filium ex duabus et in duabus naturis, hoc est diuina et humana in una persona consistentibus et in sua proprietate differentiaque manentibus esse credendum et praedicandum[2].'

[1] See note 3, p. xxv *supra*.

[2] Labbe, ed. 1729, x. p. 1389. Dr Swainson (p. 301) objects that "the text of

889. Another of Hincmar's suffragans Riculfus of Soissons[1] directed his clergy in the same way to learn by heart 'Sermo fidei catholicae cuius initium Q. u. s. e.,' thus reverting to the older title.

In the Monastery of Corbey in the diocese of Rheims were trained two distinguished men who valued the Quicunque, Anskar (see p. xxx *infra*) and Ratramn, and their testimony can be supported by a MS. written in that Monastery, S. Germain 257 (C).

868. In his book on the Procession of the Holy Spirit Ratramn[2] quoted clauses 20—22 from the Creed under the title 'Libellus de Fide b. Athanasii Alex. Epi.' But he also quoted the *Fides Romanorum* under that title, so that we must expect to find a confusion between the two Faiths[3].

Province of Sens. Diocese of Paris. 868. A contemporary of Ratramn, Aeneas Bishop of Paris, in his treatise against the Greeks quoted clauses 20—26 as from the 'Fides Cath. S. Ath. Epi. Alex.' (*adv. Graec.* c. 19).

Since the Monastery of S. Germain des Prés was in this diocese we may fairly quote in support of this testimony the MS. Paris B.N. 13,159 (P_1) which used to belong to that Monastery,

the Sermon is scarcely adequately represented." But Adalbert was writing for his Metropolitan, not for 19th century critics. It is true that in a further reference to the Ascension and final Judgment he uses the phrase 'resurgent cum corporibus.' But, as we have seen, Hincmar did this himself when he was quoting the Quicunque freely in his Ferculum Salomonis. I cannot agree with Dr Swainson that "the questions mooted by Godeschalk are passed over" in this profession. Surely the opening quotation of cl. 25, the summary of the first part of the Creed, reminds one of Hincmar's treatise 'De una non trina deitate.' For the distinction between *deitas* and *diuinitas* is one which Hincmar desired to have expressed. With Morinum (=Térouanne) we may connect the Boulogne MS. 20 of the Stavelot commentary, which comes from the Abbey of S. Omer in that diocese. See chap. II. *infra*.

[1] Riculf. *Const.* 5. Harduin, VI. p. 415.

[2] *c. Graec. Oppos.* II. 3.

[3] Some sixty years before, the Latin Monks of Mt Olivet appealed to a 'Faith of S. Athanasius' in defence of the Procession from the Son, but as the doctrine is taught in one form of the Fides Romanorum it is impossible to identify the document with certainty, though the probability is in favour of the Quicunque.

and Paris 1,451 (P_2) which used to belong to the Abbey of S. Petrus Fossatensis (S. Maur), some two leagues from Paris.

Diocese of Orleans. Theodulf, Abbot of Fleury and Bishop of Orleans (†821), directed the use of the Creed in two series of *capitula.*

(1) "Wherefore we admonish you, O priests of the Lord, that ye should hold in your memories and understand with your hearts the Catholic Faith, that is the Credo and Q. u. s. e."[1] This series has been condemned as spurious on the ground that it contains also directions "how presbyters were to be treated," and how a bishop was to do penance, which Theodulf had no right to issue. But this objection falls to the ground if these *capitula* are regarded as decrees of a provincial synod presided over by Theodulf[2].

(2) In an address to his clergy he admonished them both "to learn the Catholic Faith and preach it most diligently to the people every one of you in his own church."

In his book 'On the Holy Spirit' Theodulf quotes cll. 21—26 as from a Symbol of Athanasius, and he is the first writer to call the Quicunque by this title. This lends more weight to the notice in the catalogue of the Abbots of Fleury which ascribes to him, "an exposition of the Symbol of S. Athanasius which is chanted by the monks daily at prime after the three regular psalms."

For the place of this missing commentary there are no less than three claimants, the so-called Oratorian[3], Stavelot[4], and Orleans[5] commentaries: but this question will come before us again.

From Theodulf (†821) we turn to his friend Benedict, Abbot of S. Anianus in Languedoc, 'the Wesley of his age,' who in a letter to Guarnarius, his son in the faith, quotes clauses 3—6 of the Creed[6]. He has been arguing against subtle metaphysical speculations, especially of the Scots, and proceeds to condemn the

[1] Labbe, IX. p. 198, *ed.* 1729.

[2] *D. C. B.* Art. 'Theodulf.'

[3] Sw. p. 291; printed in Om. *E. H.* p. 327.

[4] Printed below; cf. Om. *E. H.* p. 63.

[5] Cuissard, *Theodulfe*, p. 73.

[6] Baluz. *Miscell.* II. 97.

phrase *trina deitas.* The authenticity of the letter has been denied, but without proof of its 'supposititious character[1].'

Province and Diocese of Lyons. c. 820. Agobard, the learned Archbishop of Lyons (†840), in his book against Felix of Urgel the Adoptianist, quotes cl. 2 as the writing of Athanasius. The context implies that he regarded the Quicunque as a Rule of Faith. There are close parallels to other clauses in his writings.

Florus the Deacon, fl. 834, afterwards a priest of this diocese, wrote about the Creed to Abbot Hyldrad who asked him to correct a copy of the Psalter. He wished that only Canticles should be added to a Psalter and that a separate book should be made of 'Hymns, Symbol, Lord's Prayer, Faith, Compunctum (= Computum ?), prayers, etc.' But he had corrected the Symbol, Lord's Prayer, Catholic Faith, and hymns for addition to the Psalter if Hyldrad preferred to have it so.

We may compare the evidence of a letter which Florus wrote in the name of the Church of Lyons against the teaching of John the Scot[2]:

'Qui talem doctorem mirantur, et libenter audiunt se esse Christianos, meminerint se fidem catholicam, fidem ueram sentiendi de Deo integram sibi inuiolatamque seruandam.'

Province of Cologne. Diocese of Liège. With the *capitula* of the Synod of Rheims in 852 it is interesting to compare a similar series of canons which were put together during the reign of Lothaire, Emperor 840—855, from pre-existing materials.

The second of these *capitula* runs thus: 'Fidem enim (etiam ?) S. Athanasii episcopi in hoc opere censuimus obseruandum, et simbolum apostolorum con (cum) tradicionibus et exposicionibus sanctorum patrum in his sermonibus.' It was formerly printed at the end of the Epistola de Baptismo of Jesse, Bishop of Amiens c. 800, with which it had no connection.

The rivers Meuse and Rhine were made the boundaries of the kingdom of Lothaire by the treaty of Verdun, so that the diocese of Liège suggests itself as the possible home of this document.

[1] Ffoulkes, *The Athanasian Creed Reconsidered.* Hayes, 1872, p. 80.

[2] *Magna Bibl. Patrum,* Col. Agripp. 1618, IX. 1, p. 1023.

The reference to 'expositions' is particularly interesting, and may perhaps include the Stavelot commentary.

With the Abbey of Prum in the Forest of Ardennes we must connect the Articles of Enquiry of Regino, Abbot 892—899. One is: 'Si sermonem Athanasii de Fide s. trinitatis cuius initium est Q. u. s. e. memoriter teneat.'

These testimonies are supported by the Psalter of Lothaire which formerly belonged to the Abbey of S. Hubert in the Forest of Ardennes. The title of the Creed is 'Fides catholica tradita a s. Ath. Alex. Epo.' A chronicle of the Abbey, written in the 12th century, records that it was presented by Louis le Débonnaire on the occasion of the translation of the relics of S. Hubert in 825, which is the date given doubtfully in the Palaeographical Society's publications[1]. Some verses in honour of Lothaire suggest the year 833 when he became sole Emperor[2].

Province and Diocese of Hamburg and Bremen. The diocese of Bremen till 860 belonged to Cologne; but in that year it was united with Hamburg under the great missionary bishop Anskar. At the age of 21 he came from the monastery of Corbey in Picardy to be a teacher in the daughter-house of New Corbey founded by S. Louis near Cassel. His biographer records that on his death-bed he admonished the brethren to sing "the Catholic Faith composed by Blessed Athanasius." This notice of chanting the Quicunque is interesting.

With this diocese we may connect the celebrated Golden Psalter (Y) in the Imperial Library at Vienna. It contains a copy of Latin verses with which a King Charles presents the book to a Pope Hadrian. Dr Waterland following Lambecius, a librarian of the last century, supposed that the King was Charlemagne and the Pope Hadrian I. in the year 772. But the objections to this view are strong. More probably it was Charles the Bald who had it made for Hadrian II. (867—872). He certainly gave this Pope valuable presents, though a Psalter is not mentioned among them. It is supposed that the Pope died before it reached Rome, and that the King then gave it to the Church of Bremen[3].

[1] Vol. III. plates 69 and 93. [2] Om. *E. H.* p. 167.

[3] W. p. 75. Sw. p. 373. Om. *A. C.* p. 202 supports W.

Province and Diocese of Mainz. This extensive province included the dioceses of Worms, Halberstadt, Wurzburg, and Bamberg, with the important Abbeys of Fulda, S. Gall, and Reichenau. Haito[1], Abbot of Reichenau, sometime Bishop of Basle († 836), charged his priests to learn 'the Faith of S. Athanasius,' and recite it by heart on the Lord's day at Prime. Reichenau was the mother-house of Murbach Abbey, from which comes the celebrated copy of the Fortunatus commentary, Junius 25, in the Bodleian Library at Oxford. In fact all the 9th century MSS. of that commentary belong to this province, and if Haito had come across one of them he would have been acquainted with a form which virtually includes the whole Creed.

Again, we may support his testimony by referring to one of the treasures of the Abbey of S. Gall, Psalter 20[2], of the early years of the 9th century. Between these Abbeys, Reichenau at the west and S. Gall some miles to the south of the Lake of Constance, communication was easy.

It is not a great gap that we must bridge to get back to the time of Boniface, Archbishop of Mainz († 755), among whose writings is found a sermon *de Fide,* which seems to be the product of his age if not of his pen. It contains the following parallels to the Quicunque. 'Necessarium est fratres carissimi...fidem rectam et catholicam sine dubitatione firmiter tenere, quia ad aeternam beatitudinem nemo peruenire potest nisi Deo placeat, et nullus Deo placere potest nisi per fidem rectam. Fides namque omnium bonorum fundamentum est, fides humanae salutis initium est; sine hac nemo ad nobilitatem filiorum Dei peruenire potest. ...Ista est fides catholica, ut credamus in unum Deum Patrem omnipotentem...Filium, Spiritum Sanctum ex Patre procedentem et Filio...Pater aeternus Filius aeternus Spiritus Sanctus aeternus... sicut Christus tertia die resurrexit a mortuis sic omnes homines boni et mali in nouissimo die cum propriis corporibus resurgere debent[3].'

[1] I came across a copy of these capitularies of Haito in a S. Gall MS. 446, saec. x. fol. 205: 'Quarto, ut fides sancti Athanasii a sacerdotibus discatur et ex corde die dominico ad horam primam recitatur (*sic*).' See W. p. 27.

[2] The printed Catalogue adds: "Die Initialen des Codex erinnern noch an die brodirten und Fisch-Buchstaben der Langobardischen HSS des VIII. Jhr. no. 348, 350, 731."

[3] Ed. Giles: Oxford, 1844. But the editor of the letters of Boniface in the *Mon. Germaniae Hist.* does not appear to include this sermon among his works.

The first passage contains a free quotation of the words of Fulgentius (Aug. *Op.* VI. p. 1101) which were used by Alcuin in his *De Trin.* I. 2, and were adapted by the scribe of the Milan MS. of the Fortunatus Commentary[1]. Boniface added to what was evidently a 'locus classicus' on Faith the definition 'recta et catholica' with the warning 'sine dubitatione firmiter tenere,' reminiscences of clauses 10, 38.

Province of Milan. Diocese of Bobbio. An interesting testimony to the Quicunque is found in a 'Libellus de Trinitate' which has been printed by Dr Caspari (*Kirchenhistorische Anecdota*, p. xxv) from a Milan MS. which formerly belonged to the monastery of Bobbio (Ambr. D. 268 *inf.*, saec. VIII/IX). This 'Libellus' is considered by Dr Caspari to contain both in form and words a reminiscence of the Quicunque, for it combines teaching on the Trinity with teaching on the Incarnation, and the following sentences find parallels in clauses of the Creed. It begins thus: 'Pater deus, filius deus, spiritus sanctus deus. Haec unita substantia, unita uirtus, unita natura. Generator pater, generator filius, generator et spiritus sanctus atque sanctificator......(filius) Qui tamen habet has duas substantias in se: primum, quod est substantia patris, id est uerbum, quod est ipse, [secundum, quod est substantia matris, id est] animam et carnem.'

Bobbio was the centre of opposition to Longobardic Arianism. Perhaps this fact may explain the interest taken by the author of this 'Libellus' in the Quicunque, in which he would find a thorough confutation of that heresy. We may remember too that the scribe who found and copied the Trèves fragment came from this district, and that the MS. Milan O. 212 (p. xx *supra*), which contains an important text of the Quicunque, was written in the monastery of Bobbio itself.

Ps. Gennadius, De Fide. Another testimony to the Quicunque belonging to this period, or an earlier, has been found by Dr Caspari[2] in a 'Book of the Faith' wrongly ascribed to Gennadius of Marseilles. The form of Creed contained in it is parallel in

[1] W. p. 252.

[2] p. xix: from Munich Cod. lat. 14,461 and 14,468, saec. IX., the latter written by order of Baturicus Bishop of Regensburg in the year 821.

form to the Quicunque, and the part which relates to the Resurrection and return of Christ to judgment reminds one strongly of it, and, we may add, of the Fortunatus Commentary.

Synodus Orietana. In the *Spicilegium Casinense*[1] I find the following extract from a MS. at Monte Casino, no. 439, f. 102, relating to a synod named thus, Synodus Orietana, in the year 880 or 881. The bishop Theodosius after a long scriptural address to the clergy directs that they should all learn by heart the Catholic Faith: 'Primum statum est; ut compresbyteris nostris. seu etiam diacones. et uniuersus clerus. fidem catholicam memoriter teneant. necnon et simbolum. et orationem dominicam; spiritaliter intelligant.'

The editor (p. lxxxvii) identifies the place with Oria in Calabria (afterwards joined with Brindisi).

He quotes a similar capitulary of Atto Bishop of Vercellae (Mg. 134, p. 29)[2], 'Primo omnium fidem catholicam omnes presbyteri et diaconi seu subdiaconi memoriter teneant.' This also seems to have hitherto escaped notice.

§ 4. *External evidence alleged for the two-portion theory.*

We must now turn to the external evidence of three MSS., Vienna 1261, B. M. Cleopatra E. 1 (the Profession of Denebert), and Paris 3836 (the Colbert-Trèves fragment), upon which the two-portion theory is based.

(1) Vienna 1261 is a collection of sermons and writings attributed to S. Augustine. It was written in the 12th century, though it no doubt contains materials of an earlier date. There are two distinct references to the Quicunque under the title 'Fides Catholica.' In the first the preacher quotes clause 3, and proceeds to illustrate his point from the analogy of the sphere, light, and heat of the sun, which form a trinity. In the second the preacher quotes clauses 1—6, 24 ('qui' for 'et'), 26 *a* ('quicunque ergo cupit

[1] Vol. I. p. 380.

[2] This Atto (†960) appears to have compiled his *capitula* from those of Theodulf of Orleans and the canons of Councils of Toledo.

saluus esse et catholicus haec teneat et credat et uita uiuet'). He quotes S. Paul's words (Acts xiv. 22) on the tribulations and temptations through which we must enter the kingdom of heaven, and concludes with a vivid description of the Last Judgment.

The free quotation of S. Paul suggests the inference that the Quicunque also is quoted freely. It would therefore be dangerous to rely on this sermon of an uncertain date for any reconstruction of the earliest text, unless the variants had other support; and in our future investigation we may ignore it.

(2) The Profession of Denebert, Bishop-elect of Worcester, was made to Ethelhard, Archbishop of Canterbury, about the year 798. It consisted of a promise of obedience with a short exposition of the Catholic and Apostolic Faith as Denebert had received it. He quoted from a written original clauses 1, 3—6, 20—22, 24, 25 of the Quicunque; and promised further to observe the decrees of the Popes, and the six Catholic Synods and their rule of faith. Since he undertook to be brief and would find the doctrine of the Incarnation fully expounded by these Synods, it cannot safely be said that he knew no more of the Quicunque than he quoted in this passage.

'Insuper et orthodoxam catholicam apostolicamque fidem sicut didici, paucis exponam uerbis, quia scriptum est, Quicunquė uult saluus esse ante omnia opus est *illi* ut teneat catholicam fidem. Fides autem catholica haec est ut unum Deum in Trinitate et Trinitatem in Unitate ueneremur; neque confundentes personas neque substantiam separantes: alia enim est persona Patris alia Filii, alia Spiritus Sancti, sed Patris et Filii et Spiritus Sancti una est Diuinitas, aequalis gloria, coaeterna maiestas: Pater a nullo factus est, nec creatus, nec genitus. Filius a Patre solo est; non factus, nec creatus sed genitus: Spiritus Sanctus a Patre et Filio, non factus, nec creatus, nec genitus, sed procedens. In hac Trinitate nihil prius aut posterius, nihil maius aut minus, sed totae tres personae coaeternae sibi sunt et coaequales: ita ut per omnia, sicut supra dictum est, et Trinitas in Unitate, et Unitas in Trinitate ueneranda est[1].'

It may be pointed out that Paris B. N. 1451, of the same date

[1] Haddan and Stubbs, *Councils and Eccles. Documents*, III. 525.

791 (see p. xix) contains a list of Popes, with a notice of the first six Councils and the Quicunque; and that the readings correspond with the quotations of Denebert (clause 22 *om.* est, clause 25, trin. in un. et un. in trin.). May he not have quoted from another MS. of this same collection[1], having the complete text of the Quicunque before him? Some clergy from Britain attended the Council of Frankfort in 796[2]. Perhaps they brought some such MS. back with them. The creeds of other English Bishops, of the 9th century, preserved with his profession, have, as Dr Swainson has suggested (p. 286), a Sabellian sound. It is obvious that Denebert had that heresy in view in making his selection of clauses of the Quicunque. Hincmar and Benedict d'Aniane with the same object before them quoted the same clauses.

(3) The Colbert-Trèves fragment (c. 730) is part of a sermon in which clauses 27—40 of the Quicunque (with the exception of cl. 35) have been incorporated. It is found in a Paris MS., B. N. lat. 3836, which contains the S. Blasien collection of Canons[3]. The MS. is of the 8th century and written in Lombardic characters. The scribe seems to have been a travelled man, who had visited Rome; for he gives a list of books of Scripture which were read in the Church of S. Peter. But he was illiterate and, it would seem, not acquainted with the Quicunque; since he uses this fragment, which he copied at Trèves, to illustrate the Definition of Faith of the Council of Chalcedon. Such ignorance, if the scribe was an Italian, is not surprising: the Creed was only known locally as yet even in Gaul. Of the original fragment which he found we have lost all trace. Trèves was a frontier town of old Gaul and had suffered many things from barbarian invaders in former centuries. The same fate came again, and in 882 it was sacked by the Normans. The present librarian of the

[1] Prof. Maassen (p. 613) refers to two MSS. of a similar collection which I have not been able to trace. "Eine ganz ähnliche wenn nicht dieselbe Sammlung scheinen erhalten zu haben der von Sirmond benutzte Cod. Tilianus Engolismensis, und der von Hardouin oft genannte Cod. Hardyensis."

[2] Mansi, *Conc.* XIII. 901 (Carol. Magni Ep. ad Elipand.).

[3] Maassen, p. 511. This collection was made in Italy but soon spread abroad; another MS. of the same collection, Darmstad. 2336, was found at Cologne in the 8th century and may have been written there.

Town Library, Herr M. Keuffer[1], has only been able to find one MS. in a similar hand, a copy of Prosper with marginal notes, written in 719 or within a few years of the same date.

He compares the barbarism 'omnes homo' of the fragment with the genitive 'mortes' in the MS. of Prosper, and adds; "diese Abschwächung des unbetonten *i* ist indessen ganz im Sinne des romanischen Lautgesetzes und würde ev. für eine neustrische Entstehung auch unseres Prosper sprechen."

The MS. has been photographed for the Palaeographical Society[2]; and from their transcription I give the text.

Immediately before our fragment come the words:

EXPLICIT SINODVM MVNDANVM, ID EST VNIVERSALE, APVT CALCEDONA.

Immediately after it:

INCIPIT DE SINODO NICAENO SCRIPTA PAPE DAMASI AD PAVLINVM ANTHIOCENAE VRBIS EPISCOPVM.

HAEC INVINI TREVIRIS IN VNO LIBRO SCRIPTVM SIC INCIPIENTE DOMINI NOSTRI IHESV CHRISTI, ET RELIQVA. (27) DOMINI NOSTRI IHESV CHRISTI FIDELITER CREDAT. (28) Est ergo fides recta ut credamus et confitemur quia dominus ihesus christus dei filius deus pariter et homo est. (29) deus est *de* substantia patris ante secula genitus *et* homo *de* substantia matris in saeculo natus. (30) perfectus deus, perfectus homo ex anima rationabili et humana carne subsistens. (31) aequalis patri saecundum diuinitatem minor patri secundum humanitatem. (32) qui licet deus sit homo, non duo tamen, sed unus est christus. (33) unus autem non *ex eo quod sit in carne conuersa diuinitas*, sed *quia est in deo adsumpta dignanter humanitas*[3]. (34) unus *christus est* non confusione substantiae sed unitatem personae. (36) qui *secundum*[4] *fidem nostram* passus *et mortuos* ad inferna *discendens, et*

[1] Private letter of June 30, 1893.

[2] Vol. III. plates 8 and 9.

[3] Cf. the construction in a sermon of Eusebius of Emesa (Faustus?) *ad missam*: 'non quod uerbum mutaretur in carnem, sed quia carnem suscipiendo, ex diuinitate et humanitate una persona facta est.'

[4] In the MS. the *a* of *saecundum* has been erased.

die tertia resurrexit, (37) *adque* ad celos ascendit, ad dexteram dei patris sedet, *sicut uobis in simbulo tradutum est;* inde *ad* iudicandos uiuos et mortuos credimus et speramus eum esse uenturum. (38) ad cuius aduentum *erunt* omnes homines *sine dubio* in suis corporibus *resurrecturi* et reddituri de factis propriis rationem, (39) *ut* qui bona egerunt *eant* in uitam aeternam, qui mala in ignem aeternum. (40) haec est fides *sancta et* catholica, quam *omnes homo qui ad uitam aeternam peruenire desiderat scire integrae debet et fideliter custodire.*

The variations from the usual text, which I have italicised, are all easy to explain as rhetorical amplifications. The preacher turns the precise antithesis of cl. 33 into more flowing relatival sentences. Moreover at cl. 37 he makes a reference to the Apostles' Creed. He alters 'resurgere habent' into 'erunt resurrecturi,' naturally enough in parallelism to 'reddituri,' and weights his phrase with 'sine dubio.' The use of 'habeo' with the infinitive for the synthetic future has been much discussed. It was often used in African Latin[1] from the 3rd century, and by Gallican writers in the 5th; so that it proves nothing against the date of the text which contains it. It is more likely however that a preacher would shrink from it, than that a supposed 9th century compiler would substitute it for the future participle, if he were using this sermon as the basis for his text of the Creed. The omission of cl. 35 seems to have been intentional, and to have led to a slight alteration of cl. 36, where 'omnino' is omitted and 'Christus est' is supplied, in cl. 34, from the omitted clause as antecedent to the relative 'qui.' The illustration from the constitution of man, contained in cl. 35, was misused by the Eutychians in their own interest, and came to be regarded with disfavour by Catholic writers. The preacher probably omitted it for this reason. Supposing the sermon to be some 50 or 60 years older than the copy of A.D. 730, we are brought to a date at which Eutychianism was widely prevalent. Dr Heurtley has shown that "Bede mentions this [heresy] as the occasion of the assembling of the great synod

[1] Correspondence in *Guardian*, Oct. 12, 1892. It occurs several times in Codex Bezae and in other forms of the Old Latin Version. It is fully discussed and amply illustrated by Dr Rendel Harris, *Codex Bezae*, pp. 130 ff.

of Hethfield [in 680], and mentions it in such terms as to imply that it was one of the pressing dangers of the day, to which the Church generally—not merely the English branch of it—was exposed[1]."

May I go a step further back and suggest as the possible author of the sermon, Nicetus, Archbishop of Trèves 527—566, a friend of Venantius Fortunatus? Two interesting letters of his have been preserved, in which he draws near to the language of the Creed. The first is to Queen Chlodosainda on her husband's Arianism[2], the other to Justinian on his lapse into a form of Eutychianism. He bids Justinian remember his baptismal vow: 'Unum Filium manentem in duabus substantiis cum Patre et Spiritu Sancto non duos Christos testatus es.... talis Pater qualis et Filius[3].'

This suggestion is destitute of proof, but it seems to be worth while to make it, in case we should find more writings of Nicetus. In his letter to the Queen he mentions Bishops Germanus, Hilary and Lupus; so that he had the tradition of the Lerins school[4].

§ 5. *The three assumptions underlying the two-portion theory.*

The two-portion theory further depends on three questionable assumptions[5]: (i) that the silence of such men as Paulinus and Alcuin, and Alcuin's pupil Rabanus Maurus, shows their ignorance of the Quicunque; (ii) that the authority of such a document from the hand (as was supposed) of Athanasius would constrain any one who knew anything of it to use and quote it; (iii) that the completed Creed would be a useful weapon against Adoptianism.

[1] Bede, *Hist. Eccl.* IV. 17. Quoted by Heurtley, *Hist. Earlier Form.*, 1892, p. 126.

[2] Galland, III. 776. In die resurrectionis nec manere nec apparere potuit qui Trinitatem in Unitate non crediderit.

[3] Galland, *ibid.* I owe these refs. to Sw. p. 272.

[4] A friend of his, Florianus, Abbot of Romanus (Diocese of Milan), was a pupil of Caesarius of Arles, *Mon. Germ. Hist.* III. Ep. Austrasicae.

[5] Sw., ch. xxv. xxvii. Lumby, pp. 235—257.

i. It must be admitted that Rabanus Maurus and Meginhard of Fulda are strangely silent at a time when, with the multiplication of Psalters, the Creed was coming more and more into use and was known to their contemporary Haito at Reichenau. Walafrid Strabo, Haito's successor, came from Reichenau to Fulda, and went back in 838. But the use of the Creed may have been only local as yet. None of the episcopal charges recorded would be binding on Rabanus. And his knowledge of some phrases at all events of the Creed may perhaps be attested by the following parallels: (α) oportebat ita insinuari Trinitatem ut, quamuis nulla esset diuersitas substantiae, *sigillatim* tamen commendaretur distinctio personarum[1]. (β) una substantia una natura una maiestas una gloria una aeternitas et Patris et Filii et Spiritus Sancti[2].

If, however, we turn from the pupil to his master Alcuin, we find good reason for doubting if the latter is really silent, as has been confidently asserted.

A work on the Procession of the Holy Spirit attributed to Alcuin, in which seven clauses of the Quicunque are quoted, is found in a MS. of the early part of the 9th century. It was presented by Bishop Dido (†891) to the Church of Laon (Laudunum), a suffragan bishopric of Rheims. There are slight differences in the style of this work as compared with undisputed works of Alcuin; and on account of these Sirmond ascribed it to an unknown author. But as the editor in Migne's edition points out they are not enough to discredit the traditional authorship. Certainly the Procession Controversy had been raised before Alcuin's death. Bishop Stubbs[3] quotes this book as among his dogmatic works.

The clauses quoted are in Migne LXXXII. p. 750 (cl. 20—22); p. 756 (cl. 7, 24—26).

Apart from these precise quotations, the parallels found in his works are very close. When he writes in a letter to Charlemagne that "the faith of the Holy Trinity must be taught with the utmost diligence: and the coming into this world of the Son

[1] Rabani *Opp.*, Migne, cx. p. 210.

[2] *Ibid.* p. 212.

[3] Art. 'Alcuin' in *D. C. B.* Sw. p. 300 wrongly condemns W. for making no reference to this work of Alcuin: W. p. 26 quotes it doubtfully.

of God, our Lord Jesus Christ, for the salvation of the human race[1]," even Dr Swainson admits that "his thoughts run curiously enough into the channel of the Quicunque[2]." In the same way his book on the Trinity includes the doctrine of the Incarnation. The very title of Bk. I. c. ii., 'On the Unity of the Trinity and the Trinity of the Unity,' might be a quotation from cl. 25, which is itself a summary of the preceding clauses. Dr Swainson[3] notes further "that the order of everything in the Quicunque, as well as many of its words and phrases[4], are found in this work: bear in mind that the Quicunque, or Faith of Athanasius, is not even once referred to in it, and then ask, Are the two documents entirely independent of each other?" But Dr Swainson's conclusion that the Quicunque is a summary of the compilation of Alcuin, and that he knew nothing of it, cannot be upheld in the light of accumulated evidence. Alcuin or a disciple of his, had he composed the Creed, would surely have written cl. 22 differently; compare *ad Fred. Quaest.* 2, p. 740: 'Proprium est Spiritui Sancto quod non ingenitus nec genitus est sed a Patre et Filio aequaliter procedens.' And in cl. 29 the language of a later period than the "Apollinarian times," to which the Quicunque seems to belong[5], would have been found as in Alcuin's Book *adv. Elip.* I. 9, p. 879: 'Diuinitate consubstantialis Patri, humanitate consubstantialis matri[6].' In letter 94 the phrase *perfectus in diuinitate et perfectus in humanitate* shows the same tendency to elaborate statement, as compared with the plain *perfectus deus perfectus homo* of the Quicunque.

The same must be said about the parallels to the phrases of the Quicunque in the speech of Paulinus at Friuli. The repetition of the words *naturaliter*, *personaliter* shows the scholastic manner in which, if it lay before him, he would wish to paraphrase the Quicunque: 'Inseparabilia sunt semper opera Trinitatis, et nihil est in sancta Trinitate diuersum aliquod aut dissimile uel

[1] Ep. xxxiii. (Mg.). [2] p. 405. [3] p. 412.

[4] *Ad Fred. Quaest.* 1, unitas in substantia, trinitas in personis. *ib.* 12, Vere alius est Pater quam Filius in persona, sicut Filius alius est in persona quam Pater, et Spiritus Sanctus alius est in persona quam Pater et Filius.

[5] W., p. 157.

[6] Cf. W., p. 145.

inaequale. Non diuersum naturaliter, non confusum personaliter, nihil maius aut minus. Non anterior, non posterior, non inferior, non superior, sed una et aequalis potestas, par gloria sempiterna et coaeterna, consubstantialisque maiestas. Unum namque sunt essentialiter Pater et Filius et Spiritus Sanctus .... Spiritus quoque Sanctus proprie Spiritus Sanctus est, et non est personaliter Pater uel Filius, sed ex utroque procedit, et tamen non sunt tres dii sed unus est Deus.'

Again on the Incarnation of the Son: 'Consubstantialis Deo Patri in sua id est diuina, consubstantialis etiam matri sine sorde peccati in nostra id est humana natura. Et ideo in utraque natura proprium eum, et non adoptiuum Dei Filium confitemur, quia inconfusibiliter et inseparabiliter, assumpto homine, unus idemque est Dei et hominis Filius. Naturaliter Patri secundum Diuinitatem, naturaliter matri secundum humanitatem: proprius tamen Patri in utroque, quoniam sicut dictum est non sunt duo filii, alter Dei et alter hominis, sed unus Christus Iesus propter unam personam, Dei et hominis Filius, Deus uerus et homo uerus in anima rationali et uera carne. Perfectus homo secundum humanitatem, perfectus Deus secundum Diuinitatem.' The vagueness of such references may be best explained by considering further what measure of authority the Quicunque could be said to possess at that time.

ii. The supposed authority of the document is the second assumption with which we have to deal.

The question of authority is both vague and difficult. We can distinguish between two phases of the influence which the Quicunque might win. In the first it would be known as a treatise or hymn on the Faith, whether recommended by the name of Athanasius or not, on the same level of interest and importance as the Fides Romanorum. We may compare the degree of authoritativeness which the Te Deum possessed for Caesarius of Arles, or which the hymn for Palm Sunday by Theodulf of Orleans, "All glory, laud and honour," possesses for ourselves. Afterwards, when the Quicunque had been taken up by the Bishops as an accredited expansion of the Apostles' Creed, and had been added with the Te Deum to the Psalter, it would possess the same measure of authority which the Te Deum as it stands in our Prayer-book has for us at the present time. Before the Reformation the Quicunque was itself regarded in some English dioceses as a Canticle rather than a Creed. The Bishops of Worcester and Durham, Walter de Cantelupe and Walter de Kirkham, in the 13th century recommended their clergy to study "the Psalm Quicunque." With this limited range of authority it was quoted by one champion of orthodoxy in the Adoptianist Controversy—Agobard, Archbishop of Lyons, who cites the second clause as the teaching of Athanasius. This was only a warning against defiling the faith. The obvious inference is that the other clauses did not contain doctrinal statements sufficiently precise for his special purpose.

iii. The reticence of Agobard is in itself an argument against the assumption that the Quicunque would be a useful weapon against Adoptianism. But it may be worth while to discuss the question more fully.

The history of Adoptianism is still at many points obscure. Its chief representatives, the Spanish Bishops Felix of Urgel and Elipantus of Toledo, seem to have come under Nestorian influences. It is probable that Latin translations of writings Nestorian in character (e.g. of Theodore of Mopsuestia) were read in Spain[1]. And the Brothers of Cordova, who supplied Elipantus with learned material of controversy, and were blamed by Alcuin as the source of evil, may have been infected with heresy of that type by Eastern Christians who had followed in the wake of the Arab invasion.

The Adoptianists claimed to be merely carrying out to their logical conclusion the received doctrines of two natures and two wills in Christ. But the ground of controversy had been shifted from the sphere of the natures to the sphere of the personality, "whose unity had hitherto been rather taken for granted than made the object of a definite conception[2]." It follows that the teaching of the Quicunque, which represents the level of Christology before the Council of Chalcedon, in what Dr Waterland

[1] Harnack, *Dogmengesch.* III. p. 253.

[2] Dorner, *Person of Christ* (trans.) II. 1, p. 252.

called "Apollinarian times," would be quite easily acceptable by them. For they acknowledged the perfectness of both natures in Christ, held together by unity of Person; but they imagined a process by which the Son of Man was by an act of grace 'adopted' and constituted a true Son in Him who, as the pre-incarnate Word, was the 'proper Son'; and they held that this process was only completed by the Resurrection and Ascension. So that the orthodox theologians were in truth contending for the very foundation of the Christian faith, the reality of the Incarnation, which was thus called in question. This was the meaning of their constant assertion, 'uerus homo, uerus deus'—a phrase ready to hand in the Fides Romanorum[1], though not in the Quicunque; and of their frequent use of the technical terms which we find in the contemporary commentaries on the Quicunque, 'non adoptiuus, non putatiuus, sed proprius.' Paulinus in his speech at Friuli laid great stress on the willing self-humiliation of the Incarnate Word who deigned to grow, to hunger, to thirst, to be weary, in the same human nature[2] in which He rose and in which He was exalted to the right hand of the Father. It is also noticeable how Paulinus gives just that variation of the words—"consubstantial with the Father in His own, that is the divine nature; consubstantial also with His Mother...in our, that is the human nature"—which makes them a weapon against Eutychianism, but which, as Dr Waterland (p. 145) has pointed out, is not found in the Quicunque.

A careful consideration of the history of this controversy leads therefore to the conclusion that the Quicunque was useless by itself as a weapon against heretics who could take up its phrases and give them a different turn. All depended on the way in which these phrases were applied: and when we find Paulinus actually using them with the necessary variations, what can we

[1] In Charlemagne's letter to the Spanish Bishops the phrase of the Quicunque is expanded with the help of the Fides Romanorum. "Perfectus in Divinitate Deus, perfectus in humanitate homo, Deus ante omnia saecula, homo in fine saeculi, uerus in utraque substantia Dei Filius, non putatiuus sed uerus, non adoptione sed proprietate."

[2] This point is emphasized also in the Fides Romanorum, in the 9th century form of the Creed of Pelagius (Sw. 275), and in the notes added to the Fortunatus Commentary in S. Gall 27, and in the Stavelot Commentary.

infer but that he knew and prized the Creed? For the commentaries which survive from that period prove that the Quicunque could not have been altered from the form found in the Trèves fragment to the form suggested by Paulinus, without showing the marks of the controversy in the shape of technical terms. It never was, it never could be "looked upon as a most satisfactory exposition of the doctrines in debate in Friuli[1]."

As a matter of fact, Adoptianism was soon discredited and died out in France. The Council of Arles in 813 did not find it necessary to dwell at any length, in their Canon of the Faith, on the debateable points of that controversy, beyond asserting "in one person the propriety[2] of two natures," a very distinct development of the teaching of "unity of person." Dr Lumby himself admits (p. 235) that in this year the great subject of interest was ecclesiastical discipline, which was debated by no less than five councils. But even if they had desired to expound their faith at greater length, the Quicunque, as we have seen, would not have been "so helpful a document."

It has been shown, then, that these three assumptions have no foundation in fact: that the silence of Alcuin and Paulinus is not proved; that the Quicunque had no general authority as a document to which all theologians were bound to refer; and that it was useless as a weapon against Adoptianism. Deprived of their support the two-portion theory completely breaks down; while our conclusion from the evidence of 8th and 9th century MSS. and testimonies remains unshaken—namely, that the entire Creed was known and used from the beginning of the 8th century. We are now free to turn to the early commentaries in the hope of throwing fresh light on the previous history of the Creed.

[1] L., p. 244.

[2] The term 'proprietas' in old Latin meant 'characteristic,' in law Latin 'ownership.' In the former sense it is used theologically in the plural, 'proprietates utriusque naturae'; in the latter sense in the singular, 'proprietas duarum naturarum.'

CHAPTER II.

EARLY COMMENTARIES.

THE commentaries on the Quicunque have a very varied interest. In the first place, they testify to the extent of the use of the Creed and to the importance attached to it in the Middle Ages. The increased number of the commentaries known to us, and of the recensions in which they are preserved, has rendered obsolete the adverse argument which Dr Swainson (p. 464) founded upon their paucity as compared with the commentaries upon the Apostles' Creed. I have made as full a list as I could from the information given by Dr Swainson and Mr Ommanney, and from such limited research in libraries as has been possible to myself. But the list is doubtless still incomplete, and will be supplemented in the future when attention has been directed to the importance of the enquiry.

In the next place, the theological opinions stated in the commentaries might be made the groundwork of an interesting study, which would bring into relief the features of dogmatic teaching which made the Quicunque popular, and caused its insertion into early Psalters before its use was directed by Synodical and Episcopal rules. Then there is the interest which is attached to particular names in the list of reputed authors, Theodulf of Orleans, Abelard, S. Bernard, Wyclif.

At present, however, we shall confine ourselves to that special point of view which is of most importance at the present time, while the course of the history of the Creed is disputed. It may be stated as a question as follows: What form of text is imbedded in the earliest commentaries, and is that form independent of any known MS.? We need only discuss the evidence of those commentaries which may be assigned to the 9th century or to an earlier date; and we shall take them as far as possible in a reversed chronological order.

1. *The Bouhier Commentary.* The Bouhier Commentary is found in three MSS.: (1) in Troyes 1979 (saec. X) with works of Alcuin, Rhabanus Maurus, and S. Augustine; (2) in B. M. Add. MSS. 24,902 (saec. X/XI) with treatises by S. Augustine; and (3) in Troyes 1532 (saec. XII) with Gregory's *Liber Pastoralis*, the works of Prosper and Augustine, and the Creed of Pelagius. Thus the fact that in the first of these it is attributed to S. Augustine can easily be explained. An interesting statement is made by the author, whoever he may be, in his preface, that he had seen the Creed attributed to S. Athanasius in old MSS. But this testimony must be further discussed in dealing with the Oratorian Commentary on which the Bouhier is founded. Mr Ommanney's conclusion[1] that the Bouhier has been drawn from the Oratorian, "inasmuch as the common matter almost invariably appears in the former in a condensed and abbreviated form," is indisputable. Additional proof of this may be drawn from the preface, all the personal statements being omitted or changed in the condensed form of it found in the Bouhier Commentary: e.g. *in ueteribus codicibus inuenitur* for *eum uidi...in uet. cod.*

As I assign the Oratorian Commentary to the end of the 8th or beginning of the 9th century, I cannot assign an earlier date than the 9th century to the Bouhier Commentary. The text of the Quicunque cited in it shows late readings, which I have noticed in the *apparatus* to the text of the Creed (p. 4 *infra*).

2. *The Orleans Commentary.* The Orleans Commentary[2] was found by M. Cuissard, under-librarian of the town of Orleans, in a MS. (No. 94), which had formerly belonged to the Abbey of Fleury. He followed M. L. Delisle in assigning it to the 9th century. In the same MS. he found scraps of Theodulf's treatise on Adoptianism and what seemed to be his exposition of the Mass. So he was led to ascribe to Theodulf the authorship of the Com-

[1] Om. *E. H.* p. 14.

[2] *Théodulfe Évêque d'Orléans: sa Vie et ses Œuvres*, par Ch. Cuissard. Orléans, 1892.

mentary. The list of the Abbots of Fleury, quoted by Baluze[1], says that Theodulf wrote his Commentary under the title 'Explanatio Symboli S. Athanasii,' which agrees with the title 'Symbolum' in his book *De Spiritu Sancto*, quoted above, p. xxviii, but does not agree with the title 'Explanatio Fidei Catholicae' of the Orleans MS.

There seems to be little doubt that this is the MS. seen at Fleury by the authors of the *Histoire Littéraire de la France*, who speak of Theodulf's Commentary[2]; though the pagination is now different, because the MS. was cut in various places, and parts of it were stolen by Libri[3]. But even this corroborative evidence does not make the authorship certain, because the commentary displays none of the marks of learning shown in acknowledged writings of Theodulf. No doubt the copyist is to blame for the many clerical errors and for grammatical mistakes, but the laboured explanations and the loose use of certain terms are unworthy of the author of the *De Ordine Baptismi*. In that treatise Theodulf uses the phrases 'suscipere, assumere humanitatem,' whereas this commentary has 'percipere,' 'apprehendere,' 'accipere.' The quotations from the Gospels show no dependence on the Theodulfian recension represented in the Bishop of Salisbury's Latin Vulgate. There are most interesting points of connection with other commentaries—Fortunatus, Troyes, Stavelot, Paris. But in some cases the sentences quoted are not at all improved by alteration, e.g. on clause 34 the note expanded from Fortunatus. The note on clause 36 shows dependence on an 8th century sermon, printed by Caspari (*Kirchenhist. Anecdota*, I. p. 157) from Cod. Einsiedl. 199, saec. VIII/IX, 'Dicta Abbatis Pirminii.'

Deinde corpus Christi iacuit in sepulchro; et dum illut sacrum corpus in sepulchro iaciret, anima Christi discendit ad infernum. Inde eripuit Adam, primum hominem, et omnes patriarchas et prophetas et iustus, qui propter originalia peccata ibidem detinebantur. Unde dominus dicit: *Ero mors tua o mors; ero morsus tuus inferne.* Quia dominus noster, Jesus Christus, morsus inferni fuit, quia parte abstulit, parte reliquid; illos iustus abstulit, illos peccatoris reliquit. Quia illa diuinitas dei, que inpassibilis est, hoc est uerbum, cum patre erat in celo et cum corpus in sepulchro et cum anima

[1] *Miscell.* II. 492. [2] IV. 473.
[3] Letter from M. Cuissard, October 29, 1892.

Christi in infernum, quia sola humanitas sine diuinitate mundum redimere non poterat. Deinde alligauit diabulum et expoliauit infernum.

I have reprinted this commentary from M. Cuissard's book, p. 7 *infra*. He does not give the whole of the text of the Quicunque.

3. *The Stavelot Commentary.* The Stavelot Commentary in a slightly altered form is generally known as the Commentary of Bishop Bruno of Würzburg[1]. This prelate, who was consecrated in 1034, was not possessed of much originality. His commentary on the Psalter was a mere compilation from the notes of previous editors, and his work on the Lord's Prayer has been found in a Salzburg MS. of the 9th century, written before his birth, as well as among some doubtful works of Alcuin. To the Stavelot Commentary he merely added three passages from the Commentary of Fortunatus, while he also enlarged the note on clause 14. The variations of MSS. which had not his additions puzzled Waterland[2]; but Mr Ommanney[3], finding a MS. of the 10th century from Stavelot Abbey in the British Museum (Add. MSS. 18,043), was able to clear up the mystery and give the earlier form its new name.

The Abbey of S. Remacle at Stavelot in the Forest of Ardennes was founded in the 7th century[4] under the rule of S. Columban, which was afterwards exchanged for the rule of S. Benedict. The diocese of Maestricht, to which it at first belonged, came to an end in the 9th century, and then the Abbey was attached to Liège[5]. For a time it was united with Corbey Monastery under one abbot[6]. At the end of the 9th century it was plundered by the Normans and lay desolate till the year 938, when it was restored by an Abbot Odilo[7]. Its school, which had flourished in the 9th century, was again made famous by a teacher, Notker, whom Odilo summoned to help him from S. Gall. This Notker is not to be confused with the celebrated Notker Labbeo

[1] Mg. 142. [2] p. 52.

[3] Om. *E. H.* p. 67.

[4] *Gall. Christ.* III. 939.

[5] Wilitsch, *Geog. and Statistics of the Church*, Eng. trans. p. 400.

[6] Büsch. VI. 25, quoted by Wilitsch.

[7] This Odilo was Abbot of Cluny and of Lerins; see Vincentius Barralis, *Chronology*, b, p. 151.

who presided over the school at S. Gall. But we may trace in the work of their scholars at S. Gall and Stavelot the fruit of a common interest in the Quicunque.

Notker Labbeo himself was greatly interested in popularizing the Psalter and Canticles. He translated the Psalms into Old High German, using many Latin expressions and idioms; also the Canticles and scraps of Catechism. Two translations of the Quicunque belonging to his school have recently been printed[1].

The Notker who came to Stavelot is probably the author of the Life of S. Remacle, a copy of which has been preserved at S. Gall[2]; and from the period of literary activity which he inaugurated at Stavelot we may date the beginnings of the celebrated Library[3], many MSS. from which have come into the possession of the British Museum[4]. These facts throw light on the history of the earliest MS. of the Stavelot Commentary, Add. MSS. 18,043, which is a glossed Psalter from Notker's school[5]. Here however the commentary on the Quicunque is not written in the margin, but added on a separate page.

Of its previous history we are still in ignorance. The internal evidence points to the 9th century as the date of its composition. The wording of the note on clause 27, 'non adoptiuum sed proprium Dei Filium,' corresponds with the wording of the letter of the Council of Frankfort[6]. Perhaps it is one of the commentaries referred to by the synod held in the diocese of Liège c. 840—855, in their second canon. 'Fidem enim S. Athanasii episcopi in hoc opere censuimus obseruandum, et simbolum apostolorum con tradicionibus et exposicionibus sanctorum patrum in his sermonibus[7].'

The subject-matter of the commentary is well thought out, and it was very popular in succeeding centuries, whether with or

[1] In the series *Germanischer Bücherschatz*, IX. X. 'Die Schriften Notker's und seine Schule.' Paul Piper, Freiburg, 1883.

[2] MS. 565, saec. XI/XII.

[3] Gottlieb, *Mittelalt. Bibliotheken*. Leipzig, 1890, p. 283.

[4] This Notker seems to have become Bishop of Liège.

[5] It is mentioned in a catalogue of the library of Stavelot, made in 1105 in the margin of a magnificent Bible, now B. M. Add. MSS. 28,106.

[6] Om. *E. H.* p. 77. But Mr Ommanney's conjecture that it might be the missing commentary of Theodulf of Orleans lacks support.

[7] Cf. p. xxix *supra*.

without the prestige of Bishop Bruno's name. Together with the Fortunatus and Oratorian Commentaries it was used as the foundation of several composite commentaries, one of which, under the name of the hermit Rolle of Hampole, was widely used in England in the 14th century.

The form of this commentary found in Boulogne MS. 20, in the margin of a Gallican Psalter written in Caroline minuscules, differs considerably from that in other MSS.[1] Mr Ommanney[2] informs me that it contains sentences which are quoted in two Milan commentaries of the 10th and 12th centuries, as well as quotations from the Troyes and Fortunatus Commentaries.

Some Latin acrostics at the beginning of the Psalter show that it was written by the Monk Heriuerus for the Abbey of S. Bertin at S. Omer, in the time of Abbot Odbertus, A.D. 989—1008: and in the Chartulary of the Monastery under the year 1005 mention is made of other MSS. written for this abbot. S. Omer was in the diocese of Morinum in the province of Rheims, whose Bishop Adalbert in 870 quoted the Quicunque in the profession of Faith which he made to Hincmar. We can account for an extended use of the Creed in that diocese, but we have yet to learn how the commentary was brought either to S. Omer (dioc. Morinum) or to Stavelot (dioc. Liège).

I have printed the whole of this commentary (p. 12 *infra*) from the B. M. Add. MS. 18,043, together with some of the additions in Boulogne MS. 20. The text of the Creed is printed in small capitals.

4. *The Paris Commentary.* The Paris Commentary was found by Mr Ommanney (*E. H.* p. 23), in Paris, B. N. lat. 1012, saec. X. This MS. belonged formerly to the Abbey of S. Martial at Limoges, and contains a series of expositions and instructions on Baptism, the Apostles' Creed, etc. Some of the notes of the exposition of the Quicunque are found also in the margin of a Psalter in the British Museum, Reg. 2 B. V. saec. X, but these show traces of polish. The style is simple and there is no teaching

[1] This Psalter is referred to by Dr Swainson, p. 357; and I owe my further information to the kindness of the Rev. J. H. Fry, Chaplain of S. John the Evangelist at Boulogne, who transcribed it for me.

[2] Letter of May 22, 1894.

in it which gives any definite evidence as to the date of its composition. Mr Ommanney points out that there are quotations from Gregory the Great and from Gennadius.

The form of the text of the Creed is complete with the exception of cl. 4, the second half of which is omitted, and of cl. 27, which is paraphrased. All the readings in the Paris MS. are old, whereas the Psalter, Reg. 2 B. V. (H), shows some later readings. Thus the character of the notes and the form of text point to the 8th century as the date of the commentary.

5. *The Oratorian Commentary.* The Oratorian Commentary is found in three MSS.;

(1) Troyes 804, saec. X. (discovered by Mr Ommanney and printed *E. H.* p. 327), which contains works by S. Augustine, Fulgentius, and Theodulf[1], also the Troyes Commentary on the Quicunque, and commentaries on the Lord's Prayer and Apostles' Creed. I cite it as Or_1.

(2) Vat. 231, saec. X/XI. This MS., which belongs to Queen Christina's collection, came probably from the Abbey of Fleury. The commentary was discovered by Card. Mai and printed *Script. Vet. N. Coll.* IX. 396, with a most interesting preface. Mr Ommanney told me that he examined the MS. carefully, and could not find the title which Mai gives, *Symboli Athanasii Explanatio.* I cite this as Or_2.

(3) Turin LXVI. mentioned by Dr Swainson (p. 379) as of the 15th, and (p. 459) as of the 13th century.

This commentary is by far the most learned if not the most original of all. It begins with a preface[2] in which the writer, apparently addressing a synod, states that he has carried out their instructions to provide an exposition of the work on the Faith which he says "is constantly recited in our churches and continually made the subject of meditation by our priests." He

[1] A friend has found out that these are: Theodulfus *de Catechum. et Bapt.*, *Expos. Missae ex Patribus*, *Expos. Fidei ex Patribus.* It would be interesting to know more about them.

[2] This preface is only found in Vat. 231 (of the two MSS. which have been collated), but it appears in all the MSS. of the Bouhier Commentary in a condensed form.

complains of the ignorance prevailing among the clergy, of the difficulty which they find in getting books for their sacred offices—a Psalter or a Lectionary or a Missal. Since some have no desire to read or learn, it is the will of the synod that at least they should be compelled to meditate on this exposition of the Faith which he has illustrated from the Fathers. Ignorance of God on the part of a priest should be accounted sacrilege, like blasphemy in a layman. He goes on to speak of the tradition that this work had been composed by the blessed Athanasius: he had examined the headings of many old MSS., and had come to the conclusion that it was composed to meet the Arian heresy.

His exposition contains extracts from S. Augustine's works (including those on S. John and on the Trinity), Prosper, S. Leo's Epistles, the translation by Dionysius Exiguus of S. Cyril's Synodical Epistle, Fulgentius, Pelagius I., Vigilius of Thapsus, and the Creed of (the heretic) Pelagius, with the definition of the VIth General Council (681).

On account of the extract last mentioned Mr Ommanney supposes that the commentary was composed towards the end of the 7th or the beginning of the 8th century. But beyond this single reference there is no fear expressed of the heresy of Monothelitism. On the other hand there is very distinct emphasis laid on the assertion of the Lord's Unity of Person as if in fear of a revived Nestorianism. The phrase which we find in the Troyes Commentary, *singularitas personae,* a more precise phrase than the *una persona* of the Creed itself, is repeated again and again; in the note on cl. 28 with a quotation from S. Augustine, Ad Volusianum c. 3; on cl. 32 where he adds a quotation from Fulgentius, De fide ad Petrum c. 17; and on cl. 34. This points unmistakeably to the period of the Adoptianist controversy, and supports in a remarkable way the suggestion made by Dr Swainson (p. 460) that the commentary might be the lost commentary of Theodulf.

The catalogue of the Abbots of Fleury (quoted above p. xlvii) says that Theodulf composed an '*Explanatio symboli s. Athanasii.*' As we have seen, Card. Mai ought not to have assigned this title to this commentary, as it is not found in his MS. But the title *Symbolum Athanasii* is given to the Creed in Theodulf's book

On the Holy Spirit, which is a collection of extracts from the same series of authors as are quoted in the commentary, e.g. Fulgentius, Cassiodorus, Vigilius.

The whole tone of the preface is worthy of Theodulf, whose earnestness and learning are beyond question. Moreover, as we have seen, the 'capitulary' ascribed to him, enjoining the use of the Creed and directing that the clergy should learn it, appears to be the decision of a synod. Is it fanciful to suggest some connection between the remarks in that preface on clerical ignorance and the stern denunciation of it in the Canons of the VIth Council of Toledo: 'Ignorantia mater cunctorum errorum maxime in sacerdotibus Dei uitanda est?' The author of the preface would know this, as it is found in the Collection of Dionysius Exiguus from which he quoted Cyril's Synodical Epistle. Theodulf, be it remembered, was of Spanish extraction, and in his poem *Paraenesis ad Episcopos* says much the same about the condition of the clergy: so that from this point of view he might well have been the author.

The question has been complicated by M. Cuissard's discovery of the Orleans Commentary, which he ascribes to Theodulf, but which is unworthy of him (see p. xlvii). Certainly the MS. comes from Fleury, and this perhaps gives a clue which may some day be worked out more fully. The Orleans Commentary is partly based on the Troyes Commentary and is therefore a connecting link between the library of Fleury Abbey and the MS. Troyes 804, which contains the Troyes Commentary and the Oratorian Commentary and works of Theodulf. We have seen that the Vatican MS. may also have come from Fleury, so that the chain of evidence is as complete as we can hope to make it at present.

Turning to the question of texts embedded in these two commentaries, we find that the Orleans (cited as Orl.) shows a 9th century text, while the Oratorian in the Troyes MS. (Or_1) has an older form, though the scribe of the Vatican MS. (Or_2) has a tendency to alter readings: e.g. cl. 33 *carne...deo* Or_1, *carnem... deum* Or_2. Some of the variations to which Dr Swainson calls attention are simply vagaries of the author. The joining of cl. 15. 17 and 16. 18, thus making as it were two compound clauses, was obviously done for the sake of shortness, as he had only one note to add on the whole group; and we may apply the same remark to the parallel passage in the Fortunatus Commentary.

The old readings appear in cl. 25 *trinitas in unitate et u. in t.*; cl. 21 *pariter*; cl. 33 *carne...deo*; cl. 36 *ad inferna*; cl. 37 *ad dextram Patris*; in each of which cases the Orleans has late readings, while in cl. 28, 33, 36, 37 it is supported by the Bouhier Commentary.

Mr Ommanney[1] draws attention to the fact that the Oratorian Commentary was widely known and used in the Middle Ages. Together with the Stavelot Commentary it is used in two composite commentaries; one found in the margin of an Oxford MS., Bodleian Library, Canonici Bibl. 30; the other known by the name of Richard Rolle of Hampole, an Augustinian hermit of Yorkshire (†1349).

I have not reprinted this commentary but I have quoted the readings of the two earlier MSS. in the *apparatus* to the text of the Creed.

I give here the Preface to the Oratorian Commentary Vat. 231, comparing with it certain passages from the Bouhier and Hampole Commentaries.

Iniunxistis mihi illud fidei opusculum, quod passim in ecclesiis recitatur, quodque a presbyteris nostris usitatius quam cetera opuscula meditatur, sanctorum patrum sententiis quasi exponendo dilatarem, consulentes parrochiae nostrae presbyteris, qui sufficienter habere libros nullo modo possunt, sed uix et cum labore sibi psalterium, lectionarium, uel missalem adquirunt, per quos diuina sacramenta uel officia agere queant; et, quia cum inopia librorum plerisque neque studium legendi aut discendi suffragetur, idcirco uultis ut saltem hanc fidei expositionem meditari cogantur, ut aliquanto amplius de Deo possint sapere et intellegere. Quia maxima omnium ista pernicies est, quod sacerdotes qui plebem Dei docere debuerant, ipsi Deum ignorare inueniuntur; nam sicut laico blasphemia, ita sacerdoti uoluntaria Dei ignoratio in sacrilegium deputatur. Hoc namque opusculum non quidem est altis sermonibus obscurum, nec laciniosis sententiis arduum, cum paene plebeio conscriptum sit sermone; sed tamen si adiunguntur ei pro locis necessariis tractatorum[2] fidei uerba, plurimum iuuat ad fidei notitiam.

	BOUHIER.
Traditur enim quod a beatissimo Athanasio Alexandrinae ecclesiae	*Traditur quod a beatissimo Athanasio Alexandriae ecclesie antistite is-*

[1] Om. *E. H.* p. 38.

[2] MS. tractorum.

antestite sit editum: ita namque semper eum vidi praetitulatum etiam in veteribus codicibus; et puto quod idcirco tam plano et brevi sermone tunc traditum fuerit, ut omnibus catholicis etiam minus eruditis tutamentum defensionis praestaret aduersus illam tempestatem quam uentus contrarius, hoc est diabolus excitauit per Arrium. Qua tempestate nauicula, hoc est Christi ecclesia, in medio mari, uidelicet mundo, diu tantis fluctibus est uexata, sed non soluta aut summersa. Quia ille imperauit uento et mari qui se eidem ecclesiae promisit usque ad finem saeculi affuturum. Quicunque ergo ex huius maris fluctibus saluari desiderat, et in profundum abyssi, aeternam uidelicet perditionem, demergi pauescit, teneat integre et inuiolabiliter fidei ueritatem.

tud fidei opusculum sit editum: sicut *etiam in ueteribus codicibus* invenitur *pretitulatum.*

Quod idcirco tam brevi et plano sermone tunc traditum fuisse cognoscitur, ut omnibus catholicis etiam minus eruditis tutamentum defensionis praestaret....

HAMPOLE.

Haec ratio fidei catholicae *traditur etiam in ueteribus codicibus a beato Athanasio Alexandrino* scripta *et* quia *iccirco tam plano et breui sermone tradita fuit, ut* in *omnibus catholicis et* hymnis *eruditis tutamen defensionis praestaret aduersus illam tempestatem quam uentus contrarius hoc est diabolus* concitauit, *per quam tempestatem* ....
qui fugere desiderat, hanc *fidei ueritatem integre et inuiolabiliter teneat.*

6. *The Troyes Commentary.* The Troyes Commentary was found by Mr Ommanney in the Public Library at Troyes in MS. 804, which is probably of the 10th century. It is based in the first part on the Commentary of Fortunatus, but in the second it deviates from it widely. The writer deals very freely with the text of the Creed.

The date is not easy to determine. Mr Ommanney[1] speaks of "the entire omission of the terminology of the Praedestinarian and Adoptianist controversies," and "the distinct employment of that in use when Monothelitism was the great subject of discussion," and would date it in the middle of the 7th century. But though we do not find any very precise technical terms, such as 'non adoptiuus,' there are several indications of opposition to Adoptianism, which would bring it down to the end of the 8th century.

Felix of Urgel was at one with his orthodox opponents in admitting the whole doctrine of the two Natures and two Wills. But he spoke of our Lord in His human nature as Adopted Son, and therefore incurred the suspicion of introducing a double

[1] *E. H.* p. 33.

personality. This danger would account for the strong assertion on cl. 33 of the singularity of His person, and a more emphatic condemnation of Nestorianism than is found in Fortunatus. Felix held also that our Lord assumed human nature in the state to which Adam's fall had reduced it, not indeed as tainted by original sin, but as subject to mortality and other consequences of sin; a view which is strongly condemned in the words on cl. 30, 'perfectum hominem absque peccato de uirgine suscipere dignatus est, ut per eandem naturam, quae in paradiso decepta mortem incurrerat, rursum eundem diabolum non potentia diuinitatis sed ratione iustitiae uinceret.' This conception of the Atonement is both deep and true.

As the process of Adoption was not held to be completed until the Resurrection, the emphatic iteration in this and the Stavelot Commentary (as in the 9th century forms of the Fides Romanorum and the Fortunatus Commentary), that the Lord rose in the same flesh in which He died, may be supposed to guard against Adoptianist error. Paulinus made the same point in his speech at the Council of Friuli.

Another hint of the date of the Troyes Commentary is found in the reference to the genealogy in S. Matthew's Gospel, which was distinguished by Felix from that recorded by S. Luke as giving Christ's descent according to the flesh, while S. Luke gave the descent according to the spirit[1]. The commentary confutes this view by pointing to the true contrast between the Divine Generation and the fleshly, just as Paulinus, in the speech to which I have referred, contrasts the human birth in time with the Divine birth irrespective of time.

On these grounds we may assign the commentary to the period during which Adoptianism was a growing heresy, c. 780—820.

I have reprinted the commentary (p. 21 *infra*) from Mr Ommanney's collation, giving the text of the Creed in small capitals and quotations from the Fortunatus Commentary in italics.

Before we pass on to the consideration of the most important of all the commentaries, the Fortunatus Commentary, it will be convenient to sum up our conclusions as to the dates of the com-

[1] Dorner, *Hist. Person of Christ*, II. p. 256.

mentaries hitherto described and the forms of the text of the Quicunque imbedded in them.

I assign the Bouhier and Orleans Commentaries to the middle or end of the 9th century. They contain late readings of the Quicunque. The Stavelot Commentary seems to belong to the beginning of the 9th century. It contains a reference to the Adoptianist controversy, and its text of the Quicunque shows some early readings (e.g. cl. 28 pariter; cl. 36 *om.* tertia die).

The internal evidence of the Oratorian and Troyes Commentaries, and probably of the Paris Commentary as well, points to the 8th century, and they give all the early readings of the Quicunque. The Troyes Commentary contains, it is true, only an abridged form of the text of the Quicunque. This will be considered later on in its relation to the abridged form found in the Fortunatus Commentary. The other commentaries contain the entire Creed and confirm the evidence adduced in the first chapter to prove that it was known in the 8th century.

7. *The Fortunatus Commentary.* The so-called Fortunatus Commentary has been handled somewhat roughly by recent criticism, and has not been allowed to take its proper place in the argument for determining the date of the Creed. Besides being the earliest known, it is the one which is most freely quoted in others. Waterland was only acquainted with two MSS. (*o* and *m*), but we now hear of some fifteen. On a short visit to S. Gall and Munich I was able to examine and collate three new MSS. which I found through the catalogues. I also found two new MSS. of the shorter form which is contained in the margin of the Psalter S. Gall 27. When one MS. only of such a document survives from a given century, we have no guarantee that others existed at that date. But we have now to deal with seven MSS. which belong to the 9th century, and we may reasonably imagine that other early MSS. have perished or are still in hiding. The argument from internal evidence for the early date of the archetype is proportionately strengthened. Of the seven, four may be connected with the Province of Mainz; since Junius 25 (*o*) comes from Murbach Abbey, a daughter house of Reichenau which with S. Gallen, Bamberg, and the Tegernsee seems to have belonged to that Province.

1. *o*. Oxford. Bodleian Library. Junius 25. Saec. IX *in*. A miscellaneous collection of documents including a glossary of Old German words, and at the end, in what is said to be a later hand, a sermon on the Apostles' Creed. The connection with Murbach Abbey is proved by the repeated mention of Abbot Dandolo.

2. *b*. Bamberg. A. 11. 16. Saec. IX/X. Found and collated by Rev. W. D. Macray. I do not know what else the MS. contains.

3. b_1. Bamberg. B. 11. 16. Saec. XII. Found by Mr Macray. I have copied the collation in Dr Swainson's copy of his own book in the Library of the Divinity School at Cambridge. I do not know by whom it was made.

4. *g*. S. Gall 241. Saec. IX. A miscellaneous collection of documents including letters of S. Jerome and Pope Damasus. The commentary has no title and was copied by a very illiterate scribe.

5. *G*. A S. Gall MS., now lost, which was found and printed by M. Goldast in his book *Manuale Biblicum*, Frankfurt, 1610. Goldast's MS. copy has been preserved in the University Library at Leyden (Cod. Leidensis Vossianus in 4°. no. 30, fol. 144). The librarian, Dr W. N. du Rieu, has identified the MS. from which it was taken with S. Gall 241, the MS. last named, and has been followed in his opinion by Card. Pitra, who has published a (somewhat inaccurate) transcription in his *Analecta sacra et classica* (v. p. 27). This suggestion seems to me quite untenable, for reasons which I have given at length in an Additional Note. The text agrees in general with that of *o*.

6. *t*. Munich. Cod. lat. 19,417. Saec. IX. From a Monastery on the Tegernsee, with a tract on the Nicene Council and a work of Chrysostom on the natures of animals.

7. *v*. Vienna 1,032. Saec. IX. Contains a treatise on the Catholic Faith by S. Isidore, the Nicene and Athanasian Creeds, followed by this commentary on cl. 1—19. Dr Swainson (p. 323 f.) examined the MS. and found that "turning over the leaf the subject is entirely changed: the volume begins to treat on the

difference between the historic and spiritual interpretations of Scripture."

8. *p.* Paris. B. N. Cod. lat. 2,826. Saec. IX *ex.* This like the following MS. (no. 8) was found and collated by Mr Ommanney (*E. H.* p. 47). It is said to contain writings of Isidore and Alcuin, Gregory's sacramentary, the Canons of the Council of Aix (817), etc. (the Canons in a different hand).

9. p_1. Paris. B. N. Cod. lat. 1,008. Saec. X *ex.* Om. *E. H.* p. 47, "a kind of manual for the use of priests."

10. *n.* Munich. Cod. lat. 14,508. Saec. X. Is interesting as having old readings, and at the end an apostrophe like that in the Milan MS. of the Creed (Milan O. 212). 'Lacta mater eum qui fecit te. Lacta eum qui tibi fructum fecunditatis dedit conceptos....'

The Fortunatus Commentary follows one on the Lord's Prayer; and in the same MS. are found (f. 106) the capitulary of Theodulf of Orleans, and his tracts on Baptism and Confirmation. In the Vésoul MS. (no. 15) the commentary is followed by the same capitulary.

11. *m.* Milan. Ambros. M. 48. 79. Saec. XI. A collection of commentaries on the Apostles' Creed, Lord's Prayer and Catholic Faith. This is the only MS. in which the commentary is ascribed to Fortunatus. A new collation was made for me in June 1893 by Prof. Robinson and Mr A. E. Brooke.

12. *f.* Florence (see Zaccharia, *Excursus Litterarius per Italiam,* p. 307). Saec. XIV. Quoted by Swainson, p. 426.

There are four other MSS., of which I have not been able to obtain collations:

13. Paris, B. N. 17,448. Saec. XI *in.* A copy of no. 9 *supra.*

14. Paris, B. N. 2,316. Saec. XII. The reference to this I owe to M. L. Delisle.

15. Vésoul 73. (Cat. d. Départements VI.) Saec. XI.

16. Paris, B. N. 3,786, fol. 223 *v.* A collection of sermons referred to by Dom Morin, *Science Catholique*, July, 1891.

We must add to these MSS., which contain the full form of the Fortunatus Commentary, three others in which we find what is clearly a later adaptation of it. These are—

i. g_1. S. Gall 27. Saec. IX.[1]
ii. n_2. Munich Cod. lat. 3,729. Saec. X.
iii. Munich Cod. lat. 14,501. Saec. XII.

These are Psalters in which the Fortunatus Commentary has been broken up to provide marginal notes to the Quicunque, which is here given continuously and in full. The following summary shows at a glance the relation of the adapted form (B) of the commentary to the original. Above the line are the numbers of the clauses of the Creed, words of which are commented on in the earlier form (A). Below the line and in blacker type are the numbers of clauses on which B has a new note. The sign ∧ represents that B has abridged the note of A, probably from exigencies of space; the sign ∨ denotes that B has enlarged the note of A. For the rest the notes in B are the same as in A.

A	1	.	3	4	5	6	7	8	9	10	.	.	13	.	15	.	17	.	19^a	.	.	.	23	24^a
B		**2**		∧																**20**	**21**	**22**		

A	25	.	.	28	29	30	31	32	33	34	35	36	37	38	39	40
B					∧	**30**				∧	∧	∧	∨	**38**	**39**	**40**

The note on cl. 30 in A is expressly a confutation of Apollinarianism. That in B seems to be directed against Adoptianism, though the scribe makes no mention of any heresy by name. His words are: 'Perfectus quidem deus in diuinitate, perfectus homo in humanitate, unus et uerus propriusque dei filius.' The word 'proprius' is a technical term in the Adoptianist controversy.

The author of B omits the explanation of 'in seculo' in cl. 29, which has an important bearing on the date of A. To this we shall return presently.

The Creed does not begin to appear in Psalters until the very end of the 8th century. This fact taken together with the apparent allusion to the Adoptianist controversy inclines us to regard B, found as we have seen in a 9th century MS., as a 9th century adaptation of A.

[1] Dr Swainson (p. 356) copied some of the notes in S. Gall 27, but did not recognize the relation of this form of the commentary to the fuller form.

With the materials which we have thus collected it is possible to discuss the history of the text of the Fortunatus Commentary more fully than was done by Dr Swainson.

1. With regard to the external evidence we have 9th century MSS. of the full commentary. But besides this we have also a 9th century MS. of an adaptation of the commentary in the margin of a Psalter. This at any rate would seem to throw back the archetype of all these MSS. at least as far as the 8th century. More than this we are not entitled to say.

2. But the internal evidence points back to a much earlier date. (*a*) Apollinarianism is the latest heresy mentioned by name. There is no reference to the Procession controversy of the 8th century nor to the Monothelete controversy, which in the 7th century was a struggle for life or death. Eutychianism, which revived in the 6th and 7th centuries, is ignored, and only a mild warning is given against the error of Nestorius (p. 35, l. 18)[1]. On the other hand Sabellius, Arius, and Apollinaris are in turn branded as false teachers, and the explicit warnings against their errors, which the Quicunque contains, are carefully noted. These facts would incline us to suppose that the commentary was written not long after the Creed itself. (*b*) Another indication of time has been found in the note on cl. 29, 'in seculo, id est in isto sexto miliario in quo nunc sumus.'

This 'sixth milliary' must mean the 6th period of a thousand years from the Creation. On the analogy of the record of the Creation in six days men argued that with the close of the 6th milliary would come the end of the world and a period of sabbath rest.

In the 3rd century Cyprian, *Ad Fort.* § 2 (Hartel, p. 317), writes to Fortunatus: "Six thousand years are now nearly completed since the devil attacked man."

Cyprian may have used the chronological system of Julius Africanus, who had written a summary of chronology down to the year 221 A.D. Julius calculated that Christ was born in the year 5500 from the Creation of the world. His 'sixth milliary' would end in the year 499 A.D. In the following century Eusebius

[1] It is noticeable that in the Troyes commentary founded on this, apparently when the Adoptianists had revived his heresy, Nestorius is mentioned by name.

(† 336), who appropriated most of the conclusions of his predecessor Julius, found reason to postpone the date three hundred years, fixing the date of the Birth of Christ in the year 5200 from the Creation. Thus the 6th milliary would come to an end in the year 799 A.D. But the Eusebian reckoning does not seem to have been so widespread as that which closed the 6th milliary at or near the end of the 5th century[1].

Epiphanius[2] († 403) again seems to have made an independent calculation differing slightly from that of Julius, setting the Birth of Christ at 5479, which would bring the close of the 6th milliary back to the year 478 A.D.

From the beginning of the 5th century the breaking up of the Roman Empire, the invasion of Italy, of Gaul, and of Africa by barbarian armies, brought with gloomy foreboding of fresh disasters to the Roman arms anxious anticipations of the Last Judgment. Perhaps this led to a revival of interest in the earlier date reckoned by Julius.

Sulpicius Severus begins the second chapter of his *Sacred History*, which is dedicated to S. Augustine, with the statement: "The world was created by God nearly six thousand years ago."

S. Augustine uses similar language in his book *On the City of God*, written between A.D. 413 and 426. He says: xviii. 40, 'ab ipso primo homine,...nondum sex annorum milia compleantur.' Again, speaking of the binding of Satan mentioned in the Apocalypse, he offers as an alternative explanation: xx. 7, 'aut quia in ultimis annis mille ista res agitur, id est, sexto annorum miliario, tanquam sexto die, cuius nunc spatia posteriora uoluuntur.'

It is true that he was careful to teach that the exact date of the Second Advent must remain unknown, distinguishing perhaps

[1] In a Donatist chronology ('Liber genealogus' dated 427) which Mommsen has printed in *Mon. Germ.* IX. pp. 154 ff., it is clear that 6000 years from Adam are to be completed towards the end of the 5th century.

The following lines from Commodian show how common was the view at an earlier period that the duration of the world was to be 6000 years:

Instr. I. xxxv. 6. Finitis sex milibus annis inmortales erimus.
Ibid. II. xxxix. 8. Sex milibus annis conpletis mundo finito.
Apol. 791 f. Sex milibus annis prouenient ista repletis,
Quo tempore nos ipsos spero iam in litore portus.

[2] *C. Haeres.* XXX. 30 and LXVI. 50, quoted by Routh, *Reliquiae Sacrae*, II. p. 460, in his notes on the *Chronicon* of Julius Africanus.

between the six milliaries in the history of the world and the six ages in the history of man. Of the 6th age he says: xxii. 30, 'sexta nunc agitur, nullo generationum numero metienda, propter id quod dictum est: *Non est uestrum scire tempora, quae Pater posuit in sua potestate.*'

Thus in the 5th century the 6th milliary had a well defined meaning, and it was expected shortly to come to an end. When this prediction had been falsified men were puzzled.

"The question," says Dr Swainson[1], "assumed a polemical aspect. Taking (it may be from the Christian writers) the hint as to the ages of the world, the Jewish Rabbis began to insist that, according to the Hebrew chronology, only five ages of the world had passed; and therefore they argued that the Messiah had not come. 'We insist,' says Julian, Bishop of Toledo, 'that the 6th age is passing, and therefore that the Messiah has come.' But the bishop was obliged to consider that the time had to be reckoned not *in annis sed generationibus*; for, although he wrote in the year 686 of our era, he made out that already 6011 years had passed since the world was created. Thus he was obliged to confess, 'God only knows when it will end.'"

At the beginning of the 8th century Bede, *de temporibus*, c. 22, calculated the date of Christ's birth at 5200. With this agree some calculations in the MS. Paris, 1451, which was written about A.D. 796. In his bigger book *de temporum ratione* Bede denied that the end of the 6th milliary would bring the end of the 6th age.

We come back to the question, what did the author of the Fortunatus Commentary mean by the phrase '6th milliary,' which he used as definitely as S. Augustine?

It is important to remark (*a*) that the author of the B recension omitted the statement as if it had lost its point; (*b*) that the late MS. Milan M. 79, saec. XI, adds an explanation from Isidore, *Orig.* v. 38: 'secula enim generationibus constant et inde secula quod sequantur. abeuntibus enim aliis alia succedunt.'

This seems to show that the phrase would be most natural to a writer of the 5th century, and therefore if we find it in a document we should incline *ceteris paribus* to date that document before 499.

[1] Sw. p. 434.

It is however just possible that a later writer might have used the phrase, looking to 799 as the date of its close[1]. But this is not nearly so probable as the former view.

Having made it probable that the commentary was written in the 5th century, we have now to ask whether it is possible to identify the author. There have hitherto been two claimants for the honour of having written it.

(1) We have for convenience retained the title the *Fortunatus Commentary*. We may accordingly first consider the grounds on which it has been attributed to this author.

The Milan MS. (M. 79) contains on fol. 26 *v.* an exposition of the Apostles' Creed with the heading, *Incipit expositio a fortunato presbytero conscripta.* It also contains three commentaries on the Quicunque, the 3rd of which is headed *Item expositio fidei catholicae fortunati.* Not unreasonably this Fortunatus has been identified with the Fortunatus Presbyter, the author of the commentary on the Apostles' Creed on f. 26. He is a well-known author, whose full name was Venantius Fortunatus, and who was sometime Bishop of Poictiers, and a great friend of Gregory of Tours. Dr Waterland thought he could trace in the two commentaries "great similitude of style, thought, and expressions"; and he found in Fortunatus's poems phrases which seemed like poetical renderings of phrases in the Quicunque. But the biographer of Fortunatus has left no record of the commentary on the Quicunque among his works; and the special case, built up on mere similitude of style and scraps of poetry, is much weaker than Waterland's sound general conclusion, that "the tenor of the whole comment and the simplicity of the style and thoughts are very suitable to that age, and more so than to the times following."

(2) Goldast's S. Gall MS. ascribed the Creed to a Euphronius Presbyter. Goldast himself supposed that this writer was a monk of the time of Charles the Great and the Adoptianist controversy. But he gave no reasons for this opinion, and I can myself find none. Dom Morin[2], who knew of Goldast's discovery through Card. Pitra's reprint of the Leyden MS., and of its (as I think, mistaken) identification with S. Gall 241, went further and

[1] See Addenda, p. xi.

[2] *Science Catholique*, July 1891, p. 676.

discussed the claims of more than one Euphronius to be the author. Somewhat hastily rejecting Euphronius, Bishop of Autun (450—490), as "évidemment trop tôt," and also the "Euphronius presbyter" who brought a letter from Pope Gelasius to Arles in 494, he fixed his choice on Euphronius, Bishop of Tours (555—572), a friend of Venantius Fortunatus. Not understanding, however, that the interpolation on clause 2 in the Milan MS. M. 79 was unique, he proceeded to question whether Fortunatus had borrowed from an earlier composition by Euphronius, as in his commentary on the Apostles' Creed he had borrowed from Rufinus, or whether 'Euphronius' might not be simply a mistake for 'Fortunatus.' Unfortunately Dom Morin did not know the argument of Dr Waterland on the general history of the Creed, or he might have been led to consider more favourably the claims of Euphronius of Autun, mentioned as 'Euphronius presbyter' by Gregory of Tours (*Hist.* II. 15). This Euphronius was the friend of Lupus of Troyes, of Faustus of Riez, and of Sidonius Apollinaris[1]. Together with Lupus he wrote a letter on 'Ecclesiastical Order[2].' And he joined Faustus in condemnation of a priest, Lucidus, who held Pelagian and Origenist opinions.

In Lucidus's recantation of his errors, addressed to Faustus, Euphronius and others, is a passage which throws light on one of the most characteristic passages of the commentary, whether it be from the pen of Euphronius or only a product of his age.

Lucidus condemns anyone "who says that the patriarchs and prophets or the greatest of the saints had lived in paradise even before the time of redemption; who says that fires and hell are not."

The commentary, l. 143, explains definitely that the descent of Christ into Hell was to effect the release of the patriarchs and prophets and all the just who were there detained for original sin.

This was a common explanation of the descent into Hell, and it reappears in the sermon of Pirminius, quoted above, p. xlvii, and in the Orleans Commentary. The more precise phrase 'pro origi-

[1] iv. *Ep.* 25, VII. 8, IX. 2.

[2] W., p. 47, knew of Goldast's work (or of some other MS. which attributed the commentary to Euphronius) through the 2nd edition of Paraeus' book. See Add. Note.

nali peccato' is exchanged for the vaguer 'propter originalia peccata' in Pirminius, and the unintelligible 'propter illa orientalia delicta' in the Orleans Commentary. No argument can be based on the coincidence, but it is of interest if we are right in identifying the author of the commentary, which gave such instruction on the release of the patriarchs, with the Bishop who obtained from an opponent so emphatic a contradiction of the opposite view. And this theory can be supported by the series of parallel phrases[1] which I have collected in my notes on the commentary from the writings of Faustus and of another member of the Brotherhood of Lerins, Eucherius. If the Creed came originally from Lerins, as I shall hope to make at least very probable, it would seem natural to look for the author of the first commentary in a later generation of the same circle of theologians. Further, this theory of authorship, if it bears the test of future investigation, may be held to support in its turn the interpretation of the Canon of Autun as referring to the Quicunque under the title 'Fides S. Athanasii.'

3. Lastly I have to deal with the form of text of the Quicunque embodied in this commentary. If we may trace this form back to the fifth century it becomes most important. The problem we have to deal with is the omission of cl. 2, 12, 14, 20—22, 24 *b*, 26, 27[2].

The authors of the two-portion theory appear to have regarded this abridged text as a sort of 9th century essay in the combination of the two portions, these omitted clauses being subsequent additions. But this view would lead to great difficulties. It would become necessary to date all the MSS. containing the entire Creed later than 820, but this, as we have seen, we cannot do. Again if this abridged form of the Creed (contained, as we have seen, in seven 9th century MSS. of the commentary) had an independent existence at the beginning of that century, it is marvellous that it is not preserved in any MS. which contains the Creed with-

[1] They used the same explanations of 'faith' and 'Catholic,' and the same terms *proprietas*, *conditio*, etc.

While they both taught the Procession of the Holy Spirit from the Son, the doctrine was not put forward at all controversially.

[2] I do not regard cl. 16, 18 as omitted clauses, because in l. 53 there is a clear reference to them.

out the commentary. Surely the only reasonable conclusion is that the existence in the 9th century of this slightly abridged form of the entire Creed, even granting that the author was ignorant of the omitted clauses, is fatal to the two-portion theory.

But it is necessary to enquire very carefully why the commentator should have omitted these clauses if they were part of the original Creed. Comparing the Fortunatus with the Troyes Commentary we find that both omit cl. 2, 12, 20—22, 26, 27; Fortunatus is alone in omitting 14, 24 *b*.

As regards cl. 12, 14 the leading ideas 'uncreate, incomprehensible, omnipotent' (which occur in cl. 8, 9, 13) are explained, and it does not fall within the scope of the argument to enlarge on the guarding clauses.

As regards cl. 26, 27 there is no positive statement made in them which requires explanation.

The omission of cl. 2 is more important. The B recension (S. Gall 27) has inserted, as we have seen, a new note: 'Qui catholicam fidem recte credendo et opere exercendo neglegit, hereticus est et schismaticus: huius interitus sine dubio manebit.' This does not explain any of the terms used in the clause, which was evidently regarded as intelligible in itself. But the author of the new note draws no sharp distinction between heresy and schism. May we not extend this argument and infer that the author of the original commentary also found the terms of cl. 2 intelligible, and therefore passed it without a note? It forms indeed one sentence with cl. 1, and while the Quicunque was regarded as an instruction would be included in that clause. When however the Creed was inserted in Psalters and its clauses were pointed for singing as a Canticle, cl. 2 was detached without regard to its grammatical connection. In this detached form the scribe of S. Gall 27 finds it, and must needs say something about it.

We come lastly to the section 20—22. The note on cl. 4, l. 9, 'est enim gignens, genitus, procedens, etc.' may be held to have explained sufficiently the teaching contained in this section, and to have rendered any further comment superfluous. Moreover if this section did not originally form part of the Creed, its origin will have to be accounted for. I have drawn up a table exhibiting parallels to its phrases from the canons of councils of Toledo, the

Creed of Damasus, and the notes on cl. 4 in the Fortunatus and Troyes commentaries. In the case of Toledan canons I have only given the dates at which each phrase makes its appearance.

	Quicunque vult	Councils of Toledo
20.	Pater (a nullo) factus	633
	nec creatus	increatum 638 non creatum 675
	nec genitus	uel 633 non 675
21.	Filius (a Patre solo est)	
	non factus	633
	nec creatus	638
	sed genitus	633
22.	Spiritus Sanctus (a Patre et Filio)	
	non factus	
	nec creatus	633
	nec genitus	633
	sed procedens	a 589 ex 633 de/ab 638 ab 675 de/ex 693

	Creed of Damasus	Fortunatus	Troyes
20.	Patrem esse qui genuit	Pater gignens (qui genuit)	Pater gignens (qui genuit)
		ingenitus	ingenitus
		(eo quod a nullo est genitus)	a nullo est genitus
21.	Filium qui genitus	Filius genitus (quem genuit pater)	Filius
		a patre solo est genitus	a patre solus est genitus
22.	Spiritum Sanctum	Spiritus Sanctus	Spiritus Sanctus
	non genitum		
	neque ingenitum		neque ingenitus
	non creatum		
	neque factum		
	sed de Patre Filioque procedentem	a Patre et Filio procedit	procedit ex Patre Filioque

It will be seen at once that the theory that the section has been compiled out of the note in either of the commentaries is an extremely improbable explanation. Nor is it likely that the Creed of Damasus is the source. This is rather to be sought in the writings of S. Augustine[1].

[1] *De Trin.* v. 14, 15; xv. 17. He brought men to the edge of the later controversy on the Procession of the Holy Spirit. When that had been raised, it would be difficult for enthusiasts to content themselves with the preposition *a* (patre et filio), as in the Quicunque and the Fortunatus Commentary. They would wish to

As the result of this examination of the omitted clauses we may fairly decide that the author was acquainted with the whole Creed, but quoted only those clauses which he wished to explain.

To sum up our conclusions on this commentary; we have found (1) that the MSS. point us back to the 8th century; (2) that the internal evidence inclines us to place it in the 5th century; (3) that there is some slight evidence for identifying the author with Euphronius, Bishop of Autun; (4) that the commentary may fairly be taken as a witness to the entirety of the Creed which forms its subject-matter.

On the second and third of these points we may look for further light from future investigation.

Note on G, a lost MS. *of the Fortunatus Commentary.*

In the year 1610 Melchior Goldast, a well-known writer on literary and political subjects, published this commentary at Frankfurt in a small book called *Manuale Biblicum siue Enchiridion S. S. Scripturae a Catholicae Apostolicae ueteris Ecclesiae Patribus compendiatum, et nunc primum ex uetustis membranis* MSS. *collectum, et dicatum V. ac R. Patri, D. Iohanni Muntzenbergio Priori Carmelitarum in Conuentu Francofurdiano.* Apud Egenolphum Emmelium.

The contents included Poems by Prudentius, Sedulius, Helpidius, Theodolus, Theodulf of Orleans. The Gloss on Prudentius and the poem by Theodulf were taken from S. Gall MSS.: the MS. from which the latter was taken has been identified with cod. 197, saec. IX/X.

Then followed 'S. Galli eremitae et confessoris Compendium uet. et noui Testamenti, Armenii et Honorii b. monachorum Diligentia (now S. Gall 191, saec. X), B. Siluii Versus, Euphronii Presbyteri Expositio Fidei Catholicae B. Athanasii,' followed by a fragment *Stephanus Episcopus in Encyclis* from the same MS., a poem by Walafrid Strabo, Abbot of Reichenau, an anonymous poem, and a confession of sins by Cyrinus, Episcopus Frisingensis, which again is stated to be taken from a S. Gall MS.

The description given by Goldast in the Preface is as follows: 'Euphronius Presbyter. Neque de hoc constat, cuiatis fuerit. Suspicor tempore Caroli

use the *ex* of the interpolated Constantinopolitan Creed. It is interesting to remark that the Troyes Commentary, quoting the note on cl. 4 (l. 9), substitutes *ex* for *a*. Eucherius however (*De Just.* i. 1), and Julianus Pomerius (*de uita contempl.* i. 18), a pupil of Faustus, had used *ex* uncontroversially in the 5th century. The use of the Canons of Toledan Councils varied to a great extent between *a*, *ex*, and *de*.

Magni uixisse, quum haeresis Feliciana per Germanias Gallias et Hispanias agitaretur. Nam in dubio Scholasticus aliquis Lector in Coenobio fuit. Nos ex codice monasterii S. Galli exscripsimus.'

Some years ago I found two copies of this book in the Cambridge University Library, and I was able at once to clear up a difficulty which had perplexed Dr Waterland[1]. For he found the first sentence of this commentary quoted by D. Paraeus in the second edition of his book on the Quicunque, under the name of Euphronius. He noted that the first words agreed with the copy in the MS. Junius 25, which he ascribed to Fortunatus, and could not understand the agreement. Obviously between the dates of his editions (1627, 1635), Paraeus had read Goldast's book, which Waterland never saw, though the copies in the University Library may have come there in his time.

A careful comparison of Goldast's edition with a collation of S. Gall 241 convinced me that Goldast was quoting from another MS. now lost, and on my visit to S. Gall in 1894 I followed up the enquiries which I had already made by correspondence with the Librarian, Dr Fäh, to whose kindness and courtesy I owe more than I can say. But the MS. was not to be found there. In the vain hope of obtaining some clue I continued the search in the public Library at Frankfurt, where I thought that some MSS. of Goldast's might be hidden. I have also written in vain to the libraries at Berne and Zurich, where some of the MSS. from S. Gall are preserved. Curiously enough within a few weeks of my return to England Prof. Robinson observed that Card. Pitra had recently printed the same commentary in his *Analecta Sacra et Classica* from Goldast's MS. copy which has been preserved in the University Library at Leyden (Cod. Leidensis Vossianus Graecus in 4°. n°. 30, fol. 144). The Librarian, Dr W. N. du Rieu, had identified this copy with S. Gall 241, but he is now prepared to recognize the force of the objections which I can urge against that view. In the first place, the S. Gall MS. 241 has no title, and it is impossible to believe that Goldast invented the ascription to Euphronius. In the second place, the following important variations are sufficient to distinguish between the original MSS., though there are many cases where in the printed book (*Manuale Biblicum*) it is plain that Goldast has modernized the spelling and in other small ways altered the readings: e.g. on cl. 19 he has combined the questions *Quid sit pater quid sit filius.*

Variations between Goldast's MS. *and S. Gall* 241.

(*o*=Junius 25. *G*=Goldast's MS. *g*=S. Gall 241.)

Sw. p. 436, l. 3. > ecclesia uniuersa *o G*. uniuersa eccl. *g*.
6. *om* et colamus *G*.

[1] p. 46.

14. spiritu] spiritus *o G.*
25. > est solo genitus *o G.*
28. claritatis *o G*, claritas *g.*
64. *om.* atque docente *o G.*
74. *om.* dei filius et homo est *g.*
78. in psalmo *o G*, psalmus *g*+de Christo domino *g.*
86. genitus sit *o G*, genuit filium *g.*
95. +salua uirginitatis gratia *g.*
103. homo]+id est uerus deus uerus homo *g.*
129. conditionis *o G*, conditioni est *g.*
162. celestis *g*, caelestem patriam *o G.*

I hold therefore that Goldast was quoting from a lost S. Gall MS., the discovery of which, if it may yet be found, will be of some importance for the history of the commentary, and, indirectly, of the Creed itself.

CHAPTER III.

DATE AND AUTHORSHIP OF THE CREED.

Internal Evidence. It has long been agreed that the Quicunque was not written by S. Athanasius. All the Greek MSS. are plainly translations from the Latin text[1]. Part of the phraseology shows the influence of S. Augustine, part is plainly Gallican. The Apollinarian heresy is condemned in terms which show considerable development since the days of S. Athanasius. The Creed cannot be earlier than the beginning of the 5th century. But at this point there is a wide divergence of opinions. Are we to look to Africa or to Gaul for the home of the author? Does it belong to Apollinarian, Nestorian, Eutychian or later times? A detailed examination of the internal evidence will help us to give general answers to these questions, and prepare the way for an argument based on the scanty remains of external testimony.

(1) It was S. Augustine who first used freely the method of expressing the equality of the Three Persons in the Trinity by ascribing to each the same attributes, 'uncreate, eternal, omnipotent,' while at the same time he asserted the Unity of the Divine Being by repeating each of these attributes in the singular as referring to the One God. Both S. Ambrose and Faustinus had tried it before him, but very cautiously, and it was never fully illustrated and explained till he wrote the 5th Book of his work *On the Trinity*. Fulgentius afterwards weakened it through the addition of the word 'God'—thus: "one eternal God"—which Waterland rightly calls "a very insipid and dull way of expressing it[2]." Moreover, it was S. Augustine who first brought into clear light the Western doctrine of the Procession of the Holy Spirit,

[1] W. p. 96.

[2] W. p. 214.

which is taught in the Quicunque (clause 22) with the preposition *a*. The Monks of Lerins became staunch supporters of the doctrine. Faustus, in his book *On the Holy Spirit*, uses the prepositions *ex* and *de*, e.g. II. 1. 13, 'mitti a patre et filio dicitur et de ipsorum substantia procedere.' An ancient hymn used by them at Lauds has:—

> Genitori genitoque sit laus, honor, gloria,
> Procedenti ab utroque adiuncta memoria,
> Per quem clero populoque uitae dantur praemia.

There are close parallels in the Creed to sentences in Augustine's *Enchiridion* (c. 420 A.D.), and his 2nd book against Maximinus (c. 427 A.D.). In the year 426 he was in communication with the Bishops of Gaul about a heretical priest named Leporius, who had repented of his error which was akin to Nestorianism. The African Bishops desired to see him restored to the communion of the Gallican Church, and sent him back to Gaul with a profession of faith[1] which is interesting because it contains a full confession of the unity of Christ's person in the perfection alike of Godhead and Manhood. We may therefore argue confidently that the development of the subject in the Quicunque belongs to the same period and not to the times of later Nestorianism.

On the other hand, there are phrases in the Quicunque which seem to be distinctively Gallican. The use of the term *substantia* as the equivalent of *essentia*, though he admits it in some of his later writings (e.g. *c. Max.* II. 1), is actually condemned by S. Augustine in his book *On the Trinity*. He says decidedly: *de Trin.* VII. 5. 1, 'In Deo substantia proprie non dicitur.' He would even use it as a synonym for *persona* (= ὑπόστασις). This was to revive the old misunderstandings between Eastern and Western theologians on the use of the term ὑπόστασις, which came to a head at the Council of Alexandria (362), when S. Athanasius mediated between them[2], showing that the Western use

[1] Hahn, p. 227, ut manente in sua perfectione naturaliter utraque substantia sine sui praeiudicio et humanitati diuina communicent et diuinitati humana participent.

[2] See S. Greg. Naz. *Orat.* 21. 35.

una substantia (= *μία οὐσία*), was not Sabellian, and that the Greek use *τρεῖς ὑποστάσεις* (= *tres personae*) was not Tritheistic.

When the term *persona* came to the front together with the clearer idea of the personality which the Church owes in great measure to S. Augustine, many of the old difficulties due to the imperfect moulding of Latin theological phraseology dropped out of sight. But the old use of *substantia* (= *οὐσία* = *essentia*), which had been consistently maintained in Gaul[1], was continued, and may be regarded as a Gallican contribution to the Quicunque.

Again, there is no closer parallel in Augustine for the phrase *perfectus deus perfectus homo* than Sermon 258: 'perfectam uerbi diuinitatem...perfectam hominis...ueritatem.' S. Vincentius (c. 19) has the exact phrase, which is derived, as Dr Bright[2] shows, ultimately from S. Athanasius, c. *Apollin.* I. 16; cf. *Orat.* III. 41. The Creed of Pelagius has a parallel phrase: 'ut dicamus duas esse perfectas atque integras substantias, id est deitatis et humanitatis quae ex anima continetur et corpore.' So that we may say that the phrase was brought into the Quicunque from a Gallican rather than an African source.

While we find an implicit condemnation of Apollinarianism in cl. 30, 33, there is no reference to the heresies of Eutyches and Nestorius. Dr Waterland[3] has shown this very clearly: (1) "There is not a word directly and plainly expressing two natures in Christ, or excluding one nature, which critical terms against the error of Eutyches are very rarely or never omitted in the Creeds drawn up in Eutychian times, or the times immediately following." (2) "This Creed makes no mention of Christ being consubstantial with us in one nature as He is consubstantial with the Father in another." (3) The ablatives *carne*, *Deo*, which are the older readings of cl. 33, would seem to have been altered into accusatives *carnem*, *Deum*, to "strike more directly at the Eutychian principles," which admitted a change of the Godhead in the flesh, not into flesh. (4) The illustration of

[1] S. Hilary of Poitiers, *De Synodis* 12, Essentia est res quae est, uel ex quibus est, et quae in eo quod maneat subsistit. Dici autem essentia, et natura, et genus, et substantia uniuscuiusque rei poterit. Proprie autem essentia idcirco est dicta, quia semper est. Quae idcirco etiam substantia est, quia res quae est, necesse est, subsistat in sese......

[2] *Lives of Three Great Fathers*, p. 41.

[3] W. p. 144.

cl. 35, "As the reasonable soul, etc.," was used freely by S. Augustine, S. Vincentius and others, but in the heat of the Eutychian controversy it was laid aside[1], because these heretics misused it, pleading for one nature in Christ as soul and body make one nature in man. On these grounds it may be asserted that the Quicunque was not written in Eutychian times. Neither is there, says Dr Waterland (p. 149), "a word of the Mother of God, or of one Son only,...or of God's being born, suffering, dying: which kind of expressions the Creeds are full of after Nestorius' times, and after the Council of Ephesus (431)."

Thus the internal evidence may with some reason be regarded as pointing to the years 426—431 as the date of the composition of the Creed.

(2) A further suggestion may be made, that in this rule of faith special care was taken to guard against the heresy of Priscillianism. Priscillianism was a sort of hazy Sabellianism, with a mixture of Manichean elements and a tendency to an Apollinarian denial of the Lord's human soul. From Spain it had spread widely, especially in the garb of monasticism; and at the beginning of the 5th century all monks who came from Spain were closely examined in their faith. *The Faith of Bacchiarius*, found in the Milan MS. (O. 212 *sup.*) with an early text of the Quicunque, was the defence of such a monk to the Bishops of Gaul, on the doctrines of the Trinity, the humanity of Christ, the resurrection, etc.[2].

Some of the works of Priscillian have recently been discovered in a Würzburg MS. and edited by Dr Schepss[3].

Three passages will suffice to show what Priscillian with great vehemence[4] declared to be Catholic teaching, but they bear out Orosius' judgment on their heretical tendency[5]: "Trinitatem autem solo uerbo loquebatur, nam unionem absque ulla existentia

[1] Vigilius of Thapsus apologizes for it (p. lxxxix *infra*). In the Trèves fragment the preacher omits it.

[2] Neander, *Ch. Hist.* (trans.) IV. p. 507.

[3] Vienna, 1889. *Corpus Script. Eccl. Lat.* Vol. XVIII.

[4] This vehemence seems overstrained, so that one is inclined to doubt his sincerity. Some members of the sect were very deceitful (Neander, IV. p. 511).

[5] Orosii ad Augustinum Commonitorium, Schepss, p. 154.

aut proprietate adserens sublato 'et' patrem filium spiritum sanctum hunc esse *unum Christum* docebat."

1. *Lib. ad Damasum Episcopum* Tract. II. § 45 Cuius symboli iter custodientes omnes hereses doctrinas instituta uel dogmata, quae sibi altercationem non ingenia, sed studia fecerunt, catholico ore damnamus, *baptizantes,* sicut scribtum est, *in nomine patris et fili et spiritus sancti;* non dicit autem 'in nominibus' tamquam in multis, sed in uno, quia unus deus trina potestate uenerabilis, *omnia et in omnibus Christus est* sicut scribtum est: *Abrahae dictae sunt repromissiones*[1]. § 47 Nobis enim Christus deus dei filius passus in carnem secundum fidem symboli baptizatis et electis ad sacerdotium in nomine patris et fili et spiritus sancti tota fides, tota uita, tota ueneratio est.

2. *Benedictio super Fideles,* § 142 Tu enim es deus, qui cum in omnibus originibus uirtutum intra extraque et supereminens et internus et circumfusus et infusus in omnia unus deus crederis, inuisibilis in patre, uisibilis in filio, et unitus in opus duorum sanctus spiritus inueniris.

3. Tract. VI. § 99 Denique deus noster adsumens carnem, formam in se dei et hominis, id est diuinae animae et terrenae carnis adsignans, dum aliud ex his peccati formam, aliud diuinam ostendit esse naturam, illudque *arma iniquitatis* peccato, hoc *iustitiae arma* demonstrat in salutem nostram uerbum caro factus.

The first two of these passages are evidently Sabellian, the third Apollinarian. In the Quicunque we find the best possible antidote to error of this kind, the combination of careful teaching on the Trinity with teaching on the Incarnation. We find the balanced antitheses by which alone the Trinity of eternal distinctions can be expressed, "not confounding the persons." From this point of view cl. 7—19 are seen to be, not "unnecessary amplifications" as Bishop Thirlwall once called them[2], but guarding clauses really needed. Any expansion of the fundamental antithesis, Unity in Trinity, must run into subsidiary antitheses. We find

[1] We may note also that Priscillian in his Creed, if the one MS. is correct, wrote 'Holy Spirit' after 'Holy Church,' thus throwing doubt on his belief in the personality of the Holy Spirit.

[2] Speech in Convocation. Feb. 9, 1872.

further in the Creed (cl. 30) the vindication of Christ's true humanity in contrast to Priscillian's Apollinarian tendency. Moreover the teaching of the dignity of human flesh which was wrongly despised by Manichean teachers is upheld in the Creed, inasmuch as we are taught that He took our human nature upon Him, and we hope for the redemption of our bodies in the Resurrection (cl. 38).

The assertion of free will (in cl. 1) may possibly be due to fear of Priscillianist ideas of astral influences constraining human wills, but more probably it shows the general interest maintained in Gaul in the chief point of the Pelagian controversy.

External Evidence.

We may now leave the internal evidence and follow up the path of external evidence from the 8th to the 5th century. We come upon three or four sign-posts—decrees of councils, a sermon, and a treatise, which make use of the Quicunque for the instruction of the faithful. The paucity of external testimony need not surprise us, when the character of the times is taken into account. Dr Waterland's words are still true, "the injuries of time, of dust, and of moths, and above all the ravages of war and destructions of fire, have robbed us of the ancient monuments and left us but very thin remains; that a manuscript of the 4th century is a very great rarity, of the 5th there are very few, and even of the 6th not many[1]."

(1) The Canon of Autun. We shall begin with the mention of the Faith of Athanasius in the celebrated Canon of Autun. Some new light may be thrown on this hitherto dubious reference.

Without doubt a synod was held at Autun some time between 663 and 680 under Bishop Leodgar. Some of its disciplinary canons have been preserved in the so-called Angers collection[2], which seems to have been made at the beginning of the 8th

[1] p. 139.

[2] This collection was first used by Sirmond from an Angers MS. now lost. The Canons of Autun are also found in the Herovall Collection which is based on the Angers.

century, or within 50 years from the date of the synod. Three out of the seven MSS. extant of this collection contain also on a separate page a Canon on the Faith, which is called the first (hira prima). These three are:—

1. P Cod. lat. Paris, 1603. fol. 7. Saec. IX.[1]
2. E Cod. Phillippsii nunc Berolinensis, 1763. fol. 3. Saec. IX.
3. X Cod. Vindob. 2171. fol. 1′. Saec. IX.

This first Canon runs as follows:

CANONES AGUSTODINENSIS HIRA PRIMA[a].

Si quis presbyter aut diaconus subdiaconus[b] clericus[c] symbolum, quod Sancto inspirante Spiritu apostoli tradiderunt, et fidem Sancti Athanasii[d] presulis irreprehensibiliter non recensuerit[e], ab episcopo condamnetur[f].

[a] Cañ Agūst hir̄, 1. E. Cān. Agustudunensis hr̄ 1. X.
[b] *om.* subdiaconus E. [c] clericus] *pr.* aut E.
[d] Athanasi P. [e] recensiuerit P.
[f] condempnetur X.

It seems reasonable to suppose that this canon on the Faith was made at the same synod as the disciplinary canons and was put first in the record, and that there has been some mistake about the numbering of the disciplinary canons which follow[2]. At the end is found the subscription of Leodgar on behalf of the other Bishops present.

The only real difficulty lies in the question whether the Faith of S. Athanasius referred to was the Quicunque or some other. It is true that Ratramn of Corbey quoted the *Fides Romanorum* as *Libellus de Fide Athanasii*, while he gave the same title to the Quicunque. But the Quicunque received the title *Fides Athanasii* by common consent, as some twelve 9th century MSS. show: but this cannot be asserted of any other document. We may add that, if our suggestion that Euphronius of Autun was the author of

[1] My collation of P is taken from Ommanney, *E. H.* p. 89, of E and X from *Monumenta Germaniae Historica.* Legum sectio iii., Concilia, tom. I. p. 220.

[2] In the Paris MS. the disciplinary canons are numbered 1, 8, 6, 5, 10, 21. Hardouin, *Conc.* III. p. 1016, from another MS. quotes seven, as follows, 1, 5, 6, 8, 10, 14, 15.

On the whole question see also Maassen, p. 213, and pp. 821—833, Om. *E. H.* pp. 88—119, Sw. p. 269.

the Fortunatus Commentary be accepted, we have an example of the designation of the Creed by the title *Fides Cath. b. Athanasii* in the very city in which the synod was held.

(2) 633. Fourth Council of Toledo. Some 40 years before the Synod of Autun a Council was held at Toledo which may be quoted as typical, and for our present purpose as the most important, of a series of councils in the canons of which appeared scattered quotations of the Quicunque. Dr Swainson (p. 245) has analysed the evidence of the whole series and acknowledges that the substance of many clauses is embedded in these doctrinal statements. But he attempts to explain it away by a theory (p. 246) that "the framework of the Athanasian Creed is historically of later date than the Catholic Faith which it contains: the setting is of later date than the gems." Apparently by "the setting" he does not mean only the damnatory clauses, but all that we might call joining clauses, e.g. 26, 27, 28 (Sw. 28, 29, 30), which he says "nowhere appear." This theory leaves him in an awkward dilemma from which there is no escape.

Either the Quicunque in its completed form was compiled from the confessions of this series, which would destroy his theory of two portions separately composed and in the 9th century united; or he must explain the inexplicable phenomenon of the growth in Spain and Gaul of two parallel forms of Creed based on S. Augustine, which in Spain produced as it were a single, and in Gaul a double flower.

The parallels in the earlier Spanish confessions give the wording of the Quicunque quite as exactly as the later. This is just what we should expect to find if in every case these confessions were quoting from a written document which had no more authority than it possessed by its intrinsic merits, being, as Dr Swainson says (p. 252) in this connection, "neat, concise, attractive," in contrast to their "clumsy, verbose, wearisome" effusions.

On the Canon of 633 I am prepared to stake my whole argument. Dr Swainson has not noticed that with the parallels, not to say the quotations, of the Quicunque, are interwoven quotations of a document known as the 'Creed of Damasus[1].' I have

[1] I owe this suggestion to Prof. Robinson. For the text of this Creed see note I.

printed the former in italics, the latter in small capitals. This fact leads directly to the inference that the authors of the Canon were quoting in both cases from written documents. That the Quicunque had taken its present shape is proved by the fact that its clauses are quoted in the proper sequence of numbers. And we can account for the apparent omission of cl. 33, with the characteristic phrase *assumpsit humanitatem*: the phrase of the 'Creed of Damasus,' which is also the phrase of the Te Deum, was preferred: *suscipiens hominem.*

There is another point which must be noticed. Isidore, Archbishop of Seville, who presided over this Council, wrote an important book *On the Offices of the Church,* in which, especially in vol. II. c. 23 'de Regula Fidei,' Dr Swainson searched in vain for quotations of the Quicunque, concluding that it "was not known to him, or, if known, it had no authority." Certain parallels may indeed be found, but they are much less close than those in the canon of the council and we may pass them over, only remarking that Isidore would certainly not feel constrained to quote the Quicunque if he knew it. But there are two letters of his to which Dom G. Morin has again called attention (*La Science Catholique,* July, 1891, p. 675): Ep. 6 (to Duke Claudius) 'Sub anathemate prohibitum legitur in Symbolo, et in illo Sancti Athanasii de fide catholica, diminuere uel addere aliquid.' Again: Ep. 8 (to Bishop Eugenius) 'Sicut illud Sancti Athanasii de fide Sanctae Trinitatis Sancta Ecclesia approbat, et custodit, quasi sit fidei catholicae articulus: Quod nisi quisque fideliter firmiterque crediderit, saluus esse non poterit.' It is true, Dom Morin adds, that Oudin and other critics have questioned the authenticity of these two documents, but with interested motives and without a single reason which is in the least convincing.

The evidence of the Canon of 633 is quite sufficient to support the authenticity of these letters so far as quotation of the Quicunque is concerned.

I here print the Canon from Cod. Nov. saec. X, in the *Spicilegium Casinense,* I. p. 300. I have set in the margin the clause-numbers of the Quicunque.

633. Secundum diuinas scripturas et doctrinam quam a sanctis
Patribus accepimus Patrem et Filium et Spiritum Sanctum unius deitatis
atque substantiae confitemur in personarum diuersitate Trinitatem cre-
4 dentes, in diuinitate unitatem praedicantes *nec personas confundimus*
20 *nec substantiam separamus. Patrem a nullo factum* uel *genitum* dicimus:
21 *Filium a Patre non factum sed genitum* asserimus; *Spiritum* uero
22 *Sanctum nec creatum nec genitum sed procedentem* ex *Patre et Filio*
28 profitemur. Ipsum autem *Dominum nostrum Iesum Christum Dei Filium*
29 et Creatorem omnium, *ex substantia Patris ante saecula genitum*, descen-
disse ULTIMO TEMPORE pro redemptione mundi A PATRE, QUI NUNQUAM
DESIIT ESSE CUM PATRE. Incarnatus est enim ex Spiritu Sancto et sancta
gloriosa Dei genetrice Virgine Maria, et natus ex ipsa, solus autem
Dominus Iesus Christus; unus de sancta Trinitate, anima et carne
(33) PERFECTUM, sine peccato, SUSCIPIENS HOMINEM, manens quod erat, *assu-*
31 *mens* quod non erat: *aequalis Patri secundum diuinitatem, minor Patre*
secundum humanitatem; habens in *una persona* duarum naturarum
(35) proprietates; naturae enim in illo duae, *Deus et homo*, non autem duo
Filii et Dei duo, sed idem una persona in utraque natura, perferens
36 *passionem* et mortem *pro nostra salute:* non in uirtute diuinitatis sed
infirmitate humanitatis. *Descendit ad inferos*, ut sanctos qui ibi tene-
bantur erueret: DEUICTOQUE MORTIS IMPERIO resurrexit, assumptus
37 deinde in coelum *uenturus* est in futurum ad iudicium uiuorum et
mortuorum: cuius nos MORTE ET SANGUINE MUNDATI remissionem pec-
catorum consecuti sumus, RESUSCITANDI AB EO IN DIE NOUISSIMO, IN
ea QUA NUNC UIUIMUS CARNE, et in ea qua resurrexit idem dominus
39 forma, percepturi ab ipso alii pro iustitiae meritis *uitam aeternam*, alii
PRO PECCATIS SUPPLICII AETERNI sententiam. *Haec est catholicae* ec-
40 clesiae *fides;* hanc confessionem conseruamus atque tenemus: *quam*
*quisquis firm*issime custodierit perpetuam salutem habebit.

(3) Caesarius of Arles was born at Chalons and educated by Bishop Silvester. As a young man he entered the monastery of Lerins, where he was ordained and soon made his mark as a preacher. His austerities undermined his health and he was sent to recruit at Arles, where he so won the affections of the people that on a vacancy he was unanimously elected Bishop (503—543). During his episcopate he presided over important Councils, and became one of the leading theologians of Southern Gaul. A critical edition[1] of his works is much needed, but the task is one of exceptional difficulty. Not only did Caesarius himself quote other

[1] The edition promised by Dom G. Morin (O. S. B. of the Abbaye of Maredsous), and founded in part on the collections of Bishop Fessler, may be looked for with much interest.

writers without acknowledgment, but his own sermons after his death were edited under other names. In the Benedictine edition of S. Augustine's works, among the Ps.-Augustinian sermons, no. 244 is one which contains some quotations of the Quicunque which deserve notice, together with an interesting form of the Apostles' Creed. The Benedictine editors ascribed it without hesitation to Caesarius: 'Caesarium re uera sapit.' Unfortunately they gave no reasons for their subjective opinion on the style, and have been copied in their reticence by the authors of the *Histoire Littéraire de la France*[1], by Dr Caspari[2], who quotes the sermon in notes on an *Expositio Fidei* related to it, and by Dr Arnold[3] in his recent monograph on Caesarius. The question of authorship has however been discussed by Dr F. Kattenbusch[4], who in his *History of the Apostles' Creed* has compiled a learned argument from the internal evidence of all the 102 sermons attributed to Caesarius by the Benedictine editors. The sermon literature of the 5th and 6th centuries is indeed a confused mass, but the probability that the greater number of the 102 sermons are really Caesarian is quite sufficient to establish the general principles laid down by Dr Kattenbusch for the identification of the authorship. They brought him to a settled conviction in favour of the attribution of this sermon to Caesarius[5], and on independent lines both Dom G. Morin[6] and a friend of his have come to the same conclusion. I will quote only the traits of style which Dr Kattenbusch and Dom Morin both point out. These are: (*a*) the first words: Rogo et admoneo vos fratres carissimi; (*b*) the characteristic expressions: 'qui fuit latro sit *idoneus*'; 'qui fuit bilinguis *boniloquus*...qui positi sunt in carcere requirite...pedes eorum lavate...et lecta ipsorum praeparate...si haec quae suggessi fratres implere uoluistis...*praestante Domino*.'

This unanimous testimony is reassuring; but the MS. tradition of the sermon still calls to be made the subject of fuller investiga-

[1] *Hist. Litt.* III. 207.

[2] *Kirchenhistorische Anecdota*, I. 283.

[3] Leipzig, 1894.

[4] *Das apostolische Symbol.* Leipzig, 1894. p. 165.

[5] p. 165, "Es ist überraschend wie sicher man sich davon überzeugen kann, dass dasselbe in der That dem C. gehören müsse."

[6] Letter of Dec. 23, 1894.

tion[1]. I have printed the portion which contains quotations from the Quicunque from the Benedictine text with variants from S. Gall 150, saec. VIII (G). Dr Caspari mentions another MS., Cod. Monac. 14,470, VIII/IX; but I find that it entirely omits this portion of the sermon.

The problems connected with the *Expositio Fidei* referred to above, which has been printed independently by Dr Caspari and Mr Ommanney, belong rather to the history of the Apostles' Creed. Caspari calls it a secondary product, a compilation from Sermon 244 and others. He concludes that it was made about the end of the 6th or beginning of the 7th century. Dom Morin is doubtful, and the question cannot be decided without further investigation. I will quote the text of the first of Caspari's two Paris MSS. A third MS., which omits the first quotation of the Quicunque, I have found in Junius 25 of the Bodleian Library.

A.

Ommanney, *E. H.*, p. 396, from 4th App. to S. Aug. (Ps.-Aug. Sermon 244).

Rogo et admoneo uos fratres
1. carissimi ut *quicunque uult*
saluus esse fidem rectam[a] *catho-*
(40) *licam* discat, *firmiter*[b] *teneat, in-*
*uiolatam*que conseruet[c]. Ita ergo
oportet unicuique obseruare ut
credat Patrem credat Filium
15. credat Spiritum Sanctum. *Deus*
Pater Deus Filius Deus et Spiritus
16. *Sanctus* sed *tamen non tres Dii*
7. *sed unus Deus. Qualis Pater*
talis Filius talis et Spiritus
Sanctus. Attamen credat unus-
31. quisque fidelis quod Filius *aequalis*

[a] +et G. [b] firmiterque G.
[c] conseruat G.

B.

Ibid. p. 393, from Paris 3848 B.
Expositio Fidei.

Rogo uos et admoneo, fratres
1. carissimi, *quicunque uult saluus*
(40) *esse fidem rectam catholicam*
2. *firmiter teneat inuiolatamque* con-
seruet; quam si quis digne non
habuerit, regnum Dei non possi-
debit.......Credite et in Ihesum
Christum......natum ex Maria
uirgine, hoc est sine matre de
(29) Patre, *Deus ante saecula,* et
homo de matre sine patre carnali
in finem saeculorum......
(13) Credite et in *Spiritum Sanctum*
*Deum omnipot*entem, unam ha-

[1] Prof. Loofs (*Götting. gel. Anzeigen* 1894, 9) has severely criticised the work of Dr Kattenbusch on the ground that it did not include a fresh examination of the evidence to be drawn from MSS. It was impossible for Dr Kattenbusch to travel so far outside the limits of his investigation, but we may hope that some one will undertake the task.

est *Patri secundum diuinitatem* et *minor* est *Patre secundum humanitatem* carnis quam de nostro assumpsit; Spiritus uero Sanctus ab utroque procedens.

bentem substantiam cum Patre
et Filio. Sed tamen intimare
15. debemus quod *Pater Deus* est et
Filius Deus est *et Spiritus sanctus*
16. *Deus* est, et *non* sunt *tres Dii sed*
unus est Deus. Sicut ignis et
calor et flamma una res est....Ita
ergo Patrem et Filium et Spiritum
Sanctum unum Deum esse confitemur, non tres Deos, sed unum,
ut dixi, unius omnipotentiae,
(6) *unius diuinitatis*, unius potestatis.
Et tamen Pater non est Filius et
Filius non est Pater nec Spiritus
Sanctus aut Pater aut Filius. Sed
Patris et Filii et Spiritus Sancti
una aeternitas, una substantia,
una potestas inseparabilis......
(38) Credite communem omnium corporum resurrectionem.

The problem presented by these varying forms is hard to solve. Each of the sermons must be studied as a whole in its completeness. The type of Apostles' Creed in both is early Gallican, omitting *creatorem caeli*, *omnipotentis* after *Dei Patris*, and inserting *credo* (*et in I. C.*) in the 2nd Article. But A includes *descendit ad inferna*, *sanctam* (*ecclesiam*), *sanctorum communionem*, *uitam aeternam*, while B omits these and *passus*, *mortuus*, and has *corporum* for *carnis* (*resurrectionem*). Thus the type in B seems the earlier. Such marks of priority of date can be explained by the supposition that a scribe was combining with other materials the sermon of Caesarius. This supposition, as Caspari says, suits the great reputation of the popular preacher and the extraordinary spread of his sermons in the 6th and 7th centuries. But Dom Morin[1] thinks

[1] Letter of Dec. 23, 1894. With the testimony of Caesarius we may connect the following parallels in the writings of Columban (†615), the founder of the monasteries of Luxeuil and Bobbio.

(Q. v. cl. 1.) Instructio. Credat itaque primum omnis qui *uult saluus esse* in primum et in nouissimum Deum unum ac trinum, unum subsistentem trinum substantia, unum potentia, trinum persona...

(25) ...ubi habes in ueritate *trinitatem in unitate et unitatem in trinitate.*

This looks like a quotation of the Quicunque, because clause 25 has no complete parallel in Augustine. Columban used the Rule of Caesarius, probably his

that Caesarius himself may have written both forms at different times, since it was his custom to use up and alter old material. If this latter suggestion could be proved one might proceed to the conjecture that the Creed in B was that of his mother Church of Chalons, and the Creed in A that of his second home at Lerins.

We may tabulate the quotations and reminiscences of the Quicunque thus: A 1, (2), 7, 15, 16, 31, 40; B 1, (2), (6), (13), 15, 16, (29), (38), (40).

Dom Morin, following Bishop Fessler, also attributed to Caesarius the 'Address to the Clergy' which has been variously attributed to Pope Eutychius, S. Leo IV. and Ratherius of Verona[1]. In the Munich MS. lat. 5515, saec. XII/XIII, it is found with the rubric: *Sermo beati Caesarii episcopi in praesentia cleri....* The index on the outer cover has: *Item sermo beati Caesarii episcopi ad clerum.*

The following reference to the Quicunque is found on fol. 118: "Sermonem Athanasii episcopi cuius inicium est 'Quicunque uult' memoriter teneat[2]."

But in the *Revue Bénédictine*, Sept. 1895, p. 390, Dom Morin writes: "En dépit de l'inscription...et des expressions césariennes qu'on y retrouve d'un bout à l'autre cet écrit pastoral si intéressant contient aussi 'des traits de l'époque carolingienne qui écartent absolument la paternité de saint Césaire.' (A. Malnory. St Césaire. Paris, 1894, p. 285)."

Is it not possible that the Munich MS. preserves an earlier form?

Thus we find the Quicunque used in a sermon in the early part of the 6th century for the instruction of the faithful, and we are encouraged to trace its history back even further.

(4) Avitus, Bishop of Vienne, 490—523, was born of a senatorial family in Auvergne. He carried on a continuous war against Burgundian Arianism. His force of character won back King Sigismond to orthodoxy, and at a conference held at Lyons in

sermons also, and may have been indebted to him for knowledge of the Quicunque, or to his disciple and successor Attalus who was trained at Lerins.

[1] It is preserved in substance in the *Ordo ad Synodum* of the Roman Pontifical, part III. W. p. 30, attributes it to Ratherius.

[2] Dr von Laubmann (Letter of October 22, 1895) has kindly examined the MS. for me.

499 with some Arian Bishops in the presence of King Gundobad he showed much tact as well as learning. His extant works consist of letters, sermons, theological treatises, and poems; for he was a poet of some mark in his age.

In a work on the Divinity of the Holy Spirit he uses the words of clause 22 of the Quicunque, 'quem nec factum legimus, nec genitum nec creatum'; and again, 'Sicut est proprium Spiritui Sancto a Patre Filioque procedere, istud Fides Catholica, etiamsi renuentibus non persuaserit, in suae tamen disciplinae regula non excedit[1].'

The quotation of clause 22 is so exact, taking both sentences together, that it is hard to believe that Avitus was not quoting from a written copy of the Quicunque. But I have not been able to find another quotation. In one of the fragments of his books against the Arians occur the words: 'In Christo Deus et homo non alter sed ipse: non duo ex diuersis sed unus ex utroque mediator. Gemina quidem substantia sed una persona est.' But these only show that his thoughts were moving on lines parallel to the Quicunque.

(5) Vigilius of Thapsus. A mist of obscurity hangs still round the life of Vigilius and renders doubtful the authenticity of the writings attributed to him. It was his custom to publish dialogues and other treatises under the names of distinguished teachers, Athanasius, Idacius Clarus, Ambrose, Augustine; and his own name was in uncritical times forgotten. A new edition of his works is much needed. The edition by Father Chifflet needs revision in the light of fresh MSS.[2]

He was Bishop of Thapsus in the Byzacene province of Africa, and in 484 attended a conference at Carthage convened by the Vandal King Hunneric. With other orthodox Bishops he subscribed a profession of faith drawn up by Eugenius[3], Bishop of

[1] Mg. LIX., p. 385.

[2] I have noted the following:

c. Arrianos, Grenoble, 258, saec. XII.

c. Felic., Dijon, 150; Phillipps, 241.

c. Eutych. (Anxie te quidem) Orleans 270, 276; Camb. Univ. Lib. Dd. VI. 6.

De Unitate et Trinitate, Camb. U. L. Ff. II. 32. 3; Phillipps, 241; cf. Cod. 509.

[3] Eugenius was sent to the desert of Tripoli, from which he was recalled in 492 by King Trasimund only to be again exiled, when he fled to Gaul.

Carthage, and was exiled. We next hear of him at Naples[1], where he wrote his 12 Books *On the Trinity*. Finally he made his way to Constantinople where he wrote against Eutyches. During his stay at Naples he became acquainted with the Old Roman Symbol; possibly also with the Quicunque, for the parallel passages in his writings show close agreement with clauses in both parts, and he appears to quote a confession of faith containing the words 'Deus et homo,' which might be the Quicunque.

A certain MS., Codex Tuaneus, which contains (i) a treatise by Vigilius called 'Altercatio Athanasii,' (ii) the Nicene Creed and the Faith of the Council of Ariminium, (iii) the Quicunque under the title 'Fides dicta a S. Athanasio,' has been appealed to as suggesting that he may have been the author of the Quicunque[2]. But this theory rests upon very insecure foundations. Is this MS. trustworthy? What treatises can Vigilius be really proved to have written?

The internal evidence of the Quicunque is strongly against the theory. Le Quien[3] has remarked that in the Books against Eutyches Vigilius never uses the phrase 'unitas personae' though he speaks of 'unio.' Vigilius uses the illustration of cl. 35, but with a sort of apology; for the Eutychians made use of it to serve their own heresy. The Descent into Hell was expressed by Vigilius in an African form: 'Descendit ad (in) infernum[4].' He did not assert clearly the Procession from the Son: cf. *De Trin.* XI. 'ut ipse idem sit Spiritus Sanctus procedens a Patre qui est et Filii.' Dr Waterland has remarked with reason that "there does not appear in Vigilius' pieces anything of that strength, closeness and acuteness, which we find in the Athanasian Creed." His

[1] In the preface to his three Books against 'Varimadum Arrianum diaconum' he says: 'Dudum...in Neapoli, urbe Campaniae, constitutus cuiusdam Varimadi... propositionibus...respondens in uno corpore simul de unitate Trinitatis libellos digessi.'

[2] See W. p. 82. This theory was suggested by Paschasius Quesnel (*diss.* xiv. ad opp. Leon. M. p. 384), who was followed by many others, notably Köllner (*Symbolik*, Hamburg 1837, p. 78), to whom Harnack and other German writers refer. I am greatly indebted to Dr Kattenbusch for sending me a copy of Köllner's book, which is rare.

[3] *Dissert. Damasc.*, p. 10.

[4] *c. Eut.* II. 9.

borrowed Athanasian Faith, the so-called Fides Romanorum, in his 12th book *On the Trinity*, is a very inferior production.

But it is possible enough that the Quicunque got its name by association with tracts written by him under the name Athanasius, as in the Cod. Tuaneus. In the 9th century Theodulf of Orleans quoted the Quicunque as the writing of Athanasius immediately after quoting from the *De Trinitate* of Vigilius. Ratramn of Corbey also quotes the Quicunque in the same connection.

The very phrase 'Fides Athanasii' might be taken from the following passage in the second edition of a treatise against Arrius and Sabellius and Photinus, III. 11.

Probabilis igitur et omni ueritatis adsertione subnixa, utpote apostolicis traditionibus communita, ex eorum ueniens regulis Athanasii fides apparuit. Euidentius namque nobis secundum normam fidei catholicae unum Deum ostendit, non tripertitum, non singularem, non confusum, non diuisum...sed ita Patrem et Filium et Spiritum Sanctum propriis exstare atque distingui personis, ut tamen secundum communis naturae unionem unus sit Deus.

The following passage might be understood to refer to the Quicunque.

c. Eutych. i. XIII. Illud etiam solita temeritatis audacia reprehendere solent, cum audiunt Catholicos dicere Deus et homo; arbitrantes huius syllabae et interpositione, duas posse significari personas: sed quam inepte id opinentur ausculta. Quid enim est Deus et homo nisi is qui Deus est et homo factus est non amittendo quod suum erat, sed suscipiendo quod nostrum erat; cum enim praemittimus in confessione Deus, et subsequimur dicentes et homo, non solum Deum manentem sed et hominem eundem adserimus subsistentem.

The following parallels to various clauses of the Creed are interesting.

3. *c. Palladium.* perfecta Trinitas in Unitate consistens. *c. A. S. P.* Bk. III. 9 ac si Trinitas unus Deus est secundum naturae unionem, et unus Deus Trinitas est secundum personarum distinctionem.

5. *De Trin.* II. alius est P. in persona qui vere genuit, et in hoc alter est F. a Patre in persona qui uere ab eo genitus est. sed in hoc alius est in persona Spiritus.

15, 17, 13. *c. Var.* III. 2—4 Deus Pater Deus Filius Deus Spiritus Sanctus. Dominus P. D. F. D. S. S. Omnipotens P. O. F. O. S. S.

26. *De Trin.* XII. ita sentientes de Trinitate.

29. *c. Eut.* I. ante saecula genitum et in fine temporum... suscepisse naturam.

30. (α) *Adv. Eut.* IV. 18 eundem perfectum Deum perfectum hominem. (β) Cf. *De Trin.* XI.

31. *c. Eut.* II. 6 aequalis Patri secundum Deitatem et inferior est Patre secundum humanitatis naturam. Cf. *ib.* IV. 5.

32. *c. Eut.* II. 6 unus est Christus idemque Deus idemque homo.

33. *c. Eut.* I. 4 ut tamen Verbi natura non mutaretur in carnem.

35. *c. Eut.* V. 6 quid ergo inauditum, quid a Scripturis canonicis alienum et peregrinum, ut sicut credimus et experimur unum esse hominem animam rationabilem et carnem, ita credamus unum esse Christum Deum et hominem, sicut Apostoli docuerunt, et sicut nobis uiri apostolici tradiderunt?

(6) The Brotherhood of Lerins. The monastery of Lerins, on a little island near the modern Cannes, was founded in the earliest years of the 5th century by Honoratus, a nobleman from Belgic Gaul. The balmy air and cheerful aspect of the place made it beloved by all who came there, for its beauty as well as for the hallowed associations which grew up around it and were fostered by the daily round of praise and prayer. Like Eastern monks, the Brethren lived in separate cells; but they did not lose themselves in contemplation, and by 'making time for God' were trained to do great deeds. "Happy island," exclaims Caesarius, himself a member of the brotherhood, "which receiving sons made them fathers, and of novices made kings." About the year 426 Honoratus had gathered round him a distinguished band of scholars, Hilary afterwards a famous Bishop of Arles, Vincentius author of the Commonitorium, Lupus who became the saintly Bishop of Troyes, and Faustus who became 3rd Abbot of Lerins and Bishop of Riez, one of the ablest theologians of the time.

On a neighbouring island lived Eucherius, sometime high in the civil service of the Roman Empire, who as Bishop of Lyons set in later days a noble example. It was no empty compliment when Claudianus Mamertinus called him "by far the greatest of the great bishops of his age." His two sons were educated at Lerins and became Bishops.

The times were out of joint. The tide of barbarian invaders began to pour into Gaul without a check, and art and literature were swept away as by a deluge. It was a just judgment upon a corrupt civilisation. All the indignities and inconvenience which the conquered had to suffer, as Sidonius Apollinaris, Bishop of Clermont, tells us in his amusing letters, were only in exchange for the pains and penalties which citizens of the over-taxed and burdened town communities had to suffer in Roman times.

A lurid light is cast on the wild scene of conquest by such a book as Salvian's, *On the Government of God.* He reveals, under the smiling mask of much luxury and light-thinking and constant pleasure-seeking of the gay crowds who thronged theatres and streets from Arles to Trèves, the awful apprehension of coming woe, which called some to serious thought while it drove others to wickedness of more licentious living. The Christian Churches in populous towns had a great future before them. Their Bishops as leading citizens had commanding influence. But new perils were in store for Christian people, and new responsibilities were to be thrust upon their leaders, when they were called to stand defenceless in the breach before terrible barbarian kings, and plead in the name of the Most High for the safety of their people. Thus Lupus, Bishop of Troyes, prevailed over Attila. May we not trace the secret of his power to his training at Lerins in the fresh fervour of the monastic spirit, holding the Catholic Faith in unity, in peace, and in righteousness of life? Thus was fully justified the wisdom of dogmatic teaching; "so faithful," to use the words of Eucherius, "is innocence." An innocent heart feels that "it is something great to follow virtue," alike in humble daily tasks and along the path of dazzling fame.

Faustus, 3rd Abbot of Lerins, Bishop of Riez (454—493), throughout a long life of some 90 years bore the highest character for piety. He was twice exiled by Arian kings, but was recalled, to the joy of his people. By birth he was a Briton, and he was educated as a lawyer; and when his strong bent of character led him to take holy orders, he soon became distinguished as a preacher of rare eloquence and an able theologian. The suspicion of semi-Pelagianism resting on him caused his name to fall into oblivion; his book *On the Holy Spirit* was attributed to Paschasius, his sermons to Eusebius of Emesa. Dr Engelbrecht, the learned editor of his works in the Vienna series of ecclesiastical writers, has vindicated his reputation for orthodoxy. Possibly the name Eusebius[1] was attached (by himself?) to a collection of his sermons as a pseudonym, after the custom of his contemporaries Vincentius and Salvianus, who wrote under the names of Peregrinus and Timotheus. Dr Engelbrecht calls attention to a fact which is of great importance in my present enquiry, viz. that the writings of S. Augustine were much more read by the so-called semi-Pelagians than has been generally supposed. Faustus' funeral sermon on the death of S. Augustine shows that he admired the man, and stood in unconscious rather than conscious opposition to his teaching.

The parallels to the Quicunque noted in my Table (Add. Note G) are some of them very close and all of them new. But Eusebius-sermons are quoted tentatively in brackets as their authorship is disputed. There can be no doubt that they were all written by early preachers of the Lerins school, and may be relied on as offering early parallels in any case. Together with the parallels in Vincentius and Hilary of Arles they suggest the theory that all these writers knew the Creed as it had been taught them orally, and quote its phrases as current theological terms. Caesarius in the following generation quoted from a written original terms which had become stereotyped.

Vincentius of Lerins († 450) has been held by many writers, from the time of Antelmi (1693), to quote the Creed in his Com-

[1] For the Eusebius collection cf. Engelbrecht, *Studien*, p. 27. Dom G. Morin in the *Revue Bénédictine*, Feb. 1892, shows that the Durlach MS. collection of Faustus' sermons contains much of Faustus, but is really a *Homilarium* of Caesarius which was sent far and wide. He quotes a Homilarium of Silos, Brit. Mus. Add. MSS. Cod. 30,853, unknown to Engelbrecht. If this criticism can be justified, it will influence future editors of Faustus' works: but it matters little for my theory of the origin of the Quicunque whether the parallel is found in a sermon of Faustus or Caesarius.

monitorium. The parallels are close enough to warrant the conclusion that there is some relation between the Commonitorium and the Creed, and it is easier to believe that Vincentius both used and illustrated the Creed than that anyone in a subsequent century of less exact scholarship picked out his phrases and wove them into a document of this nature. There is no evidence that Vincentius was himself the author[1]. He was a poet-theologian, and the Quicunque represents rather the grammar than the poetry of theology. His intellect was imaginative rather than analytical, and there is true poetry in his illustrations; as when he compares the growth of religious thought to the growth of the body, changing, yet the same; or when he speaks of the calm harbour guarded by the strong breakwater of the Catholic Faith, within which the soul is in peace, while without are storms, raging winds, and rough waves. His promise to treat of matters of faith in another work, 'Haec in excursu dicta sunt, alias, si Deo placuerit, ulterius tractanda et explicanda,' can only refer to a more elaborate form of the Commonitorium equally diffuse in style, not to the terse, clearly cut sentences of the Quicunque. We seem to have fragments of this work in the second part of the Commonitorium.

I must here examine in detail some points noticed by Dr Swainson (pp. 224, 225): (*a*) "There is no appearance that Vincentius was quoting any particular document." This is true, but it does not exclude the supposition that he quoted by memory phrases of the Quicunque. Dr Swainson goes on to argue that "if there was any document known to Vincentius having the authority we now assign to the Quicunque, and from which Vincentius drew his language, that document would have been quoted by name." This use of the words 'document' and 'authority' is misleading. If Vincentius had seen the Creed written out, he would not have thought of it as an important 'document' in the sense in which the letter of S. Capreolus, which was read at the Council of Ephesus, of which he speaks in chap. 42, was important. The substance of the Quicunque, not synodical sanction, would give it 'authority'; for he would not know it as 'the

[1] Antelmi was misled about the archetype of the Trèves fragment, which he connected with the fact that Vincentius was born near Trèves. We have seen that it belonged to Eutychian times; but of the Eutychian heresy Vincentius says nothing.

Symbol of Athanasius,' and would only receive it as approved by his private judgment and recommended by his love and reverence for those from whom he had received it.

(β) "The Quicunque must (like the Commonitory) have been composed after the Council of Ephesus." Against this the internal evidence which I have already quoted is very strong. Vincentius (c. 12) says that Nestorius wished to make 'two Sons of God'; he on the other hand upholds the title 'Mother of God.' In the Quicunque there is no reference to these points of dispute. We find *unus est Christus*, not *unus est filius*. The Creed of Pelagius, c. 417, before the rise of Nestorianism, fully stated the doctrine of two whole and perfect substances united in one Person. It is not therefore impossible that the Quicunque should have affirmed the same some ten years later. Moreover, if cl. 29 is really pre-Nestorian, we can understand why Vincentius avoided the expressions *ex substantia Patris, ex substantia matris*, set in an antithesis without a guarding word such as 'idem.'

(γ) "Nor do I find the words *assumptio humanitatis in Deo* or *Deum*, or anything equivalent to them." Dr Swainson regards these words as having been unnecessary in the time of Vincentius, but called forth to meet Eutychianism. Now Vincentius (c. 20) uses the phrase *Deus uerbum assumendo et habendo carnem*. He also uses the term *humanitas* freely. He does seem however to shrink from the compound phrase *assumptio humanitatis*. Perhaps the reason can be gathered from c. 17 *ad fin.*, where he is arguing against Nestorius and the theory that 'postea in eum (the Man Christ) assumentis uerbi persona descenderit; et licet nunc in Dei gloria maneat assumptus, aliquamdiu tamen nihil inter illum et ceteros homines interfuisse uideatur.' I take it that he fears a Nestorian interpretation of the *assumptio humanitatis*, if the humanity is not regarded as impersonal. Further, Dr Swainson's theory that *assumptio hum. in Deo* was directed against Eutyches is contradicted by the fact that Eutyches could accept the statement, unless it was enlarged by a denial of any subsequent change of the manhood into God. This was the intention of the later change of reading *in carnem, in Deum*. Accordingly the original phrase was pre-Eutychian.

In c. 19, after a close parallel to cl. 31, which Dr Swainson overlooked, Vincentius adds of the two substances, *una consubstantialis Patri altera consubstantialis matri;* an admirable argument against Eutychianism, though written before the rise of that heresy, and one which would surely have been introduced into the Creed if it had been composed in Eutychian times, especially if the author had borrowed from Vincentius.

(δ) "Vincentius was not acquainted with the writings of Augustine." Certainly there is no mention of Augustine in his book, and the semi-Pelagian sympathies which he seems to have felt would dispose him to think less of that author than his brother monk Eucherius thought, whose experience of official life and wider outlook on the affairs of men would help him to appreciate the versatility of Augustine's genius. Vincentius (Preface) speaks of himself as one who loved seclusion. However, if he did not read Augustine for himself, he had read or heard some one else who was a student of Augustine. The terminology of some sentences is unmistakeably Augustinian. Study of the following test-clauses suggests that the Quicunque is the connecting link, and that the genealogy of the phrases is Augustine-Quicunque-Vincentius.

Cl. 28. *Aug.* Christus Jesus Dei Filius est et Deus et homo.
Quicunque. Jesus Christus Dei Filius Deus et homo est.
Vinc. Christus Filius Dei Deus et homo.

The Quicunque has 'Deus pariter': so Vincentius in another place 'Deum pariter atque hominem,' cf. Faustus, *De Sp. S.* II. 4, but not Augustine.

Cl. 29. (*a*) *Aug.* Deus ante omnia saecula.
Quic. Deus est ex substantia Patris ante saecula genitus.
Vinc. Idem ex Patre ante saecula genitus.

(*β*) *Aug.* homo in nostro saeculo.
Quic. homo ex substantia matris in saeculo natus.
Vinc. idem ex matre in saeculo generatus.

The *idem...idem* of Vincentius shows a fear of Nestorianism not present in the mind of the author of the Quicunque. Indeed the greater part of this chapter (13) is taken up with the confutation of Nestorian statements: 'duos Christos aut semper esse aut aliquandiu fuisse.'

Cl. 34. *Aug.* non confusione naturae sed unitate personae.
Quic. non confusione substantiae sed unitate personae.
Vinc. non diuinitatis et humanitatis confusione sed unitate personae.

As I have pointed out, Augustine shrank from the word *substantia* (= *essentia*), though in his Books against Maximinus he seems to use it with more freedom. But in a Christological connection (= *natura*) he was willing to use it: *In Johann. Tract.* 78. The well-known Ambrosian hymn has, 'Procede de thalamo tuo geminae gigans substantiae[1].' Both Faustus and Vincentius used the word freely in both connections. Why then did Vincentius substitute *diuinitatis et humanitatis* in this sentence, as if he would prefer the plural *non confusione substantiarum* to the singular of the Quicunque form? Because the wording of the Quicunque is pre-Eutychian, the author having no fear of the wresting of the singular in a Eutychian sense; and pre-Nestorian, so that it did not satisfy Vincentius in his endeavour to prove the coexistence of two natures with unity of person.

Honoratus, the founder of Lerins, became Bishop of Arles in 427, but died in 429. The funeral sermons preached in his memory by Hilary and Faustus are almost unique tributes to the influence of spiritual sympathy and strong character. Both of them refer to his zeal for the true faith, and to his careful instructions concerning it.

Hilarius. *Vita Honorati*, c. 38. Quotidianus siquidem in sincerissimis tractatibus confessionis Patris ac Filii ac Spiritus Sancti testis fuisti: nec facile tam exerte tam lucide quisquam de

[1] Faustus in his letter to Graecus quotes it as sung on the Lord's birthday by the Catholic Church throughout Italy and Gaul.

Diuinitatis Trinitate disseruit, cum eam personis distingueres, et gloriae aeternitate ac maiestate[1] sociares.

Faustus. Euseb. Coll. 72 *In Depositione S. Honorati* (sub eius disciplina Deo militare). Sed et modo minus potest gaudere is ...qui patriam uel parentes illius feruore contempserit...qui fideliter sanctam regulam[2] custodierit ab illo allatam et per illum a Christo ad confirmationem loci istius constitutam...Ergo, carissimi, ut adipisci possimus illa quae obtinuit, sequamur illa prius, quae docuit; *teneamus* in primis *fidem rectam*, credamus Patrem et Filium et Spiritum Sanctum unum Deum. Ubi enim est unitas esse non potest inaequalitas, et cum Filius quia Deus est perfectus consummatus et plenus sit; prorsus minor dici non potest plenitudo.

Only the first of these sermons was known to Dr Waterland, who recognised an allusion to the Quicunque, but inferred that Hilary was quoting his own composition. He was partly misled by the statement of Hilary's biographer that he wrote "an admirable exposition of the symbol," which he supposed to refer to the Quicunque, but which in truth more probably refers to the Apostles' Creed[3]. The Quicunque cannot be called an exposition of the Creed, although it is an enlargement of certain Articles[4]. The sermons of Faustus and of Nicetas which belong to this period discuss the Apostles' Creed clause by clause on a very different plan.

By the evidence of these two sermons I have been led to suppose that Honoratus himself may have been the author of the Quicunque. Surely all the fire of a true teacher's enthusiasm would be kindled in him when he addressed disciples so well informed and so earnest. A student of S. Augustine and able to

[1] Gloriae...maiestate. Is not this a reminiscence of the Te Deum in a verse which is parallel to cl. 6 of the Quicunque? It agrees with the text of the Te Deum quoted by Cyprian, Bishop of Toulon, in Cod. Colon. 212.

[2] It is worth while to point out that the word *regula* passed through the same phases of meaning as the word *fides*. It meant (1) a rule shaping a result, (2) a shaped result or creed; as faith referred to the content before it referred to the form.

[3] W. was also mistaken about a MS., now Laud. Lat. 493, which he supposed gave to the Quicunque the title Anastasii Expositio Symboli Apostolorum, Om. *A. C.*, p. 328.

[4] Heurtley, *Hist. Earlier Form.*, p. 129.

assimilate his teaching, he would give them, we may imagine, in the Quicunque a worthy instruction, a summary of their Faith. This theory of the authorship is certainly speculative, but it harmonizes with my suggestion that the warnings of the Creed were directed against the loose pietism of the Priscillianists. In such a case we are content with a probability. We do not receive the Creed as the faith of any individual teacher, but as the faith of the Universal Church. We are content to trace it to the Island-home which sent forth into the world so noble a band of confessors and martyrs. "Peace also has its martyrs," wrote Hilary of Honoratus. These men were ready to live or die for the Creed they taught, because on their lips it was no mere assertion of formal orthodoxy, but while "acknowledging the glory of the eternal Trinity," they desired with true reverence and deep devotion, "in the power of the Divine Majesty to worship the Unity."

Summary.

A short summary may enable the reader who has followed the investigation of the early history of the Athanasian Creed thus far to look back over the steps which he has been led to take. We began with the evidence of 8th and 9th century documents which contain the entire Creed. Of such there is no lack. The only thing needful is that they should be carefully collated and their evidence made accessible. I have endeavoured to contribute something to this end in the *apparatus* to the text of the Creed which follows this discussion. As a supplement I have added a list of the quotations found in writings of that period, and a chart to show at a glance which clauses were quoted (Add. Notes A and B).

The evidence of the quotations in the profession of Denebert and the Trèves fragment was then discussed, with a view to the examination of the 'two-portion theory' which has been founded upon them. I gave reasons for rejecting that theory, and offered an explanation of the limited scope of the quotations in each case.

The next stage in our enquiry led to a survey of the early commentaries on the Creed. I have further compiled a list of all that I can discover down to the 16th century (Add. Note C).

Turning to the important question of the text of the Quicunque imbedded in the earliest of them, I showed that those commentaries which must be assigned to the 9th century (Bouhier, Orleans, and Stavelot) have later readings; whereas the three commentaries (Oratorian, Paris, Troyes) which may be assigned to the 8th century have earlier readings. Thus we have a confirmation of the evidence of 8th century and early 9th century MSS. of the Creed.

The external evidence of the Fortunatus Commentary did not take us beyond the 8th century, but we saw that the internal evidence pointed to a much earlier date, probably even to the 5th century. The omission of certain clauses in the first portion of the Creed, as quoted by the author of this commentary, proved capable of a satisfactory explanation. One S. Gall MS. (now lost) has been declared to ascribe the authorship to a 'Euphronius presbyter.' I have shown that it would not be unreasonable to identify him with Euphronius, Bishop of Autun in the 5th century.

From the internal evidence of the Fortunatus Commentary we passed to the internal evidence of the Creed itself. We saw that it points conclusively to the period immediately preceding the rise of Nestorianism, and that its writer must have been a Gallican student of S. Augustine.

Retracing the path of external evidence from the 8th century, we observed that the quotations in the Canons of the Council of Toledo (633), in the sermon of Caesarius of Arles, and in the treatise of Avitus of Vienne, support the theory of the 5th century origin of the Creed in its entirety. We came, lastly, to a group of writers who were fellow-students in the monastery of Lerins, in which Caesarius had been trained. The parallels in their writings (Add. Note G) are close enough to warrant the conclusion that some one belonging to their school of thought was the writer of the Creed. Their abbot and teacher Honoratus had laid down similar lines of belief in expansion of the baptismal Creed. If, then, we must be content to remain in uncertainty about its actual authorship, yet we may with some measure of confidence trace back the history of the Quicunque to Lerins and the years 425—430 A.D.

In conclusion we may say that the chief interest of these researches is centred in the hypothesis that the Quicunque belongs to the 5th century; that is to say, to an age of original thought, the age of S. Augustine himself, and not to an age which could only make a patchwork theology out of his writings. The author seems to have adapted phrases which he had borrowed from S. Augustine as current terms, not confining himself to slavish reiteration like later writers. The Church of Gaul had then a special gift for full-toned and worthy liturgical language[1] to which the present forms of the Apostles' Creed and the Te Deum bear witness. Avitus and Caesarius, the inheritors of lofty traditions, might be expected to quote the Quicunque with appreciation as the product of their own spiritual home. But the 6th and 7th centuries were for Gaul an age of failing culture, of weakened and crude theology, an age in which such a composition is unimaginable; in which, as a matter of fact, the very faculty of appreciating its terse, incisive style and the accuracy of its definitions had failed. Gregory of Tours, earnest and orthodox as he was, while he bewailed his bad grammar, had equal reason to bewail his lack of theological perception. From Lerins a few copies were spread possibly through Euphronius to Autun, through Columban or Attalus to Bobbio. The commentaries show that it was not forgotten. After the revival of learning in the 8th century it found its way into Psalters in company with the Te Deum. Thenceforward its history is well known.

[1] Zahn, *Das apostolische Symbolum.* Erlangen, 1893. p. 9.

TEXTS AND ADDITIONAL NOTES.

I. The text of the *Quicunque uult* edited from early MSS. and Commentaries.

II. Texts of Commentaries: (1) Orleans, (2) Stavelot, (3) Troyes, (4) Fortunatus.

III. Additional Notes.

A. List of 8th and 9th century testimonies.
B. Chart showing which clauses were quoted by 8th and 9th century authors and early Commentaries.
C. A list of Commentaries.
D. Victricius of Rouen.
E. Fulgentius of Ruspe.
F. The date of the Utrecht Psalter.
G. Tables of parallels in Augustine, Vincentius, Faustus and others.
H. Chart of the Lerins Brotherhood.
I. The Fides Romanorum and the Creed of Damasus.
J. Ps.-Gennadius *De Fide*.

TEXTS. I. THE TEXT OF THE QUICUNQUE FROM MSS. OF THE 8TH AND 9TH CENTURIES.

Symbols[1]		Psalters	Saec.	Title	Descriptions Sw.	Om. E. H.
A (*a*)	Paris B.N. 3836. Trèves fragment. Canons (Coll. S. Blasien)		VIII	—	262	
B (*b*)	Milan O. 212 *sup.* Collection		VIII	None	313	
C (*g*)	S. Germain 257. Collection (lost)		VIII	Fides S. Ath. epi.	329	
D (*t*)	Paris B. N. 1152. Psalter of Charles the Bald	G	IX	F. S. Ath.	363	
E (*x*)	(Claudius C. VII) Utrecht Psalter	G	(IX)	Fides Catholica	363	
F (*z*)	B. M. Galba A. XVIII. Psalter	G	IX/X	F. S. Ath. Alex.	366	
G_1 (*u*)	S. Gall. 20. Psalter	G	IX *in.*	F. C. S. A. epi.	361	
G_2 (*l*)	„ 15. „	G	IX	F. C. edita a S. A. A. epo.	354	
G_3 (*m*)	„ 23. „	G	IX	F. C. S. A. epi.	354	
G_4 (*n*)	„ 27. „	G	IX	F. S. A. epi.	355	
H (*ac*)	B. M. Reg. 2. B. V. Psalter	R	IX/X	Hymnus A de Fide Trinitatis	374	
L	Lambeth Palace Library 427. Psalter	G	IX/X	F. C. S. A. epi.		
P_1 (*k*)	Paris B. N. 13,159. Psalter	G	VIII	None	350	181
P_2 (*h*)	„ 4858 (cl. 1—11) with Works of Eusebius		VIII	None		171
P_3 (*d*)	„ 1451. Canons (Coll. S. Maur)		VIII	F. C. S. Atanasi epi. A.	268	174
P_4 (*bb*)	„ 3848 B. Canons (Coll. Herovalliana)		IX	F. S. A. epi.	268	92
Q (*q*)	C. C. C. Cambridge 272. O. 5. Psalter	G	IX	F. C.	357	
S (*s*)	„ „ 411. N. 10. Psalter	G	IX	F. S. Anasthasii epi.	359	
U (*c*)	Vatican Pal. 574. Canons (Coll. Lorsch.)		IX	F. Catholicam	267	170

Symbols[1]		Psalters	Saec.	Title	Descriptions Sw.	Om. *E. H.*
V (*e*)	Vienna 1032. Works of S. Isidore		IX	F. C. S. Atanasi epi.	322	
Y (*y*)	„ 1861. Golden Psalter	G	IX	F. S. A. epi. A.	372	
	Psalter of Lothaire now in a private collection	G	IX	F. C. tradita a S. A. A. epo.		167
(W)	Old German Version, Wolfenbüttel		VIII/IX	None	482	129
	Commentaries.					
Fort	Fortunatus, commentary in Junius 25		IX	F. C.	423	47
Tr	Troyes, com. in Troyes 804		X	F. C.		3
Or_1	Oratorian com. in Troyes 804		X/XI	F. C.		4
Or_2	„ „ Cod. Vat. 231		X	None	459	
Bou_1	Bouhier, com. in Troyes 1979		X	F. C. S. A. epi.		11
Bou_2	„ „ Br. Mus. Add. MSS. 24,902		X/XI	F. C.		
Bou_3	„ „ Troyes 1532		XII	F. C. S. A. epi.		
Orl	Orleans, com. (fonds de Fleury) 94		IX	F. C.		
Paris	Paris, com. in Paris B. N. 1012		X	F. C.		23
Stav	Stavelot, com. in Br. Mus. Add. MSS. 18,043	G	X	F. C. S. A.		67
Den	Profession of Denebert 798 A.D. (Cleopatra E. 1)		XII	(F. C.)	285	
Tol	Conc. Toletanum 633 A.D. (Cod. Nov.)		X	None	233	

[1] A—F and H are so denoted in Dr Lumby's edition, Dr Swainson's symbols I give in brackets (*a*), (*b*), &c. See Addenda, p. xi.

I. THE TEXT OF THE QUICUNQUE FROM MSS. OF THE 8TH AND 9TH CENTURIES AND COMMENTARIES.

[1]Quicunque uult saluus esse ante omnia opus est ut teneat catholicam fidem, [2]quam nisi quisque integram inuiolatamque seruauerit absque dubio in aeternum peribit. [3]Fides autem catholica haec est ut unum deum in trinitate et trinitatem in unitate ueneremur: [4]neque confundentes personas, neque substantiam separantes. [5]Alia est enim persona patris alia filii alia spiritus sancti, [6]sed patris et filii et spiritus sancti una est diuinitas, aequalis gloria, coaeterna maiestas. [7]Qualis pater talis filius talis et spiritus sanctus. [8]Increatus pater increatus filius increatus et spiritus sanctus. [9]Immensus pater immensus filius immensus et spiritus sanctus. [10]Aeternus pater aeternus filius aeternus et spiritus sanctus, [11]et tamen non tres aeterni sed unus aeternus: [12]sicut non tres increati nec tres immensi sed unus increatus et unus immensus. [13]Similiter omnipotens pater omni-

The paraphrases in A and Paris are not included in this apparatus: see above, p. xxxvi. The following MSS. are used in this apparatus: those which are not represented in their completeness are within brackets—B(C)(D)EF$G_{1,2,3,4}$HL$P_{1,2,3,4}$QS(U)(V)(Y)(W). I have used Mr Ommanney's collations of the Paris MSS.: for those in brackets I have taken Dr Swainson's.

1—27 *deest in* A   1 Quicumque BFH   ult L   > esse saluus B   est] + enim H   > fidem cath. Den   chatolicam FP_1 Paris   2 quisque] quis B   inuiuolatamque B   *om* absque dubio P_2 *ad fin*: Incipit de Fide H   3 trinitatem] trinitate P_1 4 confudentes B; confundantes HP_3 substantia P_2 5 > enim est Den   alia persona filii alia persona spiritus sancti B   spiritus] *pr* et $G_{1,2,3,4}$ 6 sed patris et fili et s̅p̅s̅ s̅c̅i̅ *supra lin e recentiori manu* B   coaeterna] *pr* et Or; quo-aeterna $P_{2,3}$Orl Paris   7, 8, 9, 10, 13, 15, 17 *om* et L Bou Orl; et *eras* S   7, 9, 10 *om* et W Stav   13, 15, 17 *om* et B   15, 17 *om* et Stav   8 *om* et B Or_2 8, 9, 10 > 10, 8, 9 aeternus...increatus...inmensus P_3 (cf. 11, 12)   9 inmensus (*semper*) BFHG_2G_4*LQS Fort Tr Or Bou Paris   *om* et B Or_2 Paris   10 *om* et BG_2 11 et] *om* EF   tres] .III. B   unus aeternus] *def* P_2 12 > unus inmensus et unus increatus B

potens filius omnipotens et spiritus sanctus, [14]et tamen non tres omnipotentes sed unus omnipotens. [15]Ita deus pater deus filius deus et spiritus sanctus, [16]et tamen non tres dei sed unus est deus. [17]Ita dominus pater dominus filius dominus et spiritus sanctus, [18]et tamen non tres domini sed unus est dominus. [19]Quia sicut singillatim unamquamque personam et deum et dominum confiteri christiana ueritate compellimur, ita tres deos aut dominos dicere catholica religione prohibemur. [20]Pater a nullo est factus nec creatus, nec genitus. [21]Filius a patre solo est, non factus nec creatus sed genitus. [22]Spiritus sanctus a patre et filio, non factus nec creatus nec genitus est sed procedens. [23]Unus ergo pater non tres patres, unus filius non tres filii, unus spiritus sanctus non tres spiritus sancti. [24]Et in hac trinitate nihil prius aut posterius, nihil maius aut minus, sed totae tres personae coaeternae sibi sunt et coaequales: [25]ita ut per omnia sicut iam supradictum est et trinitas in unitate et unitas in trinitate ueneranda sit. [26]Qui uult ergo saluus esse ita de trinitate sentiat. [27]Sed necessarium est ad aeternam salutem ut incarnationem quoque domini nostri Iesu Christi fideliter credat. [28]Est ergo fides recta ut credamus et confiteamur quia dominus noster Iesus Christus dei filius deus pariter et homo est. [29]Deus est ex substantia patris ante saecula genitus, et homo est ex substantia matris in saeculo natus. [30]Perfectus deus, perfectus homo ex anima rationali et humana carne

14 *om* tamen B   nec tamen Bou   16, 17 > 17, 16 Or   16 tres] .III. B dii FHLQS   *om* est BP_1 18 tres] .III. B   *om* est B   19 *om* sicut P_1 singulatim L *om* et 1° CEF$G_{1,2,3,4}$HLQS Or Bou Orl Stav   et 2°] ac Or Orl Stav   christiane P_1 conpellimur BFHQS   tris P_1 aut] ac Bou_2 dominos] *pr* tres E$P_{3,4}$ Or $Bou_{1,3}$ dicere] dici P_4 relegione Paris   proibemur Q Paris   ita tres...prohibemur *in marg* G_4 20 > factus est Den   21 nec] aut Or   22 nec 1°] aut Or *om* est B$G_{1,2,3,4}$HLP_3QSU Paris Den   procedens] + patri et filio coaeternus est B, *cf symb Damasi sec*   23 *om* sanctus P_1 tres] *pr* sed Or_2; tris P_1; .III. B (*ter*) 24 et 1°] sed Or   *om* et in hac C   hac] ac P_3*; a Paris   quo-eternę P_1; quohaeternae P_3; quoaet- Or Paris   quoequales P_1; quoaeq- Q Or Paris 25 supradictum] superius dictum P_1*   trinitas in u- et u- in t-] BE$G_{1,2,3,4}$HL$P_{1,3}$Q S^{corr}UVW Or $Bou_{1,3}$ Paris Stav Den; > unitas in t- et t- in u- CDFP_4Y Fort? Bou_2 Orl 26 senciat Paris   27 *om* est P_1 domini] *hic inc* A   Iesu] $\overline{\text{Ihu}}$ BFHLQS   fideliter *pr* unusquisque *in marg e recentiori manu* Q   credat] + s. qui uult saluus esse *supra lin* S   28 *om* dei filius Or   deus] *pr* et BCG_1P_3 Paris   pariter] ABCDG_2*HL* P_1*P_4S*U Fort Tr Or Paris Stav *in marg* Q^{corr}; *om* pariter EF$G_{1,3,4}P_3$VY Bou Orl 29 *om* est $Bou_{1,3}$ ex] de AD (*bis*)   ante saecula genitus et *in marg e recentiori manu* B   *om* et BCDFP_4 Tr Or $Bou_{1,3}$ *om* est 2° ACDFH Tr $Bou_{1,3}$ in secula HP_1; a saeculo Y   30 rationabili ABCDQ* Tr Stav; racionabile P_1 Fort   umana P_3

subsistens. [31]Aequalis patri secundum diuinitatem, minor patri secundum humanitatem. [32]Qui licet deus sit et homo non duo tamen sed unus est Christus. [33]Unus autem non conuersione diuinitatis in carne sed assumptione humanitatis in deo. [34]Unus omnino non confusione substantiae sed unitate personae. [35]Nam sicut anima rationalis et caro unus est homo, ita deus et homo unus est Christus: [36]qui passus est pro salute nostra, descendit ad inferna, resurrexit a mortuis, ascendit ad caelos, sedet ad dexteram patris: [37]inde uenturus iudicare uiuos et mortuos, [38]ad cuius aduentum omnes homines resurgere habent cum corporibus suis et reddituri sunt de factis propriis rationem. [39]Et qui bona egerunt ibunt in uitam aeternam, qui uero mala in ignem aeternum. [40]Haec est fides catholica quam nisi quisque fideliter firmiterque crediderit saluus esse non poterit.

31 aequalis + est Or$_2$ (*bis*) secundum] sedum P$_3$ patri 2° AEFP$_{1,3}$ Fort Tr Or Paris 33 conuers××ione (at *ut uid eras*) B in carne...deo ABCDEFG$_2$H LP$_{1,3,4}$Q (-nae) SUV Fort Or$_1$ Paris; carne...diuinitate Tr; carnem...deum G$_1$ Or$_2$ Bou$_1$ Orl; carnem...deu× (m *eras*) G$_3$; carne...deum Bou$_{2,3}$Stav; carne× (m *eras*)...deum G$_4$; carnem...deo Y adsumptione BFHP$_3$*,$_4$E Stav; adsuptione P$_1$; adsumpsione Paris 34 unitatis persone P$_3$ 35 rationabilis B Tr; racionabilis Paris *om hunc uers* A 36 saluta U > pro salute n. passus est Or discendit B; descendat P$_3$ ad inferna] A Fort Or Stav; ad infernum Tr Paris; ad inferos B (-nos C)DEFG$_{1,2,3,4}$ HLP$_{1,3,4}$QSUVY Bou Orl Tol resurrexit] *pr* tertia die E (*cum lin* G$_4$) HL Or Bou Orl; > die tertia A Tr; *sine* tertia die BCDFG$_{1,2,3}$P$_{1,3,4}$Q*S*UVYW Fort Paris Stav Tol surrexit BP$_3$ Fort Bou cuelos F sedit BEHP$_{1,3,4}$ ad] a P$_1$ dexteram] + dei BDEFG$_{1,2,3,4}$HP$_{1,3}$QSY Bou Orl Stav patris] + omnipotentis CEFG$_{1,2,3,4}$HLP$_{1,3,4}$QSY Bou Orl Stav 37 uenturus] + est H et] ac B 38 ad ...et] *om* a e F cum] in AB 39 uitam aeternam] + ××××× (? salui *eras*) P$_3$ erunt in resurrectionem uitę P$_3$ aet.] a *eras bis* L qui 2°] *pr* et DEFH qui uero m. *secunda manu ut uid* Q *om* uero ABEFP$_1$ Paris mala] + egerunt Or 40 Haec] a *eras* L fides] + fides P$_3$ chatolica P$_3$ firmiterquae P$_3$ *om* que G$_3$ crediderit] + atque seruauerit G$_2$

II. Texts of Commentaries.

(1) The Orleans Commentary. (Orleans MS. 94, S. IX.)

In this commentary I have printed the text of the Creed, so far as it is given by M. Cuissard, in small capitals, and quotations from other commentaries in italics. Scripture quotations are not indicated. The letters in the margin refer to the commentaries quoted: Fortunatus, Troyes, Paris, Stavelot.

INCIPIT EXPLANATIO FIDEI CATHOLICAE.

QUICUNQUE UULT SALUUS—CATHOLICAM FIDEM. Qualiscumque homo sit 1
qui uult saluus esse, ante omnia, ante ullam operationem opus et necessitas
est ut teneat catholicam fidem. *Catholica* graecus sermo est in nostra
locutione *uniuersalis, fides credulitas siue credentia.* QUAM NISI QUISQUE— 2
IN AETERNUM PERIBIT. Quam fidem nisi quisque integram inuiolatamque,
hoc est, inuiolata quae non est uiolata, tenere debet; hoc non debet credere
quod *pater maior* sit *quam filius*, nec *filius minor quam pater*, nec *spiritus
sanctus* minimus: qui hoc credit absque dubio in aeternum [non][1] peribit.
FIDES AUTEM CATHOLICA—IN UNITATE UENEREMUR. Fides autem catholica, 3
credulitas siue credentia uniuersalis, haec est, ostendit quidem ut unus deus
una substantia sit, quomodo una substantia sicut dicit in ueteri testamento:
audi, Israel, dominus deus tuus deus unus est. In trinitate patrem et filium
et spiritum sanctum, trinum in personis, et unum in diuinitate, sed tamen
istas tres personas in una substantia ueneremur, sicut dicit propheta: *bene-
dicat nos dominus deus noster, benedicat nos dominus.* NEQUE CONFUNDENTES 4
PERSONAS NEQUE SUBSTANTIAM SEPARANTES. Neque confundentes personas,
sicut Sabellius, qui credebat unam substantiam et unam personam et non
credebat tres personas: ibi illas confundebat, quia illas non credebat.
Dicebat quod pater ipse sibi fuisset filius et filius ipse sibi fuisset pater:
spiritus sanctus similiter. Neque substantiam separantes, sicut Arius,
qui credebat tres substantias et tres personas. Dicebat quod Pater per se
habuisset suam substantiam et filius per se habuisset suam substantiam et
spiritus sanctus similiter. Credebat *patrem majorem quam filium et filium* S.
minorem quam patrem et spiritum sanctum minissimum. Dicebat patrem T.
quasi aurum, filium quasi argentum, spiritum sanctum quasi aeramentum.

[1] The photograph shows that this MS. omits *non*: but it is plainly required by the sense.

P. 5 ALIA EST ENIM PERSONA PATRIS ALIA FILII ALIA SPIRITUS SANCTI. *Pater
per se sonat, quia suam proprietatem personarum tenet pater eo quod genuit
filium ; filius per se sonat, quia suam proprietatem personarum filius tenet,
spiritus sanctus per se sonat, quia suam proprietatem personarum tenet,
quia ex patre et filio procedit. Pater ingenitus, quia a nullo est genitus ;
filius genitus, eo quod a patre est genitus ; spiritus sanctus nec genitus,
6 nec ingenitus, sed ex patre et filio, ex utroque procedens est. SED PATRIS
ET FILII—QUOAETERNA MAIESTAS. Una est diuinitas, una est gloria, una
7 est maiestas, una est uirtus. QUALIS PATER—TALIS SPIRITUS SANCTUS.
F. 8 Istae tres personae in una substantia consistunt. INCREATUS PATER—
INCREATUS SPIRITUS SANCTUS. Increatus pater, quia *a nullo* est *creatus*,
increatus filius, quia semper fuit cum patre et spiritus sanctus similiter.
F. 9 IMMENSUS PATER—IMMENSUS SPIRITUS SANCTUS. Immensus est, quia *non
10 *est mensurabilis*. AETERNUS PATER—AETERNUS SPIRITUS SANCTUS. Quo-
modo aeternus pater, quia aeternum habet filium, quomodo aeternus filius,
quia aeternum habet patrem, similiter et spiritus sanctus apud patrem
11, 12 et filium aeternitatem habet. ET TAMEN NON TRES AETERNI, SED UNUS
AETERNUS. SICUT NON TRES INCREATI NEC TRES IMMENSI SED UNUS IN-
CREATUS ET UNUS IMMENSUS. Unus est immensus, quia omnia creavit.
13 SIMILITER OMNIPOTENS PATER OMNIPOTENS FILIUS OMNIPOTENS SPIRITUS
14—18 SANCTUS tamen in diuinitate unus est. ET TAMEN NON TRES OMNI-
POTENTES SED UNUS OMNIPOTENS. ITA DEUS PATER DEUS FILIUS DEUS
SPIRITUS SANCTUS, ET TAMEN NON TRES DII SED UNUS EST DEUS. ITA
DOMINUS PATER DOMINUS FILIUS DOMINUS ET SPIRITUS SANCTUS, ET TAMEN
NON TRES DOMINI SED UNUS DOMINUS. QUIA SICUT SINGILLATIM UNAM-
QUAMQUE PERSONAM DEUM AC DOMINUM CONFITERI CHRISTIANA UERITATE
COMPELLIMUR. Quia sicut singillatim, sicut separatim ; unamquamque
personam deum et dominum christiana ueritate compellimur siue sugge-
19 rimur confiteri. ITA TRES DEOS AUT DOMINOS DICERE CATHOLICA RELIGIONE
PROHIBEMUR si potest dicere tres deos, semper unam substantiam debemus
20—22 tenere. PATER A NULLO EST FACTUS NEC CREATUS NEC GENITUS. FILIUS
A PATRE SOLO EST NON FACTUS NEC CREATUS SED GENITUS. SPIRITUS
SANCTUS A PATRE ET FILIO NON FACTUS NEC CREATUS NEC GENITUS SED
23, 24 PROCEDENS. Spiritus sanctus de patre et filio procedens est. UNUS ERGO
PATER NON TRES PATRES UNUS FILIUS NON TRES FILII UNUS SPIRITUS
SANCTUS NON TRES SPIRITUS SANCTI. ET IN HAC TRINITATE NIHIL PRIUS AUT
POSTERIUS NIHIL MAIUS AUT MINUS, nisi una trinitas et una substantia,
SED TOTAE TRES PERSONAE QUOAETERNAE SIBI SUNT ET QUOAEQUALES. Istae
25 tres personae in diuinitate aequales sunt. ITA UT PER OMNIA SICUT IAM
SUPRA DICTUM EST ET UNITAS IN TRINITATE ET TRINITAS IN UNITATE UENE-
26, 27 RANDA SIT. QUI UULT ERGO SALUUS ESSE ITA DE TRINITATE SENTIAT. SED
NECESSARIUM EST AD AETERNAM SALUTEM UT INCARNATIONEM DOMINI NOSTRI
IHESU CHRISTI FIDELITER CREDAT. Sed necessarium est ad aeternam
salutem, necessitas est ut unusquisque homo istam incarnationem domini
28 nostri Ihesu Christi fideliter credat. ERGO FIDES RECTA UT CREDAMUS ET

CONFITEAMUR QUIA DOMINUS NOSTER IHESUS CHRISTUS DEI FILIUS DEUS ET
HOMO EST. Deus secundum diuinitatem, homo secundum humanitatem,
tamen unus est. DEUS EST [EX ?] SUBSTANTIA PATRIS ANTE SAECULA 29, 30
GENITUS ET HOMO EST EX SUBSTANTIA MATRIS IN SAECULO NATUS. PER-
FECTUS DEUS, secundum diuinitatem, PERFECTUS HOMO, secundum humani-
tatem, tamen unus est deus et perfectus homo, EX ANIMA RATIONALI
ET HUMANA CARNE SUBSISTENS. AEQUALIS PATRI SECUNDUM DIUINITATEM 31
MINOR PATRE SECUNDUM HUMANITATEM. QUI LICET DEUS SIT ET HOMO 32
NON DUO TAMEN SED UNUS EST CHRISTUS. UNUS AUTEM NON CON- 33
UERSIONE DIUINITATIS IN CARNEM SED ASSUMPTIONE HUMANITATIS IN
DEUM. Unus ergo, unus deus, unus dei filius, quia proprius filius est;
non conuersione diuinitatis in carnem, illa diuinitas dei non potest esse
versa in carnem ut *desistat sua diuinitas, quod deus non sit*[1] et fiat caro,
quia non potest separari a deo patre, sed ipse filius, quia proprietatem
personarum filii tenet. Ipse percepit humanitatem et sic complacuit cum
humanitate, ut unus deus efficiatur, ut sicut erat perfectus, deus ex sub-
stantia patris si fieret perfectus homo ex substantia matris. UNUS OMNINO 34, 35
NON CONFUSIONE SUBSTANTIAE SED UNITATE PERSONAE. NAM SICUT ANIMA
RATIONALIS ET CARO UNUS EST HOMO ITA DEUS ET HOMO UNUS EST CHRISTUS.
Homo ex duabus substantiis constat et anima et corpore, ita deus et homo
unus est Christus. Ille quando apprehendit humanitatem nostram, tunc
fuit perfectus deus et perfectus homo. *Christus*, is sermo est in nostra F. T.
locutione unctus, sicut psalmista dicit: *Propterea unxit te deus tuus.* Ille
quando accepit humanitatem nostram, erat maculata et praeuaricata a
diabolo, et sicut eam purgauit absque ullo delicto et absque ulla macula
contagia peccati, sicut dicit Esaias propheta: *Vere languores nostros ipse* F.
abstulit et aegrotationes nostras ipse portauit. Sicut ignis, quod accipit,
purgat et non desistit quod non sit; at ipse dei filius quando accepit
humanitatem nostram, non desistat suam diuinitatem quod non sit, sicut
sol quod accepit purgat et non desistat quia ille non sit. QUI PASSUS EST 36
PRO SALUTE NOSTRA. Dominus noster Ihesus Christus non dedignauit
descendere de sinu patris ut ueniret in uterum uirginalem et acciperet
humanitatem nostram, ut sicut erat perfectus deus ex substantia patris,
ita fieret perfectus homo ex substantia matris. Sic etiam non dedignauit
passionem suscipere propter nostram salutem, ut per eius passionem libe-
raret nos, ut salui esse mereremur a potestate diaboli, *quia* Ihesus *non uenit
ministrari, sed ministrare aliis et dare animam suam redemptione pro multis.*
In tantum *se humiliauit* Ihesus Christus, sicut *fuit obediens usque ad
mortem, mortem autem crucis.* DESCENDIT AD INFEROS. Propter hoc ibidem F. T.
descendit ut patriarchas et prophetas qui ibidem iniuste detinebantur propter
illa *orientalia delicta*, ut eos *liberaret* a potestate diaboli. Memor sit illius
uerbi prophetae: *O mors ero mors tua, morsus tuus ero, inferne.* Partem

[1] Cf. Conc. Tol. XI. (A.D. 675): Nec tamen uerbum ipsum ita in carne conuersum atque mutatum ut desisteret deus esse qui homo esse uoluisset.

abstulit, partem reliquit, et postquam pugnauit cum diabolo et pergit illud
bellum et *exspoliauit infernum.* TERTIA DIE RESURREXIT A MORTUIS. Non
per carnem in qua natus, in qua mortuus, in qua sepultus, in ipsa resurrexit.
Non solum autem ille, sed *et multa corpora sanctorum, qui dormierunt,*
37 resurrexerunt in testimonium. ASCENDIT AD CAELOS. Sicut superius
diximus, qui passus est pro salute nostra, postquam omnia sustinuit, post-
quam resurrexit, amore suorum conuersatus est in hoc mundo cum suis
sanctis apostolis et in quadragesimo die ascendit ad caelos. Non dixit ad
caelum, sed ad caelos. Dixit beatus Paulus raptus usque ad tertium caelum.
Non tali modo ascendit quod Elias qui in curru igneo; alterius potestas
fuit quod ascendit non sua, sed ipse per suam potestatem et per suam
uirtutem potestatiuam ascendit. SEDET AD DEXTERAM DEI PATRIS OMNI-
T. POTENTIS. Sedere, quid aliud significat nisi *regnare* uel iudicare? Dextera
dei, quid aliud est nisi regnum dei? Qui ascendit omnis bonus est; rex est
F. et totus iustus. INDE UENTURUS EST IUDICARE UIUOS ET MORTUOS. Uiuos
38 qui ibidem inueniantur; mortuos qui transierunt per mortem corporis. AD
CUIUS ADUENTUM OMNES HOMINES RESURGERE HABENT CUM CORPORIBUS
SUIS ET REDDITURI SUNT DE FACTIS PROPRIIS RATIONEM. Ad cuius ad-
uentum illius aduentum quem superius diximus qui passus fuit. Omnes
resurgere debent cum corporibus, non cum animabus, quod per corpus
intelligitur anima, quia corpus sine anima mortuum est. Omnes resurgere
39 habent ad rationem reddendam. ET QUI BONA EGERUNT IBUNT IN UITAM
AETERNAM QUI UERO MALA IN IGNEM AETERNUM. Hoc est qui in bona
opera perseuerauerunt, ibunt in regnum dei, et qui in mala in ignem per-
T. 40 petuum. HAEC EST FIDES CATHOLICA, *quam uniuersalis ecclesia* cum (*in*)
electis suis corde credit, ore profitetur et bonis actibus operibus exsequitur.
De qua fide, quicunque et ii, qui christiano nomine censentur, quicquam
detraxerit aut credere noluerit, procul dubio Christianus (*catholicus*) *non erit,*
sed intra ecclesiam positus sub nomine Christianitatis recte catholicus ut
haereticus re(*de*)*putabitur.*

(2) The Stavelot Commentary.

		saec.
1.	British Museum, Add. mss. 18,043. Psalter from Stavelot Abbey .	x
2.	Boulogne ms. 20. Psalter from S. Omer	x
3.	Vatican Library (printed by Pinius from an unknown ms. *Liturgia Ant.* ii.)	x/xi
4.	Munich, Cod. Lat. 17,181. Abbey of Scheftlarn (defective) . .	xi
5.	,, ,, 2,580	xii ex
6.	,, ,, 14,506. Abbey of S. Emmeran	xii
7.	Trinity College, Cambridge. Eadwine Psalter	xii
8.	Durham Chapter Library, ms. A. iv. 2	xii
9.	York Chapter Library, ms. xvi. 7. 4	xii
10.	Bodleian Library, Oxford, Laud Lat. 17. From Cirencester Abbey .	xii
11.	Paris, B. N. Lat. 12,020. Not a Psalter, from Abbey of S. Germain des Prés, printed by Montfaucon (S. Athanasii *Op.* ii)	xii
12.	Balliol College, Oxford, ms. 32. Ex dono Willmi Epi Eliensis . .	xii ex
13.	St John's College, Oxford, ms. 101. Not a Psalter	xiii
14.	Venice. Swainson (p. 378) quotes a page photographed by Sir T. D. Hardy	xiii

Bishop Bruno's Edition.

	mss.	
1.	Würzburg, Cathedral Library, presented by the Bishop. (Ed. J. Cochlaeus, 1531. Le Long i. 274)	xi
2.	Rawlinson 163. Bodleian, has Bruno Eps at the top of each page; contains a prayer to St Quirynus the Patron	xi
3.	Laud Lat. 96, Bodleian, an exact copy of 2, but has not Bruno's name, and contains a prayer to S. Kilian, the Apostle and Patron of Würzburg	xi

Printed Editions.

1. 1486, readings *carne, deo.*
2. 1494—1497, all late readings. Camb. Univ. Lib. has a copy, iv Jan. 1495, Reyser. (Om. *E. H.* p. 69, refers to such a copy in the British Museum.)

Text of the Stavelot Commentary.

This Commentary is here printed for the first time from my transcription of Brit. Mus. Add. 18,043. The text of the Creed is printed in capitals, scriptural quotations in italics. The words within square brackets are omitted in Boulogne MS. 20 (B). I have given in the *apparatus* not a complete collation of B but some of the new notes to indicate the character of the divergences and a few striking readings. I have kept the capitals, not the stops.

Fides Catholica S̄C̄Ī Athanasii.

1 QUICUNQUE UULT SALUUS ESSE ANTE OMNIA OPUS EST UT TENEAT CATHOLICAM FIDEM. Hic beatus Athanasius liberum arbitrium posuit
Ps. xxxiv. 12. sicut dicitur in psalmo: *Quis est homo qui uult uitam* et in euangelio:
Mt. xvi. 24. *Qui uult post me uenire.* Similiter et hic, quicunque uult saluus esse. Non dicit uelis aut non saluus eris, sed quicunque uult, qui deus omnipotens nullum hominem inuitum aut coactum trahit ad fidem, nisi qui sua propria uoluntate uult uenire ad fidem. [Sed quicunque uult esse in corpore uel in anima necesse est ut teneat catholicam fidem, quia ante omne opus necesse est ut fides praecedat; ante omnem operationem,] ante omnem inchoationem, ante omne principium unicuique
Heb. xi. 6. opus est ut teneat catholicam fidem [dicente apostolo: *Sine fide impos-*
Habac. ii. 4. *sibile est placere deo.* Et iterum *Justus ex fide uiuit.*] Katholica graecus sermo est, latine interpretatur generalis siue uniuersalis; generalis pertinet ad omnes homines. Uniuersalis quia per uniuersum orbem est diffusa. Fides est credulitas qua ueraciter credimus id quod nequa-

2 Ibi ille doctor l. a. composuit 3 dicit et] in e. iterum in e. ipsa ueritas dicit 6 aut] nec fidem] Nisi quia sua propria uoluntate uelit uenire ad fidem 10 ante 1°] *pr* ante omnem praeparationem 13 latine] in Latinum int. gen. que per uniuersam ecclesiam tenere oportet, fides enim Latinum nomen est expressius Latinum credulitas siue credentium istam deinde istam credulitatem ante omnia nobis opus est tenere, quia fides fundamentum est omnium uirtutum et prius aedificemus fidem quod est fundamentum et super eam ceteras uirtutes, quia sine fide nullus saluus erit, dicente apostolo, impossibile est placere deo

quam uidere ualemus. Unde apostolus dicit: *Fides est sperandorum* Heb. xi. 1
substantia rerum argumentum non apparentium. Dicitur namque fides
eo quod fit inter deum et hominem. Istam fidem, istam credulitatem
ante omnia nobis opus est tenere, quia fides fundamentum est omnium uir-
tutum, quia sine fide nullus saluus esse potest.] QUAM NISI QUISQUE 2
INTEGRAM INUIOLATAMQUE SERUAUERIT ABSQUE DUBIO IN AETERNUM
PERIBIT. quam id est quam fidem quisque, id est, unusquisque. Integram,
[id est plenam et perfectam,] ut eam non scindat per heresim, [neque ab
ullo schismate corrumpat.] Inuiolatam ut eam non uiolet maledocendo
atque predicando, et si eam non custodierit integram et inuiolatam,
absque dubio in aeterna dampnatione peribit. FIDES AUTEM CATHOLICA 3
HAEC EST UT UNUM DEUM IN TRINITATE ET TRINITATEM IN UNITATE UE-
NEREMUR. [Nunc manifestat quid est fides uel qualiter unusquisque eam
credere debeat. Debemus deum credere trinum et unum, Unum in sub-
stantia et trinum in personis, Nec propter trinitatem debemus dimittere
unitatem, Nec propter unitatem debemus dimittere trinitatem.] Ut ip-
sum quem colimus unum ueneremur et trinum, [Unum propter unitatem
substantiae, trinum propter personarum uocabula, Ueneremur, adoremus
atque colamus.] NEQUE CONFUNDENTES PERSONAS NEQUE SUBSTANTIAM 4
SEPARANTES. Confundere est comisceri, quia non tantum debemus
unam personam credere sicut Sabellius hereticus affirmabat sed tres id
est patrem et filium et spiritum sanctum, Nec substantiam separare, ut
Arrius hereticus adfirmabat, dicebat enim quod sicut erant tres personae,
ita fuissent tres substantiae. Patrem asserebat maiorem filio, filium mi-
norem patre, spiritum sanctum ministrum eorum dicebat. [Substantia
dicitur eo quod ex semet ipsa subsistat; substantia uero commune est
omnium rerum quae sunt. caelum, sol, luna, terra, arbores, homines etiam
substantiae dicuntur. Deus igitur substantia est, et summa substantia et

2 Dicitur namque fides eo quod fit] Cf. Paris Com. (Om. *E. H.* p. 376): Fides dicitur ab eo quod fies in dies, and the common source in Caesarius (Ps. Aug. Serm. 264): Fides a fit, id est ab eo quod fiat, nomen accepit.

10 inuiolatam] immaculatam 13 Nunc etc.] i.e. ac si tibi aliquis interrogasset que est ista fides et tu respondisses, Haec est que ut unum deum id est in substantia, in trinitate i.e. in personis, et trinitate quod sunt illas personas, et unitate quod est illa substantia ueneranda sit i.e. adoranda atque colenda 20 comisceri] misculare 25 Substantia etc.] Dicebat patrem quasi aurum, filium quasi argentum, spiritum sanctum quasi aeramentum (cf. Troyes cl. 4), et tamen inter hos hereticos uniuersalis ecclesiae quia Sabellius in quo dicebat unam substantiam benedicebat, in quo dicebat unam personam maledicebat. Arrius in quo dicebat tres personas benedicebat, in quo dicebat tres substantias maledicebat. Et nos accipiamus de Sabellio illam unam substantiam in quo benedicebat, et derelinquamus illam unam personam in quo maledicebat. Accipiamus de Arrio illas tres personas in quo benedicebat, et derelinquamus illas tres substantias in quo maledicebat. Et teneamus nostram fidem

prima et omnium substantiarum causa, quia omnium rerum creator est.
Ex. iii. 14. Essentia igitur proprie de deo dicitur quia semper est quod est, quia in-
commutabilis est. ITEM. Substantia quid est, substantia est omne quod
est, substantia uero commune nomen est omnium rerum que sunt. Nam
deus ipse substantia est et summa substantia et prima substantia et
omnium substantiarum causa quia ipse est creator omnium rerum. Sub-
sistentia quid est, subsistentia eo sensu dicitur quo deum semper stare id
est semper esse. Non a stando humani corporis consuetudine sed a per-
5 manendo quia semper permanet esse quod est.] ALIA EST ENIM PERSONA
PATRIS ALIA FILII ALIA SPIRITUS SANCTI. Hic contra Sabellium sunt per-
sonae divisae, quia asserit unam esse, quia pater in sua persona non est
filius, sed tantum pater, nec filius in sua persona est pater sed tantum
filius, nec spiritus sanctus in sua persona est pater, nec filius, sed tantum
spiritus sanctus ex utroque procedens. [Persona dicta est eo quod per
6 se sonat.] SED PATRIS ET FILII ET SPIRITUS SANCTI UNA EST DIUINITAS
una substantia AEQUALIS GLORIA COAETERNA MAIESTAS coaequalis gloria
7 sine initio et fine et potestas. QUALIS PATER TALIS FILIUS TALIS SPIRITUS
SANCTUS. Quia sicut pater est aeternus uel omnipotens seu inuisibilis,
8 similiter est et filius et spiritus sanctus. INCREATUS PATER INCREATUS
FILIUS INCREATUS ET SPIRITUS SANCTUS. In praepositio est in hoc loco
pro non posita. Increatus pater, id est non creatus quia ipse est
omnium creator, et a nullo creatus. Ipse est omnium factor, et
a nullo factus. Increatus filius, increatus et spiritus sanctus. In-
creatus filius non creatura, sicut Arius dicebat, quia omnia simul
9 creavit cum patre, similiter et spiritus sanctus. INMENSUS PATER INMENSUS
FILIUS INMENSUS SPIRITUS SANCTUS. Inmensus, [quia eius magnitudi-
Job xi. 8, 9. nem uel quantitatem nullus mensurare potest, qui *caelo est excelsior*,
terra *profundior et latior mari*]: et est incircumscriptus, incorporeus,
inlocalis, ubique totus: et non est locus ubi non sit, sicut dicit in psalmo,
Ps. cxxxix. 8, 9, 10. *Si ascendero in caelum tu illic es; si descendero ad infernum ades;* et si iero
ad *extrema maris* ibi *me tenebit dextera tua.* Ipse est intra omnia et non
Ps. xxxiii. 6. conclusus; extra omnia et non exclusus. [Similiter et filius, qui attingit a
Wisd. i. 7. fine usque ad finem fortiter, de quo scriptum est], *Verbo domini caeli firmati
sunt.* [Pari modo et spiritus sanctus: *Spiritus domini replevit orbem
10 terrarum.*] AETERNUS PATER AETERNUS FILIUS AETERNUS SPIRITUS SANC-
11 TUS. ET TAMEN NON TRES AETERNI SED UNUS AETERNUS. Hic aeternus
pro sempiterno debemus intelligere. Aeternus dicitur deus pater quia

14 Persona dicta est eo quod per se sonat] Cf. Paris Com.: Personam dicis, quia unusquisque per se sonat.

2 id est non mensus, quia nulla creatura eum potest metiri, quia inuisibilis est et incircumscriptus 32 quia eorum separatio inuisibilis et inseparabilis est, sicut dicit in psalmo 37 Non autem sumus aeterni, sed non sempiterni quia antequam crearemur non eramus. Pater et filius patris intelligitur est sempiternus quia nec initium habet nec fine concluditur

sine initio et sine fine constat, Similiter et filius et spiritus sanctus, quia
sicut numquam non pater Ita numquam non filius ac spiritus sanctus.
SICUT NON TRES INCREATI NEC TRES INMENSI SED UNUS INCREATUS ET UNUS 12
INMENSUS. SIMILITER OMNIPOTENS PATER OMNIPOTENS FILIUS OMNIPOTENS 13
ET SPIRITUS SANCTUS. ET TAMEN NON TRES OMNIPOTENTES SED UNUS OMNI- 14
POTENS. Omnipotens dicitur quia omnia potens ; non a patiendo quod non
uult, sed a faciendo omnia quaecumque uult et nihil illi inpossibile est.
Omnipotens et filius quia quicquid potest pater, potest et filius ; nihilomi-
nus et spiritus sanctus. Ista nomina patris et filii et spiritus sancti quae
saepe dicimus relatiua sunt, quia alia ad alia referuntur. Verbi gratia ser-
uus ad dominum dominus ad seruum, magister ad discipulum discipulus ad
magistrum, pater ad filium filius ad patrem, quia nullus pater dicitur nisi
habeat filium et nullus filius nisi habeat patrem cuius sit filius. Similiter
spiritus sanctus non a se sed alicuius spiritus est. Similiter relatiue dicitur
spiritus sanctus. [Donatorem dico esse patrem donum spiritum sanctum.
ITA DEUS PATER DEUS FILIUS DEUS SPIRITUS SANCTUS. Deus proprium 15
nomen est trinitatis, pertinens ad patrem et filium et spiritum sanctum,

6 Cf. Bouhier Com. (Om. p. 364): Omnipotens dicitur Deus, quia omnia potest, non patiendo aliquid quod non uult, sed faciendo quodcunque uult; and the common source, Aug. *de Civ. Dei* v. 10.

9 The gist of this paragraph is found in Aug. *de Trin.* v. 12 and vii. 23. There is also an interesting parallel in a small treatise published by Florus Diaconus, of Lyons, against John the Scot in 850. (M. *Bibl. Pat.* IX. p. 1011. Colon. Agripp. 1618.) Florus quotes Augustine *de Trinitate*, and in several places comes near to the wording of the Commentary, e.g. 'Ipsum liberum arbitrium fides Catholica fides vera inter dona gratiae deputat....meminerit se fidem Catholicam fidem veram sentiendi de Deo integram sibi inuiolatamque seruandam.'

6 et maledictus et anathema est qui dicit, fuit aliquando pater sine filio. Similiter autem spiritus sanctus. Et tamen non tres aeterni id est in substantia, sicut non tres increati, id est quia unus est deus, ideo non tres increati nec tres inmensi, sed in quo trinus dicitur deus tres sunt dii tres inmensi et tres increati, et in quo in unum consistunt unus est deus id est in substantia 13 Et filii nomen non a se sed a patre est, et in qua die habuerit filium continuo nascitur ei nomen patris, et ipsum nomen patris non de se sed de illo filio assumit illud nomen, quia si non habuisset filium nunquam habuisset nomen patris...Ideo relatiua dicuntur, quia ad se inuicem referuntur 16 id est deus potestatis nomen est nomen proprietatis. Proprium nomen illi est pater quia solus est pater. Et si aliquis te interrogatus fuerit quid est deus, responde illi bonum quo nihil melius, potens quo nihil potentior. Et si adhuc te interrogatus fuerit quid est deus, responde illi: Ignis est deus, sicut dicit apostolus Paulus, Deus noster ignis consumens est. Ideo ignis dicitur deus quia sicut ignis comburit ligna, sic uelocius ille peccata hominum ad se conuertentium. Et si adhuc te interrogatus fuerit, responde illi. Est sicut dominus dicit ad Moysen quando mittebatur ad populum Israheliticum: Ego sum qui sum. Hec dices populo Israhel, qui est misit me ad uos

translatum ex greca appellatione. Nam deus grece theosphebos dicitur,
id est timor. Unde tractum est deus, quod eum colentibus sit timor.]
Proprium nomen est patris quia solus est pater; et proprium nomen est
filii quia solus filius est a solo patre; et proprium nomen est spiritus
sancti quia ab utroque procedit. Deus est pater, quia ipse est fons et
origo deitatis: similiter filius deus hoc non a semet ipso, quia non est a
se sed a solo patre est genitus; pari modo et spiritus sanctus non a se est
16 deus sed a patre et filio procedens. ET TAMEN NON TRES DII SED UNUS
Deut. vi. 4. EST DEUS. Sicut scriptum est: *Audi Israel. Dominus deus* tuus *deus*
17, 18 *unus est.* ITA DOMINUS PATER DOMINUS FILIUS DOMINUS SPIRITUS SANCTUS
ET TAMEN NON TRES DOMINI SED UNUS EST DOMINUS. [Dominus dicitur a
dominatione, eo quod creaturam suam dominetur regat atque gubernet,
19 similiter et filius et spiritus sanctus.] QUIA SICUT SINGILLATIM UNAM-
QUAMQUE PERSONAM DEUM AC DOMINUM CONFITERI CHRISTIANA UERITATE
COMPELLIMUR ITA TRES DEOS AUT DOMINOS DICERE CATHOLICA RELIGIONE
PROHIBEMUR. De patre si quis te interrogauerit quid est in persona
responde deus et dominus. Si autem [de filio similiter deus et dominus.
Si uero] de spiritu sancto indubitanter responde plenum deum et dominum
20 eum esse. PATER A NULLO EST FACTUS NEC CREATUS NEC GENITUS. Pater a
nullo factus quia ipse est omnium factor, nec creatus sed creator, nec
21 genitus sed genitor. Pater enim graece, latine genitor dicitur. FILIUS A
PATRE SOLO EST NON FACTUS NEC CREATUS SED GENITUS. Filius a patre solo
est non factus [quia ipse est omnium factor simul cum patre nec creatus
quia ipse est omnium creator sed genitus solus a solo patre. Et unaquaeque
persona habet proprium quod non habet alia, proprium habet in persona
pater quia solus est pater; et proprium habet in persona filius quia solus a
solo patre genitus est. Sed et habet aliquid proprium filius quod non habet
pater nec spiritus sanctus; habet aeternitatem cum patre et spiritu sancto,
et habet in tempore natiuitatem de matre quam non habet spiritus sanctus]
nec pater quia non suscepit carnem pater in sua persona, nec spiritus
sanctus sed tantum filius, ut nobis in se ostenderet duas habere naturas,
unam ante omnia saecula qua genitus est ex patre, de qua dicit Esaias:
Is. liii. 8. *Generationem eius quis enarrabit?* Aliam in tempore quia natus est ex

20 The long note on the birth in time would come better on cl. 29 or 31. Troyes has quotations from Isaiah and S. Paul on cl. 31.

10 Et sicut in primordio dominus dicit: Faciamus hominem ad imaginem et similitudinem nostram. Cum dicit nostram trinitatem demonstrauit et sicut dicit in psalmo: Benedicat nos deus deus noster benedicat nos deus et metuant eum omnes fines terrae. Audis quia ter nominauit dominum et addidit, et metuant eum. Non dicit eos sed eum ut intelligas trinum et unum esse deum 11 Dominus pater quia omnibus dominatur. Dominus filius quia hic omnia dominatur simul cum patre. Similiter autem spiritus sanctus sicut dicit in psalmo Dominus autem in caelo et in terra omnia quaecumque uoluit fecit 13 Singillatim i.e. distinctum uel separatim (cf. Fort. cl. 19)

matre de qua dicit apostolus Paulus: *Cum autem uenerit plenitudo* Gal. iv. 4.
temporis misit deus filium suum natum ex muliere factum sub lege. In
qua complacuit *plenitudinem diuinitatis* habitare *corporaliter*. De patre Col. ii. 9.
sine initio et sine fine, de matre initium habens et nullo concluditur fine.
SPIRITUS SANCTUS A PATRE ET FILIO NON FACTUS NEC CREATUS NEC GENITUS 22
SED PROCEDENS. Proprium habet spiritus sanctus quia non pater et
filius sed spiritus et procedens a patre et filio. Audis quia iste ab
ambobus, filius ab uno pater a nullo: ac per hoc aperte monstrantur pro-
prietates eorum. [Ideo igitur spiritus dei sanctus uocatur: quia patris
et filii sanctitas est. Nam cum sit et pater spiritus et filius spiritus
et pater sanctus et filius sanctus, proprie tamen ipse uocatur spiritus
sanctus.] UNUS ERGO PATER NON TRES PATRES UNUS FILIUS NON TRES 23
FILII UNUS SPIRITUS SANCTUS NON TRES SPIRITUS SANCTI. Unus pater quia
solus sibi unicum genuit filium et unus filius quia singulariter ab unico patre
genitus est. Unus spiritus sanctus quia a patre et filio unicus procedit.
ET IN HAC TRINITATE NIHIL PRIUS AUT POSTERIUS NIHIL MAIUS AUT MINUS 24
SED TOTAE TRES PERSONAE COAETERNAE SIBI SUNT ET COAEQUALES. Quia
nullus anterior et nullus posterior, nullus inferior et nullus superior, sed
coaeternae sibi. ITA UT PER OMNIA SICUT IAM SUPRADICTUM EST ET 25
TRINITAS IN UNITATE ET UNITAS IN TRINITATE UENERANDA SIT. Debemus
colere et adorare Trinitatem in unitate, et unitatem in Trinitate. QUI 26
UULT ERGO SALUUS ESSE ITA DE TRINITATE SENTIAT. Hic rogat et am-
monet ut unusquisque doctor memoriter eam teneat, et firmiter eam
credat, et alios predicando doceat. SED NECESSARIUM EST AD AETERNAM 27
SALUTEM UT INCARNATIONEM QUOQUE DOMINI NOSTRI IESU CHRISTI
FIDELITER CREDAT. Necesse est nobis ut sicut superius diximus ista
credamus. Si uero aeternam salutem uolumus habere, id est cum Christo
sine fine regnare necesse est ut incarnationem domini nostri Iesu Christi
fideliter credamus. Quomodo fideliter? non adoptiuum sed proprium Rom. viii.
dei filium, sicut dixit apostolus: *proprio filio suo* etcetera. EST ERGO 32.
FIDES RECTA UT CREDAMUS ET CONFITEAMUR QUIA DOMINUS NOSTER 28
IESUS CHRISTUS DEI FILIUS ET DEUS PARITER ET HOMO EST. Modo in-
choat enarrare secundum humanitatem Christi quid sit fides recta ut
ipsam humanitatem credamus corde, et confiteamur ore sicut dicit apo-

9 Cf. Bouhier Com.: Nam cum sit et Pater et Spiritus et Filius et Spiritus et Pater sanctus et Filius sanctus, proprie tamen ipse uocatur Spiritus Sanctus.

3 Cf. Troyes (cl. 29): Ex patre sine initio...et matre a certo initio 14 unicum ...unico] unum...uno 16 B inserts the note found in Fort. 23 doctor] presbyter eam praedicet et memoriter eam teneat 30 Et sicut ille centurio quando Christus pendebat in cruce: Vere dei filius erat iste. Non in fantasia ambulasse aut passum esse sicut Manichei dicebant, sed ueram carnem et ossa habuisse, sicut ipse dominus post resurrectionem suam ad discipulos dixit: Videte manus mea et pedes quia ego ipse sum. Spiritus carnem et ossa non habet sicut me uidetis habere. Non sine anima sicut Apollonaristae dicebant, sed ueram animam et rationabilem habuisse credamus

Rom. x. 10. stolus: *corde creditur ad iustitiam, ore autem confessio fit ad salutem.*
Deus et homo unus est, uerus dei filius quia secundum diuinitatem nihil
minus quam deus pater secundum humanitatem nihil minus extra pec-
29 catum quam homo. DEUS EST EX SUBSTANTIA PATRIS ANTE SAECULA
GENITUS ET HOMO EST EX SUBSTANTIA MATRIS IN SAECULO NATUS. Ex
substantia patris, id est ex aequalitate naturae. Ante saecula genitus id est
Ps. cix. 3. ante omnem creaturam, sicut dicit in psalmo: *Ex utero ante luciferum*
genui te. Ex utero ex mea substantia. Ante luciferum ante omnem
creaturam. Et homo est ex substantia matris in saeculo natus, id
est totus homo cum corpore et anima, in omnia nobis similis absque
peccato. Ex substantia matris, id est de aequalitate naturae matris. In
saeculo natus, id est in his temporibus, non aliunde, nisi de semine
Prov. xxiv. 3. mulieris sine coitu uiri carnem suscepit. Unde Salomon dicit: *Sapientia*
aedificauit sibi domum: hoc est Christus aedificauit sibi carnem de beata
Rom. i. 3. Maria et alibi legitur: *Qui factus est ex semine Dauid.* PERFECTUS DEUS
30 PERFECTUS HOMO EX ANIMA RATIONALI ET HUMANA CARNE SUBSISTENS.
Perfectus dicitur, id est plenus, quia nihil indiguit, perfectus homo, qui
nihil minus habuit extra peccatum quam homo. [Ex anima rationali]
Christus ueram animam habuit, ubi sapientia crescere potuisset, sicut
Luc. ii. 52. dicit in euangelio: *Iesus proficiebat sapientia et aetate;* sapientia in anima,
aetate in corpore. Et humana carne subsistens: quia humus terra dicitur,
31 de humanitate carnem assumsit. AEQUALIS PATRI SECUNDUM DIUINI-
TATEM MINOR PATRE SECUNDUM HUMANITATEM. [Aequalis patri secundum
Jo. x. 30. illud, *Ego et pater unum sumus.* Minor patri secundum humanitatem
Jo. xiv. 28. iuxta quod dicit: *Pater maior me est*, et in quo homo est minor est a
32 diuinitate.] QUI LICET DEUS SIT ET HOMO NON DUO TAMEN SED UNUS
EST CHRISTUS. Ideo si coniungi uoluit dei filius cum humana natura,
33 ut ex his duabus substantiis fieret una persona. UNUS AUTEM NON CON-
UERSIONE DIUINITATIS IN CARNE SED ADSUMPTIONE HUMANITATIS IN DEUM.
Non quod illa diuinitas quae est filius dei se conuertisset in humanitatem ut hoc quod erat diuinum fieret humanum sed assumendo nostram naturam sic est unus effectus, ut non amitteret quod erat, sed assumeret

6 aeq. naturae] de caritate patris 13 suscepit] + Fuerunt aliqui heretici qui dicebant, quod secum Christus carnem adtulisset et sic transisset per beatam Mariam quasi aqua per fistulam 15 et] sicut dicit Paulus apostolus, Qui factus est ei ex semine Dauid secundum carnem, quia beata MARIA de stirpe Dauid fuit, et inde Christus carnem assumpsit 19 Fuerunt aliqui heretici qui dicebant, quod Christus animam non habuisset. Et postea surrexerunt exinde aliqui coniuncti et dixerunt quod animam habuisset sed tamen irrationabilis fuisset sicut pecora, quia pecus quando moritur carne moritur et anima 28 Id est duae substantiae...una est persona (cf. Fort. cl. 32) 30 id est unus autem in deo non quod illa diuinitas fuisset conuersa in illa humanitate sed humanitas in diuinitate non aliud nisi ut melior fieret quam erat. Unus omnino i.e. homo transiuit in deum non uersus in unitate naturae, sed propter diuinitatem personae, ideo non sunt duo Christi nec filii, sed unus Christus et unus filius deus et homo

quod non erat. Assumpsit humanitatem et non amisit diuinitatem.
UNUS OMNINO NON CONFUSIONE SUBSTANTIAE SED UNITATE PERSONAE. 34
Non in eo naturarum commixtio est, ut uel diuinitas mutaretur in naturam humanitatis: uel humanitas conuerteretur in naturam diuinitatis; sed utrique naturae sua manet proprietas in perpetuum, tanta tamen coniunctio est naturarum, ut idem qui aeternaliter ex deo patre genitus est homo sit uerus et ille qui natus est temporaliter ex uirgine deus sit uerus. Homo propter suscipientem deum deus uerus deus dei filius; propter suscipientem hominem, homo uerus. Personam quippe filii dei, non ex duabus personis unitam, sed ex duabus naturis existere credimus: de duabus
personis compositam ut nefas uitamus.] NAM SICUT ANIMA RATION- 35
ALIS ET CARO UNUS EST HOMO ITA DEUS ET HOMO UNUS EST CHRISTUS.
Sicut enim ex carne et anima unum dicimus hominem et unusquisque habet duos homines in se, unum carnalem alium spiritalem; unum mortalem
alium immortalem; ita deus et homo unus est Christus. QUI PASSUS EST 36
PRO SALUTE NOSTRA DESCENDIT AD INFEROS RESURREXIT A MORTUIS. In quo passus est, in quo uidebatur, in quo homo erat, in quo crucifixus, in quo mortuus, in quo sepultus, in quo resurrexit: quia diuinitas inpassibilis est, sed in coniunctione personae filius dei dicitur passus et in uera natura filius hominis passus est. Descendit ad inferos, id est anima cum uerbo; quia postquam humanitas assumpta est a diuinitate non est separata a uerbo: sed ipsa anima a corpore separata est; quia si non esset separata, corpus non posset mori: et iste descensus ad solam animam pertinet.
Resurrexit a mortuis [ut nobis exemplum resurrectionis ostenderet sic ut
propheta ait: *Post duos dies suscitabit nos et tertia die resurgemus, et in* Hos. vi. 2.
conspectu eius uiuemus.] ASCENDIT AD CAELOS SEDET AD DEXTERAM DEI 37
PATRIS OMNIPOTENTIS INDE UENTURUS EST IUDICARE UIUOS ET MORTUOS.
Ascendit ad caelos [id est ipsa humanitas quae fuit passa, sic]ut angeli
dixerunt: *Viri galilei, quid statis aspicientes in caelum?* Quia secundum Acts i. 11.
diuinitatem ad nullum potest ascendere locum, sed ubique totus est. Sedet ad dexteram, dexteram autem dei non corporalem non carnalem, sicut humana habet natura, sed in hoc loco gloriam dei conuenit accipere, ac si aperte dicat: Regnat in gloria dei et sedere pro regnare dicit. Inde uenturus est iudicare uiuos et mortuos. Venturus est in eadem forma in qua crucifixus in qua mortuus in qua sepultus est in qua et resurrexit; non in ea tantum humilitate in qua antea fuit sed in gloria et maiestate et ideo in ipsa forma, ut uideat Herodes et Pilatus quem iudicauerunt ut uideant iudaei

19 passus] et in uera natura filius hominis passus 24 mortuis] quia inde eripuit illos iustos qui in debitae (indebitae?) mortis tenebantur uinculis. Cf. Troyes, Fortunatus and Orleans *ad loc.* Also Milan T. 103, S. x (B. M. Reg. 8, xiv). Et quare descendit? ut eos qui detinebantur in inferno eriperet id est iustos. Milan I. 152, S. XII. Descendit ad inferos. In sola scilicet anima ut illos qui indebite detinebantur illic eriperet et liberaret 33 Gloriam dei intelligas quamquam quodam in loco dextera dei filius intelligitur patris ut est illud in psalmo: Dextera domini fecit uirtutem

quem tradiderunt ut uideant milites quem crucifixerunt ut uideant impii
quem negauerunt. Viuos quos eius aduentus inuenerit in corpore uiuentes
Mortuos qui mortui fuerunt ab initio usque in illum diem; [Aliter uiuos id
38 est sanctos, mortuos id est peccatores cum peccatis suis.] AD CUIUS ADUEN-
39 TUM OMNES HOMINES RESURGERE HABENT CUM CORPORIBUS SUIS ET REDDITURI
SUNT DE FACTIS PROPRIIS RATIONEM ET QUI BONA EGERUNT IBUNT IN UITAM
AETERNAM QUI UERO MALA IN IGNEM AETERNUM. In aduentu Christi domini
unusquisque siue iusti siue peccatores resurgere habent cum corporibus suis.
Et redditurі sunt de factis propriis rationem. Reddere autem rationem
non fabulo uerborum sed recordatione omnium quae fecit siue bonum siue
malum, et secundum hoc unusquisque recipere debet: boni bona, mali uero
mala. Et qui bona egerunt ibunt in uitam aeternam qui uero mala in
ignem aeternum. Et qui bona egerunt ibunt in uitam aeternam quia sem-
per erunt boni sine fine in gloria regnaturi. In ignem aeternum quia sem-
per erit malis sine fine poena inferni et sine ulla misericordia cum corpore
40 et anima non consumpturi sed semper arsuri et numquam deficient. HAEC
EST FIDES CATHOLICA QUAM NISI QUISQUE FIDELITER FIRMITERQUE CREDI-
DERIT SALUUS ESSE NON POTERIT. sicut superius diximus. Hic rogat et
ammonet ut unusquisque sacerdos hoc sciat et predicet. quam id est
quam fidem, quisque aliquis. Fideliter ut de ea non dubitet; firmiter ut
nullus a tua fide te remouere possit nullo schismate uel heresi. Et si ita
non credide(ris saluus esse non poteris).

16 nunquam deficiendo semper deficiunt 22 credide] Here Add. MSS. 18,043 fails, the rest of the page having been torn off. poteris] + unde nos pius dominus non meritis nostris sed propter suam misericordiam eripere dignetur. Amen.

(3) The Troyes Commentary.

Reprinted from Mr Ommanney's transcription of the Troyes MS. 804. Saec. x.

I have printed quotations from the Creed in small capitals, and quotations from the Fortunatus Commentary in italics, neglecting Scriptural quotations.

QUICUNQUE UULT SALUUS ESSE, ANTE OMNIA OPUS EST UT TENEAT 1
CATHOLICAM FIDEM. *Fides dicitur credulitas siue credentia; Catholica* uero
uniuersalis uocatur, quod ab *uniuersa ecclesia tenere*[1] oportet. *Ecclesia*
autem est *congregatio* fidelium, *siue conuentus* fidelium *populi*. FIDES uera 3
HAEC EST, *ut credamus et confiteamur* UNUM[2] uerum DEUM IN TRINITATE
ET TRINITATEM IN UNITATE; NEQUE CONFUNDENTES PERSONAS, *ut Sabellius* 4
hereticus, *qui ipsum dixit esse patrem in persona quem et filium, ipsum
filium quem et spiritum sanctum.* FIDES AUTEM CATHOLICA EST nec personas
confundere neque deitatem separare, quoniam tres personae, una uero
diuinitas deitatis. *Est enim gignens, genitus, et procedens; gignens est pater,
qui genuit filium;* filius uero est a patre; spiritus autem sanctus nec
genitus, quia non est filius, neque ingenitus, quoniam non est pater, sed ex
patre et filio procedens. Quae tres personae *pater* uidelicet *et filius* et
spiritus sanctus, consubstantiales *sibi sunt* et *coaeternae et coaequales* atque
co-operatores, de quibus in psalmo *scriptum est: Verbo domini coeli firmati
sunt, et spiritu oris ejus omnis uirtus eorum.* In persona quippe domini
pater intelligitur, in uerbo uero ejus filius accipitur, in spiritu autem oris
ejus ipse spiritus sanctus designatur. Quae tres personae deitatis et
singillatim tres sunt et singulariter substantiae unum existunt, non
essentiae diuisae sicut *Arrius* impie praedicare ausus est, *qui sicut tres
personae* in deum *esse* credidit, ita *et tres substantias* commentatus est.
Filium dei *minorem esse dixit patri*, non de substantia ejus genitum, sed
ex nichilo temporaliter creatum; *spiritum* autem *sanctum* similiter non
creatorem sed *creaturam* plusquam minorem quam filium, *et patris et filii*

[1] The author has altered the construction and omitted to change the mood of the verb.

[2] MS. unum est uerum.

ministrum asserunt, et ideo non creatorem cum patre et filio neque uerum deum eundem spiritum sanctum, sed creaturam ut dictum est praedicare ausus est; quasi quosdam gradus impietatis suae in deum, qui unus est, arbitratus, patrem scilicet, ut aurum, filium uero, quasi argentum, spiritum autem sanctum eramentum. Nos autem impietatem ejus anathematizantes
5 credimus et confitemur ALIAM ESSE PERSONAM PATRIS, quem *ingenitum* ideo
(21) appellamus, quia A NULLO EST GENITUS, ALIAM PERSONAM FILII, quia PATRE
solus EST GENITUS, ALIAM uero PERSONAM SPIRITUS SANCTI, qui neque
(22) ingenitus, ut pater, NEQUE GENITUS, ut filius, SED ex PATRE FILIOque
6 PROCEDIT. Et in his tribus personis, PATRIS uidelicet ET FILII ET SPIRITUS
SANCTI, UNA EST essentia DIUINITATIS, AEQUALIS GLORIA, COAETERNA
7 MAJESTAS, unita *potestas* communisque operatio. QUALIS PATER, TALIS
8 FILIUS, TALIS ET SPIRITUS SANCTUS. INCREATUS PATER, INCREATUS FILIUS,
9 INCREATUS ET SPIRITUS SANCTUS; hoc *est a nullo creatus.* INMENSUS
PATER, INMENSUS FILIUS, INMENSUS ET SPIRITUS SANCTUS; quia metiri
omnino non possunt. *Incircumscriptus* pater, incircumscriptus filius,
incircumscriptus spiritus sanctus; quia non loco continentur, sed
ubique presentes existunt. Inuisibilis pater, inuisibilis filius, inuisibilis
10 et spiritus sanctus; quia uideri a nullo queant. AETERNUS PATER,
11 AETERNUS FILIUS, AETERNUS ET SPIRITUS SANCTUS, NON TAMEN TRES
AETERNI, SED UNUS AETERNUS, neque *initium* habens, neque *fine*
13 concluditur. OMNIPOTENS PATER, OMNIPOTENS FILIUS, OMNIPOTENS ET
14 SPIRITUS SANCTUS, NON TAMEN TRES OMNIPOTENTES SED UNUS OMNIPOTENS,
quia *omnia* que uult *potest. Hoc* enim *non potest*, quod non uult, hoc est
quod non expedit. *Veritas est, quia falli* omnino *non potest.* Virtus *est*,
quoniam *infirmari* omnino *non potest. Vita est, quia mori* nullo modo *potest.*
15 DEUS PATER DEUS FILIUS DEUS ET SPIRITUS SANCTUS, NON TAMEN TRES
16 DII, SED UNUS EST DEUS. *Deus* enim *nomen est potestatis, non proprietatis.
Pater nomen est patri*, quod *pater* est; *proprium nomen est filio*, quod *filius*
17 est; *et proprium nomen est spiritus sancti spiritus sanctus.* ITA DOMINUS
18 PATER, DOMINUS FILIUS, DOMINUS ET SPIRITUS SANCTUS; NON TAMEN TRES
DOMINI SED UNUS EST DOMINUS. *Dominus* autem ideo appellatur pro *eo*
19 *quod* omnem creaturam coeli ac terrę *dominetur.* SICUT enim SINGILLATIM,
ut dictum est, UNAMQUAMQUE PERSONAM ET DEUM ET DOMINUM digne
CONFITERI CHRISTIANA UERITATE COMPELLIMUR, ITA TRES DEOS uel tres
DOMINOS credere, ut praedicare, auctoritate diuina et ratione ueritatis
PROHIBEMUR. Si autem[1] quislibet quempiam ex doctoribus interrogare uoluerit, quid sit pater; ratione ueritatis et auctoritate diuina, ut dictum est; respondere illi necesse est, deus et dominus. Similiter si inquirat, quid est filius; respondere illi oportet, deus et dominus, sicut et pater. Si autem sciscitetur ab eo, quid sit et spiritus sanctus; similiter ei respondere conuenit, deus et dominus, quemadmodum pater et filius. Sed
(16. 18) *in his tribus* personis *non tres deos neque tres dominos, sed unum deum et*

[1] si autem: note of Fortunatus expanded.

unum dominum esse confirmet. UNUS ERGO PATER, qui nunquam fuit sine 23
filio, NON TRES PATRES. UNUS est FILIUS coaeternus patri, NON TRES FILII.
UNUS est SPIRITUS SANCTUS ex patre et filio procedens, NON TRES SPIRITUS
SANCTI, neque posterior aut inferior uel minor patri et filio, a quibus
procedit. ET IN HAC sancta TRINITATE deitatis NICHIL PRIUS nichil 24
POSTERIUS nichilque inferius aut inaequale, SED TOTAE TRES PERSONAE, ut
dictum est, COAETERNAE SIBI SUNT, ET QUOAEQUALES et consubstantiales
atque inseparabiles. Sed quia omnipotens deus ita inuisibilis est ut a
mortali creatura, id est, ab homine uideri omnino, sicuti est, non possit,
idcirco a mundi creatura quantulacumque comparatione ad deum nobis
adtrahere conuenit apostolica auctoritate informati qua dicit: Inuisibilia
enim ipsius mundi creatura *que facta sunt intellecta conspiciuntur*, sempi-
terna quoque ejus uirtus. Solis qui, cum sit unus in natura, tres habere
uidetur efficientias; id est, *sol*, *splendor*, *et calor*. *Tria* quidam *uocabula*,
sed *res una est*. Splendor quoque illuminat, calor uero exurit. Haec duo
ita in sole naturaliter consistunt, ut unum absque alio, et utrumque sine
tertio esse non possint; quia neque splendor sine calore, neque calor sine
splendore, neque utrumque, id est, splendor et calor sine splendore fieri
possunt. Quod etiam de natura ignis prudens contemplator colligere
potest. *Ita pater et filius et spiritus sanctus tres* procul dubio extant
personae, sed *indiuidua* majestate *deitatis* et gloria aeternitatis. FIDES 28
autem catholica haec EST, UT CREDAMUS ET CONFITEAMUR, QUIA DOMINUS
NOSTER JHESUS CHRISTUS, DEI patris est FILIUS, DEUS PARITER ET HOMO EST.
DEUS scilicet EX PATRE sine initio, HOMO uere EX MATRE a certo initio, unus 29
atque idem filius dei; AEQUALIS PATRI SECUNDUM DIUINITATEM, MINOR uero 31
PATRI juxta HUMANITATEM; coaeternus patri in diuinitatem, contemporalis
uero matri erga humanitatem, consubstantialis matri in assumptam humanitatem; similis patri per omnia secundum diuinitatem, dissimilis uero omni creaturae, consimilis autem nobis hominibus in humanitate, excelsior uero omni creaturae coeli ac terrae; unus atque idem Ihesus Christus dominus ac redemptor noster. Cuius nominis aetinologia hec est. *Jhesus Ebreo* sermone *Latine saluator* siue salutaris interpretatur; Christus autem Hebraice Messias uocatur, *Greca* uero *lingua Christus* dicitur, *Latine* uero *unctus* appellatur. *Jhesus* autem ideo nuncupatur pro *eo quod* ipse *saluum* facit *populum* suum. Christus autem secundum humanitatem ideo uocatur, quia spiritu sancto a patre unctus est, *sicut ex ipsius Christi persona Esaias* propheta *ait: Spiritus domini super me propter quod unxit me;* et *in psalmo* propheta ad ipsum Christum dominum: Sedes tua, deus, in saeculum saeculi; uirga equitatis uirga regni tui; dilexisti justitiam et odisti iniquitatem; propterea *unxit te deus, deus tuus, oleo letitiae pre consortibus tuis*. Unctus deus, filius dei, a patre et spiritu sancto, non in diuinitatis essentia, sed in humanitate assumpta. Duas quippe in Christo credimus esse naturas, duasque formas, duasque natiuitates, duas etiam uoluntates atque operationes in singularitatem personae. De prima quippe natiuitate ejus, quę secundum diuinitatem ex patre est,

Dauid propheta ex persona patris ad filium ait[1]: Ex utero ante luciferum genui te. Ex utero inquit, hoc est, de mea substantia; ante luciferum, id est ante omnem creaturam. De secunda uero generatione ejus, quę iuxta humanitatem temporalis facta est, beatus Paulus apostolus sua nos informans auctoritate, At ubi uenit, inquit, plenitudo temporis, misit deus filium suum, factum ex muliere, factum sub lege, ut eos, qui sub lege erant, redimeret, ut adoptionem filiorum reciperemus. De prima generatione, quę secundum deitatem est, *Esaias propheta* clamat: *Generationem ejus quis enarrabit?* De generatione autem ejus, que secundum carnem est, Mattheus euangelista scripsit: Liber generationis Jhesu Christi, filii Dauid, filii Abraam. De duabus uero uoluntatibus in eo ipse sibi dei filius testis est, qui tempore passionis suae patrem efflagitans ait: Pater, si fieri potest, transeat a me calix iste; ueruntamen non sicut ego uolo, sed sicut tu, pater. Similiter et de duabus operationibus qui nosse cupit, ex euangelica predicatione plenius scire potest. Idcirco autem dei filius, qui
30 uerus DEUS est ex patre, uerus HOMO dignatus est fieri ex matre, EX ANIMA
RATIONABILI ET CARNE consistentibus suis in singularitate personę, ut totum hominem ex anima rationabili et carne mortali subsistente, qui in Adam peccando perierat, per suam passionem ac mortem de mortis potestate redimeret, et per resurrectionem suam aeternae uitae participem efficeret. Non sicut Apollinaris hereticus predicare ausus est, qui eundem filium animam non habuisse asseruit; hoc tamen rationabile existimans, quod diuinitas ei sufficeret pro ratione. Catholica uero fides eundem dei filium dominum ac redemptorem nostrum, sicut uerum deum ex patre, ut dictum est, ita et uerum hominem ex matre animam habere rationabilem et carnem cum sensibus
32 suis credit et confitetur. QUI LICET DEUS SIT ET HOMO, NON TAMEN DUOS
Christos neque duas personas neque duos filios dei in eum credere oportet,
SED UNUM CHRISTUM unumque dei filium in duabus, ut dictum est, naturis;
35 singularis uero persona. SICUT enim quilibet HOMO, ex ANIMA RATIONABILI
(30) ET CARNE mortali SUBSISTENS NON DUO, SED UNUS EST HOMO, ITA et
34 Christus et DEUS ET HOMO IN UNITATEM PERSONAE, NON DUO SED UNUS EST
(31) CHRISTUS; unus saluator mundi ac redemptor humani generis: AEQUALIS
PATRI in forma dei MINOR uero ei in forma serui; creator matris suae et dominus secundum potentiam diuinitatis, creatus uero ex ipsa filius juxta humanitatem. Nam simul ex ea deus et homo absque ulla corruptione
33 gemina substantia, simplici autem persona, NON CONUERSIONE DIUINITATIS
IN CARNE, neque HUMANITATIS IN diuinitate: *id est*, neque *diuinitas, que immutabilis est*, in humanitatem conuersa est, neque humanitas in diuinitatem. Tenent igitur in eo in singularitate personae utręque naturae absque ulla conuertibilitate proprietates suas, dei scilicet quod dei est et hominis quod homo est. Sicut enim in essentiam diuinitatis unum est[2]

[1] This quotation from Ps. cxix. 3 was a proof-text in the Adoptianist controversy. It reappears in the Stavelot Commentary in the note on cl. 29. Cf. Alcuin c. *Felic.* v. 2.

[2] MS. sunt.

cum patre, ipso dicente: Ego et pater unum sumus, ita in natura humanitatis unum est cum ecclesia; quia idem Christus dominus cum ecclesia catholica, quae est sponsa ejus et caput et corpus, unus est Christus, Apostolo hoc affirmante atque dicente: Propter hoc relinquet homo patrem et matrem et adherebit uxori suae, et erunt duo in carne una. Sacramentum hoc magnum est; ego autem dico in Christo et in Ecclesia. Hoc autem ideo dominus fieri uoluit, ne in trinitate, *quod absit, quaternitas* intromittatur; quemadmodum Nestorius hereticus impie praedicare ausus est, qui dixit beatam Mariam uirginem non deum et hominem genuisse, in quo homine postea propter meritum sanctitatis diuinitatem filii dei habitasse, sicut et in ceteris sanctis. Ac per hoc, non unam, sed duas in Christo asserunt esse personas, et introduxit in trinitatem quaternitatem: cuius impia professio procul *absit a cordibus fidelium.* Nos autem credere oportet saepedictum dei filium secundum diuinitatem inuisibiliter in utero uirginis Mariae introisse, et ueram carnem ex substantia ejusdem uirginis Mariae, quam cum patre et spiritu sancto creauit, quasi quoddam uestimentum in singularitate personae suae ita unisse, ut nec deus sine homine nec homo absque deo fieri omnino potuisset; et ita in utraque natura et una persona incorruptibiliter ex ea natum. Et idcirco iam dictam uirginem Mariam non hominis tantum, sed dei et hominis, genitricem credimus et confitemur; quia dei filius, non personam hominis, sed naturam ex ea assumpsit humanitatis; quia nequaquam conceptio carnis in uirginis utero diuinitatis praeuenit aduentu, sed diuinitas praeuenit uirginis conceptum; quam humanam naturam tota trinitas in utero uirginis creauit, sed solus filius in singularitate personȩ suae suscepit atque uniuit. Idcirco autem dei filius naturam humani generis, id est, PERFECTUM HOMINEM absque peccato de uirgine suscipere (30)
dignatus est, ut per eandem naturam, quae in paradiso a diabolo decepta mortem incurrerat; rursum eundem diabolum, non potentia diuinitatis, sed ratione justitiae uinceret et prostraret, et per indebitam mortem suam debitam mortem nostram euacuaret, et credentibus sibi perpetuam uitam condonaret; quatinus et diabolus per justitiam uictus cederet, et, quos injuste retinebat, amitteret et humanum genus, non merito suo, seu libero arbitrio, sed sola gratia misericordiae saluaretur. Et ideo ob redemptionem humani generis, ut dictum est, diuinitatis suae potentia PASSUS EST, in 37
carne mortuus, et sepultus est in eadem carne. Secundum animam DESCENDIT AD INFERNUM. Secundum uirtutem diuinitatis suae DIE TERTIA in eadem carne, in qua mortuus fuerat, uiuus RESURREXIT. Post resurrectionem uero suam per dies XL. multis modis discipulis suis se uiuum exhibuit, atque ad palpandum prebuit, et ad confirmandam eorum fidem, et hereticorum destruendam perfidiam, qui eum negant ueram carnem in caelo leuasse, cibum petiit, et coram eis comedit: quadragesimo uero die post resurrectionem suam, uidentibus apostolis suis, ASCENDIT in CAELUM, et SEDET AD DEXTERAM PATRIS, id est, regnat in gloriam et beatitudinem sempiternam. Quem INDE UENTURUM ad faciendum judicium UIUORUM ET MORTUORUM in ipso mundi termino sustinemus in eadem forma humanitatis

et uera carne, in qua ascendit, sed glorificata, non infirma aut despecta, sicut in primo aduentu cum uenit occultus, ut judicaretur, sed, ut dictum est, in gloriam patris et suam, non ut judicetur, sed judicet et reddat unicuique secundum opus suum. De CUIUS ADUENTU secundo in libro apocalypsin scriptum est: Ecce ueniet cum nubibus caeli, et uidebit eum omnis oculus, et qui illum pupugerunt; ipse quisque in euangelio de suo aduentu ait; Cum uenerit filius hominis in majestate sua, et omnes angeli cum eo; et iterum ipse: Verum tamen filius hominis ueniet, putas,
38 inueniet fidem in terra? In CUIUS ADUENTU ad angelicam tubam OMNES defuncti a primo homine Adam usque ad ultimum, qui in fine mundi obiturus erit, tam pii, quam impii, tam justi quam etiam injusti secundum apostolicam auctoritatem in ictu oculi in eadem carne, in qua uixerunt, et in qua bona uel mala gesserunt, et in qua mortui sunt, RESURGERE HABENT, non naturam aut sexum mutantes, id est, neque uir in sexum femineum, neque mulier in uirili forma, sed unusquisque, ut dictum est, in propria forma atque sexu, in qua uixit et mortuus fuit, resurrecturus erit, ut in eadem carne, in qua bona uel mala gesserunt, recipiat unusquisque quod meretur. Illud tamen nobis credendum est, quod tam justi, quam et peccatores incorrupta recipiant CORPORA SUA. Hoc est, quod ultra mori non potuerunt, apostolo hoc affirmante atque dicente: Omnes quidem resurgemus, sed non omnes inmutabimur, in momento, in ictu oculi, in nouissima tuba. Canet enim tuba et mortui resurgent incorrupti, et nos inmutamur. Ideo tam electi, quam reprobi, incorrupta recipient corpora, quatinus et justi in eadem carne, in qua propter deum in hac uita poenas seu ceteros labores sustinuerunt, in ipsa recipiant a domino aeternam beatitudinem et perpetuam gloriam. In quibus erit aeterna uita una remuneratio, sed pro diuersitate meritorum dissimilis gloria. Similiter et omnes reprobi, impii uidelicet et peccatores, in propria corpora sua, in qua praue seu luxuriose uixerunt, recepturi sunt aeternam dampnationem, in quibus tamen pro qualitate uel quantitate peccatorum dissimilis erit poena, sed una dampnatio sempiterna. Hoc quippe judicium deus pater omnipotens per filium suum in hominem assumptum facturus est, sicut ipse filius in euangelio de semet ipso testatur dicens: Pater non judicat quemquam, sed omne judicium dedit filio. Non tamen ita accipiendum est, ut filius absque patre et spiritu sancto, a quibus omnino diuidi non potest, solus judicet; sed ideo ita dictum credimus, quia pater inuisibilis est, et a nullo hominum uideri potest. Et ideo solus filius, ut dictum est, judicabit, quia ipse solus formam serui accepit, in qua uisibiliter uiuos et mortuos judicaturus est. Inuisibiliter uero tota trinitas judicabit; uisibiliter autem, ut dictum est, solus filius in forma serui juste judicabit, qui ob redemptionem humani generis solus in carne assumpta injuste ab impiis judicatus est. In cujus judicio electi duabus in partibus discreti erunt, id est, perfectis, quibus dictum est: Sedebitis super duodecim sedes judicantes XII. tribus Israel. Quod enim apostolis tunc promissum est, ad omnes perfectos pertinet, qui cum domino ceteros judicabunt. Secundus uero ordo erit in illis, qui ad superiorem, hoc est, apostolorum et martyrum se perfectorum

mensuram peruenire non potuerunt, et tamen per satisfactionem poenitentię, per elymosynarum largitionem, per compassionem sanctorum, et cetera justitiae opera uitam consecuturi sunt aeternam. Talibus enim conuenit illa domini sententia qua ait: Facite uobis amicos de iniquo mamona, ut cum defeceritis, recipiant uos in eterna tabernacula; et illud: Qui uos recipit, me recipit. Reprobi uero similiter duabus distincti erunt in partibus, impiis uidelicet et peccatoribus. Impii appellantur omnes infideles, qui dominum non nouerunt, de quibus psalmista ait: Non resurgunt impii[1] in judicio. Resurgent utique, non ut judicentur, sed ut punientur; quoniam secundum apostolicam auctoritatem quicunque sine lege peccauerunt, sine lege et peribunt. De talibus ueritas in euangelio ait; Qui non credit jam judicatus est; hoc est, jam dampnatus est. Peccatores uero uocantur, qui intra ecclesiam per fidem commorantur, sed praue uiuunt. De talibus rursum psalmista ait: Neque peccatores in concilio justorum; de quibus et Paulus: Confitetur se nosse Deum, factis autem negant, cum sint abbominati, et incredibiles, et ad omne opus bonum reprobi; quos et dominus per euangelium increpat dicens: Quid prodest qui dicitis michi, domine, domine, et non facitis quae dico. Sicut enim fides, quam se mali christiani habere gloriantur, absque bonis operibus eos saluare non potest, ita bonum opus quodcunque infideles agunt, sine fide nichil illis prodest, apostolo hoc affirmante, qui ait: Omne, quod non est ex fide, peccatum est. Et ideo solos illos credimus posse saluos fieri, qui et fidem rectam absque ullo discrimine retinent, et bonis operibus, in quantum possunt, laborare non desinunt, uitantes scilicet capitalia atque mortifera crimina, sicut ait psalmista: Declina a malo et fac bonum; et alibi: Quiescite agere peruerse, discite bene facere. Quod
autem dicimus de Christo domino: INDE UENTURUS UIUOS AC MORTUOS[2], 37
uiuos intelligimus, quos dies judicii uiuos inuenerit, mortuos autem omnes, qui antea obierunt, et tunc resurrecturi erunt; uel certe, ut quidam uolunt, sicut per uiuentes electi, ita per mortuos reprobi omnes accipiendi sunt. Post futurum uero judicium, et justorum remunerationem, atque iniquorum dampnationem, quicquid in utrisque diuina sententia decreuerit, id est, in electis ac reprobis, aeternum et sine fine erit: nec mali ultra gaudia sperabunt, nec boni tristitiam formidabunt. Quoniam, sicut electi perpetua letitia fruentes ad reproborum dampnationem, ut quidam heretici uoluerunt, in aeternum reuersuri non erunt, ita et reprobi in perpetua demersi[3] ad electorum gaudia nequaquam ultra consurgent, ipso judice teste, qui ait:
ET IBUNT hi, id est, impii et peccatores IN supplicium AETERNUM, justi 39
autem IN UITAM AETERNAM. HAEC EST FIDES CATHOLICA, QUAM uniuersalis 40
ecclesia in electis suis corde credit, ore profitetur, et bonis operibus exequitur. De qua fide quicunque ex his, qui christiano nomine censentur, quicquam detraxerit aut credere noluerit, proculdubio catholicus non erit, sed intra ecclesiam positus sub nomine christianitatis recte catholicus, ut hereticus deputabitur.

[1] MS. impio. [2] + IUDICARE *corr. supra lin.*
[3] Probably *tristitia* has been omitted.

(4) The Fortunatus Commentary.

A.

			Saec.
1.	*o*	Junius 25, Bodl. Lib. Oxford, from Murbach Abbey, collated by myself	IX in
2.	*b*	Bamberg A. 11. 16, found and collated by Rev. W. D. Macray .	IX/X
3.	b_1	Bamberg B. 11. 16, found and collated by Rev. W. D. Macray .	XII
4.	(*f*)	Florence (collated imperfectly by F. A. Zaccaria, in Swainson p. 436)	XIV
5.	*g*	S. Gall 241, collated by Dr Fäh, verified by myself	IX
6.	*G*	Goldast's S. Gall MS.	(IX)
7.	*m*	Milan Ambros. M. 48. 79, collated by Prof. J. A. Robinson and Rev. A. E. Brooke	XI
8.	*n*	Munich cod. lat. 14,508, collated by Dr v. Laubmann and verified by myself	X
9.	*p*	Paris B. N. lat. 2826, collated by Mr Ommanney	IX ex
10.	p_1	Paris B. N. lat. 1008, collated by Mr Ommanney	X ex
11.	*t*	Munich cod. lat. (19,417), collated by myself	IX
12.	*v*	Vienna 1032 (clauses 1—19), collated by Dr Swainson . . .	IX

B.

1.	g_1	S. Gall 27, transcribed by friends, verified by myself	IX
2.	n_2	Munich cod. lat. 3729, collated by myself.	X

The words omitted in the B recension are shown by [ ]

Expositio Fidei Catholicae.

1 Quicunque uult saluus esse, ante omnia opus est ut teneat catholicam fidem. fides dicitur credulitas siue credentia. catholica uniuersalis dicitur, id est recta, quam uniuersa ecclesia tenere debet. Ecclesia

Expositio in Fide Catholica *o* Ex. fidei bb_1 *deest titulus gv* Euphronii presbyteri ex. fidei catholicae Beati Athanasii *G* Ex. f. c. fortunati *m* De Fide Catholica *n* Ex. super fidem Cath. *p* ......fide catholica p_1 Ex. super fides catholica *t*

1 > esse saluus *m* 2 *om.* fides...credentia *m* dicte g_1 credentia (-cia *t*)] + catholica b_1pgt catholicam uniuersalem quia catholicam *v* 3 id est] idem *v*, *om.* est b_1 rectam *v* *om.* quam...debet *n* > ecclesia uniuersa *obGp* Ecclesia] + quippe *m*

2 *Credulitas* is often used by Faustus as a synonym for *fides*, cf. *Ep.* 5 (E.). In a list of Greek words Eucherius explains *catholica* by *uniuersalis* S. Gall 27 + Qui catholicam fidem credendo et opere exercendo neglegit hereticus est et schismaticus: huius interitus sine dubio manebit

dicitur congregatio christianorum siue conuentus populorum. Vᴛ ᴜɴᴜᴍ 3
ᴅᴇᴜᴍ ɪɴ ᴛʀɪɴɪᴛᴀᴛᴇ ᴇᴛ ᴛʀɪɴɪᴛᴀᴛᴇᴍ ɪɴ ᴜɴɪᴛᴀᴛᴇ ᴜᴇɴᴇʀᴇᴍᴜʀ: et credamus
et colamus et confiteamur. Nᴇǫᴜᴇ ᴄᴏɴꜰᴜɴᴅᴇɴᴛᴇs ᴘᴇʀsᴏɴᴀs, ut Sabellius 4
errat, qui ipsum dicit esse patrem in persona quem et filium ipsum et
spiritum sanctum. non ergo confundentes personas quia tres omnino
personae sunt. est enim gignens genitus procedens. [gignens est pater,
qui genuit filium, filius est genitus quem genuit pater, spiritus sanctus est
procedens quia a patre et filio procedit. patri et filio coaeternus est et
coaequalis et cooperator. sicut scriptum est: *Verbo domini coeli firmati* Ps. xxxiii.
sunt, id est a filio dei creati, *spiritu oris eius omnis uirtus eorum:* ubi 6.
sub singulari numero *spiritu eius* dicit, unitatem substantiae deitatis
ostendit: ubi sub plurali numero *omnis uirtus eorum* dicit, trinitatem personarum aperte demonstrat, quia tres unum sunt et unum tres. Nᴇǫᴜᴇ ꜱᴜʙꜱᴛᴀɴᴛɪᴀᴍ ꜱᴇᴘᴀʀᴀɴᴛᴇꜱ, ut Arius garrit, qui sicut tres personas esse dicit sic et tres substantias esse mentitur. filium dicit minorem quam patrem et creaturam esse, spiritum sanctum adhuc minorem quam filium, et patris et filii eum esse administratorem adserit. non ergo substantiam separantes, quia totae tres personae in substantia deitatis unum sunt.]

1 *om.* dicitur g_1n_2 congregacio *t* populi *n* (Troyes) 2 et 2°] ut g_1n_2 (Troyes) 3 *om.* et 1° *G* colamur et confiatemur g_1 *om.* et colamus *Gn* 3, 5 confundantes *g** 4 personam *g*n* quem] qui *n* ipsum] + filium quem (Troyes) *forsitan recte* 5 quia] + tote *n* ∽ personae omnino g_1mnn_2tpv (*sed* -as *g**, -a *g corr.*, -nas (n *supra*) omni × no n *ras. t*) 6 enim] ergo g_1n_2p gignens] gignis *g*, gignes *n* genitus] + et mp_1 (Troyes) 7 genitus] unigenitus *t* quem genuit] qui est genita -us *in ras. n* 8 quia] qui *Ggp* *om.* a *t* patri et filio quoaeternus (co- *n*) est et (*om.* et *n*) quoaequalis et quooperator (co- *n*) *nv* *cf.* Symb. Damasi sec. pater et filius coaeterni sibi sunt et coaequales (coeq-o *t*) et cooperatores ob_1Ggmpp_1t (Troyes) (*sed* cooperationes i *ras. g*p*) 9 domini] dei *n* celi *g* 10 creati] + sunt *n* *om.* a *G* filjo *o* creatus *g* spiritu] spiritus ob_1Gfp eius] meus *n* 11 *om.* sub *G* singulare *gt* spiritus ᴍss. *omnes* dicit] dicitur *bfGmt* 12 attendit *G* sub plurali] supplurali *g*, plurari *o* uirtur *g* dicit] dicitur $fmpp_1t$ 13 *om.* aperte *G* quia] qui *G*, + et *n* 14 substantia *g* seperantes *o*, separentes *t* arrius ob_1gnpp_1v quia *mp* *om.* sicut *mft*, sic bb_1p_1, ut *f*, scilicet *G* 15 si et *m*, sicut *v*, sicut et Gb_1, *om.* et *p* 16 patrem] + filium b_1 17 patri et filio *oG* filii eum] fili eum (i *intra lin.*) *g* > administratorem esse b_1mptv, ministrum (Troyes) *om.* esse p_1 18 seperantes *obv*, separentes *t* tote ob_1g, tota *t*, toto *p* persone *t* in substantia] in s. (*ras.* 4) substantia (*ras.* 1) *g* (substantiae p. m. *ut uid.*), substantiae *n* substantiam p_1

8 Greg. Turon. *Hist.* (Mg. p. 88) shows that Avitus of Vienne confessed: filium et spiritum sanctum aequalem patri 9 *Verbo domini*...This verse is quoted by Eucherius in the same connection. He adds: pater ingenitus, filius genitus, spiritus sanctus nec genitus nec ingenitus: ne si ingenitum dixerimus, duos patres dicere uideamur: si genitum duos filios: sed potius qui ex patre et filio procedat uelut quaedam patris filiique concordia

5 (20) ALIA EST ENIM PERSONA PATRIS, quia PATER ingenitus est, eo quod A
(21) NULLO EST GENITUS. ALIA persona FILII, quia FILIUS A PATRE SOLO
(22) GENITUS EST. ALIA SPIRITUS SANCTI, quia A PATRE ET FILIO SPIRITUS
6 SANCTUS PROCEDENS EST. SED PATRIS ET FILII ET SPIRITUS SANCTI UNA
EST DIUINITAS, id est deitas AEQUALIS GLORIA, id est claritas. COAE-
7 TERNA MAIESTAS, maiestas gloria est claritatis siue potestas. QUALIS
PATER TALIS FILIUS TALIS ET SPIRITUS SANCTUS, id est in deitate et om-
8 nipotentia. INCREATUS PATER INCREATUS FILIUS INCREATUS ET SPIRITUS
9 SANCTUS, id est a nullo creati. IMMENSUS PATER IMMENSUS FILIUS IM-
MENSUS ET SPIRITUS SANCTUS. non est mensurabilis in sua natura, quia
inlocalis est, incircumscriptus, ubique totus, ubique praesens, ubique po-
10 tens. AETERNUS PATER AETERNUS FILIUS AETERNUS ET SPIRITUS SANC-
11 TUS, id est NON TRES AETERNI, SED in tribus personis UNUS deus AETERNUS,
13 qui sine initio et sine fine aeternus permanet. SIMILITER OMNIPOTENS
PATER OMNIPOTENS FILIUS OMNIPOTENS ET SPIRITUS SANCTUS. omnipotens dicitur eo quod omnia potest et omnium obtinet potestatem. ergo si omnia potest, quid est quod non potest? hoc non potest quod omnipotenti non competit posse. falli non potest quia ueritas est; infirmari non potest quia sanitas est; mori non potest quia inmortalis uita est;

1 > patris persona p_1 *om.* pater b_1 2 nulo g_1 alia] + est p filii] + est g_1 3 > est solo genitus oG, solo est genitus p_1 alia] + et filii et p *om.* sancti n quia] qui pg_1 *om.* a t > spiritus sanctus a patre et filio gnp_1 *om.* spiritus sanctus g_1mn_2pt 4 *om.* est n *om.* et spiritus sancti p_1 5 deitas] *pr* una g_1n_2 aequalis (eq- t)] qualis g aequalis (eq- g_1) claritas coeterna gloria est claritas siue potestas g_1n_2 6 maiestas 2° *intra lin. al. man.* g *om.* est v claritatis $obGfnv$] claritas $b_1gg_1n_2mpp_1t$ potestatis n 7 *om.* et 1° b_1p *om.* est b omnipotentia (a *ras.*) t^* 8 increatus et s. s.] *om.* et b_1p *om.* increatus 3° g 9 *om.* est b_1 creatus gg_1mn (Troyes) immensus t] inmensus MSS. *alii* 10 *om.* et G natura (n *super ras.*) t 11 inlocalis] *pr* et g incircums.] *pr* et gg_1mnn_2t presens o 12 *om.* et g 13 tribus] tres g 14 inicio t *om.* et G 16 dicitur] dicit g_1 *om.* eo n potens g (*bis*) optenit oG, optinet n, obtenit g 17 quid est] quidem g hoc non...ueritas est *in marg.* g_1 non potest] non potenst g_1 hoc...ueritas est *infra* g_1 *om.* quod 2° n omnipotente gn 18 conpetit og posse] esse G, post se g *om.* quia ueritas...non potest mn_2t *om.* infirmari non potest g_1n_2t infirmare og 19 sanita g] sanctus m potenst g_1 > est uita b_1

9 Eucherius *Lib. Form.* Omnipotens deus pater et filius et spiritus sanctus unus atque trinus. Unus uidelicet exstat in natura, trinus in personis. Solus inuisibilis immensus atque incomprehensibilis...ubique praesens et latens, ubique totus et immensus...Immensus est quia quantitas eius uel qualitas a nullo ex creaturis metiri possit 13 Note that the main part of cl. 11 is incorporated in the weakened form in which it appears in Fulgentius 18 *competit.* Cf. Faustus *Ep.* 5 (E.) and *De Sp. Sco.* ii. 8 Soli deo conpetit de suo charismatum dona largiri. Fulgentius *c. Fab. Frag. ex Ep. ad Cor.* 1 xii. quia deo conpetit naturaliter dominum esse

finiri non potest quia infinitus et perennis est. ITA DEUS PATER DEUS 15
FILIUS DEUS ET SPIRITUS SANCTUS. deus nomen est potestatis non proprie-
tatis. proprium nomen est patris pater, et proprium nomen est filii
filius, et proprium nomen est spiritus sancti spiritus sanctus. ITA 17
DOMINUS PATER DOMINUS FILIUS DOMINUS ET SPIRITUS SANCTUS. domi-
nus dicitur eo quod omnia dominat et omnium est *dominus dominator*. IV Esdr.
QUIA SICUT SINGILLATIM, id est, sicut distinctim, UNAMQUAMQUE PER- 19 iii.—xiv.
SONAM ET DEUM ET DOMINUM CONFITERI CHRISTIANA UERITATE COMPEL- *passim.*
LIMUR: quia si me interrogaueris quid sit pater, ego respondebo deus et
dominus: similiter et si me interrogaueris quid sit filius, ego dico
deus et dominus: et si dicis quid est spiritus sanctus, ego dico deus
et dominus. et in his tribus personis NON TRES DEOS nec TRES DOMINOS (16. 18)
sed in his tribus sicut iam supradictum est UNUM DEUM ET UNUM DOMI-
NUM confiteor. VNUS ERGO PATER, NON TRES PATRES, id est quia pater 23
semper pater nec aliquando filius: UNUS FILIUS NON TRES FILII, id est
quia filius semper filius nec aliquando pater: UNUS SPIRITUS SANC-

1 finire ogg_1pp_1 potens g_1 quia] quod g_1 pennis g_1 2 filjus o > deus et Gg *om.* deus...proprietatis m potestate non proprietate gt deus est potestatem non proprietatem f 3 > est nomen G (*bis*) *om.* est 1° bb_1gg_1nt *om.* est 2° g_1 patris...filii...sp. sancti] patri...filio...spiritui sancto v (Troyes) (*sed* spiritus sancti) nomen patri pater g 4 ita dominus p. d. f. d. et s. sanctus *infra in marg.* g 5 *om.* et p 6 dominatur b_1fn (-etur Tr.), domat g_1n_2 *om.* dominus p_1, > dominator dominus n_2 7 *om.* id... distinctim G *om.* est *sicut* b_1 distinctum obg^*v, distincte b_1g_1 (-ae m) n_2pp_1t, distinctam n 8 *om.* et 1° Gbb_1mpp_1t et 2°] ac G confitere g conpellimur obb_1gnt] *def.* v 9 quia] quodsi n si me] sint g_1 quid] qui p_1 sit] est $g_1mnn_2pp_1t$, *om.* sit g *om.* ego n 10 *om.* et g_1mnn_2t *om.* me ob_1 quid] qui gn_2 sit] est gg_1nt dico] dicam m, ergo respondebo n 12 *om.* in p_1t] ab n nec] neque n 13 sed in his b_1mpr] sed his tribus $obgg_1np_1$ *om.* iam g_1 supradixi $oGfn$ 14 confitemur n_2 patris p_1 i. e.] et g_1, idem b quia] qui obb_1 15 *om.* semper p nec] non n i. e.] et g_1 16 quia] qui opg_1

3 Faustus *De S. S.* ii. 6. Da in deo nomen speciale uel proprium, id est pater et filius et spiritus sanctus ingenitus genitus ex utroque procedens. id. *Sermon* 2. trinitatem facit proprietas nominum et numerus personarum. *Sermon* 31. proprietas est appellationis non diuersitas potestatis uel maiestatis. genitus et ingenitus personae est differentia non naturae. Fulg. *c. Fab. Frag. ad Col.* iv. Personarum uero proprietas demonstrat alium esse patrem a. f. a. s. s. 4 Faustus *De S. S.* ii. 10. uides quod sicut unus pater et unus filius ita et unus est spiritus sanctus. 14 S. Gall 27 + Istum nobis unum deum noui et ueteris testamenti ueredica demonstrat auctoritas. de hoc uno muses (moyses n_2) dicit Audi israel dominus deus tuus deus unus est et dominum tuum (unum n_2) adorabis et illi soli seruies. et dauid dicit Quis (est n_2) deus praeter dominum Pater ex quo omnia et qui non habet patrem. filius a patre genitus. spiritus sanctus de dei hore procedens et cuncta sanctificans. Note that S. Gall 27 omits the quotation on p. 29 line 10 *spiritus oris eius omnis uirtus eorum.*

TUS NON TRES SPIRITUS SANCTI, id est quia spiritus sanctus semper
spiritus sanctus nec aliquando filius aut pater. haec est proprietas
24 personarum. ET IN HAC TRINITATE NIHIL PRIUS AUT POSTERIUS: quia
sicut nunquam filius sine patre, sic nunquam fuit pater sine filio,
sic et nunquam fuit pater et filius sine spiritu sancto. coaeterna ergo
trinitas et inseparabilis unitas sine initio et sine fine. NIHIL MAIUS AUT
MINUS. aequalitatem personarum dicit [quia trinitas aequalis est et una
Rom. i. 20. deitas, apostolo dicente atque docente: *Per ea quae facta sunt intellecta*
conspiciuntur, et per creaturam creator intelligitur, secundum has com-
parationes et alias quamplures: sol, candor, et calor, tria sunt uocabula
et res una. quod candet hoc calet et quod calet hoc candet: tria haec
uocabula et res una esse dignoscitur. Ita et] pater et filius et spiritus
sanctus tres personae in deitate substantiae unum sunt et indiuidua unitas
recte creditur. [item de terrenis, uena, fons, fluuius, tria itemque uocabula
et res una in sua natura. ita trium personarum patris et filii et spiritus
28 sancti substantia et deitas unum est.] EST ERGO FIDES RECTA UT CREDAMUS
ET CONFITEAMUR QUIA DOMINUS NOSTER JESUS CHRISTUS DEI FILIUS ET

1 i. e.] et g_1 quia] qui *ot* semper] + est *m* 2 nec] non *n* aliquando] + est ? *ras. t*, + pater et *n* *om.* filius aut *p* hec g_1 *om.* est $b_1gg_1n_2$ 3 et iam trinitate *n* nichil *m* 4 sicut] sic g_1 numquam obb_1 sic] sicut *G* sicut numquam fuit pater sine filio sic nunquam filius sine patre et sic nunquam p_1 filio] filius *t** 5 *om.* ergo g_1n_2 6 *om.* inseparabilis unitas g_1n_2 seperabilis $obb_1g_1pp_1$ inicio g_1 nichil *m* 7 equalitatem $obb_1g_1mpp_1$, equalis obb_1m *om.* est et *n* 8 deitatis *o* dicente] *om.* atque docente *oG*, dicentem *m* atque] et *b* quae] que *n* facta] ficta b_1 9 intellegitur obb_1npp_1 *om.* has *n* as *p* conparationes obb_1npt 10 cadorem et calorem habet et tria (trea *sub ras.*) *n* candor] splendor (Troyes) tria] trea *ot*, tres *gG*, *pr.* et *gm* uocabula] nomina $obpp_1$ 11 *om.* et 1° *g* res una] tres una *n*, tria unum mpp_1t, + dinoscitur *g*, + ut diximus *n* uocabula...sed res una est (Troyes) candit (*bis*) $ogmpp_1$, cardet (*bis*) b_1 calit obb_1gpp_1t *om.* quod candet...una *n* tria haec... dinoscitur *in marg. o* hec *b* 12 *om.* et 1° obb_1gmpp_1 res unam *t*, *om.* res *b* dinoscitur obb_1Ggmt *om.* et 2° bb_1gmpp_1 (Troyes) 13 persone $ob_1g_1np_1t$ *om.* in deitate...sunt p_1 in substancia g_1, substanciae *g* (-e *t*) 14 recta credatur *g* item] ita b_1 terraena p_1 > fluuius fons p_1 trea ob_1G ite |||| que *n*, idemque *m* + sunt p_1 uocabulo *g*, uocabu....la *t* (*lacuna in perg.*) 15 res una] tres una *n*, tria unum bb_1mpp_1t, + sunt bb_1 sua] una *b* *om.* et 2° *oG* 16 unum] una ob_1gnp_1 *om.* ergo *t* recte *t* 17 *om.* noster mpp_1t Ihesus $ognpp_1$ (Troyes), Jesus bb_1g_1m (*semper*) Christus + Ihesus *p* *om.* dei filius et homo est b_1gmnt

11 *tria haec uocabula.* Cf. Fides b. Athanasii in Milan Cod. I. 101 (Bobbio) saec. VII/VIII, Sw. p. 327, una uirtus unus deus trea uero uocabula. 14 S. Gall. 27 + Solus humanam naturam sic accepit ut suam faceret et per illam diuinitatis quoque sue notitiam (notic- n_2) misericorditer hominibus infudisset.

HOMO EST. Jesus hebraïce, latine saluator [dicitur. Christus graece, latine
unctus uocatur. Jesus ergo dicitur] eo quod saluat populum: Christus eo
quod spiritu sancto sit delibutus, [sicut in ipsius Christi persona Esaias
ait: *Spiritus domini super me propter quod unxit me* etc.]. item in psalmo: Is. lxi. 1.
Vnxit te deus, deus tuus, oleo laetitiae prae consortibus tuis. DEI FILIUS, Ps. xlv. 7.
DEUS PARITER ET HOMO EST. filius a felicitate parentum dicitur, homo ab
humo dicitur, id est de humo factus est. DEUS EST EX SUBSTANTIA 29
PATRIS ANTE SAECULA GENITUS: id est deus de deo, lumen de lumine,
[splendor de splendore, fortis de forte, uirtus de uirtute, uita de uita,
aeternitas de aeternitate. per omnia idem] quod pater in diuina sub-
stantia hoc est filius. deus pater deum filium genuit, non uoluntate neque
necessitate, sed natura. nec quaeratur quomodo genitus sit, quod angeli
nesciunt prophetis est incognitum. [unde eximius propheta Esaias dicit: Is. liii. 8.
Generationem eius quis enarrabit? ac si diceret, angelorum nemo prophe-
tarum nullus.] nec inenarrabilis et inaestimabilis deus a seruulis suis

1 Jesus] + ergo *n* ebraice *g*, aebreica *t*, ebreo sermone (Troyes) in latino *n* grece *o*, in greca lingua, in latina (-o *n*) unctus dicitur (uocatur b_1n) b_1gn greca lingua Christus latine unctus (Troyes) *om.* Christus...dicitur *mt* 2 ergo] + saluator *p* *om.* eo p_1 populum] + suum fp_1 (Troyes) eo 2°] et g_1 3 spiritus sanctus sit *g* sit] *om.* sit obb_1f *pr.* diuinitus b_1gm (-as *n*) n_2t, diuitus *p*, diuinitatis *b*, dilibutus *g*, + ut psalmista g_1 *om.* Christi np_1 persone *o*, personam Isaias *n* 4 ait] dicit *nt* me] + euangelizare *t* *om.* propter...me p_1 item] ita $bfgmnpp_1t$, *om.* g_1n_2 in psalmo] psalmus bb_1fgnpp_1t, et psalmista *m*, ut psalmista g_1n_2, + de Christo domino $bgmnpp_1t$, + de Christo *b*, + dicit $gmnpp_1t$ 5 uncxit *m* (*bis*) (Troyes), uncsit *g* deus deus] dominus deus *f* et in psalmo propheta ad ipsum Christum dominum: sedes tua...unxit etc. (Troyes) oleum *t* letitiae *mo* (-a *t*) preconsortibus *og*, pre cons. t. (Troyes) dei] deus *nt* 6 pariter] pater bb_1np (*ras.*), *om.* pariter p_1 *om.* homo est *b* felicitate g_1 dicitur] dictus g_1 (*bis*), est dictus n_2 7 *om.* est *b* de huma *g*, humo, umo p_1] + terrae $bb_1gg_1mnn_2pp_1t$ *om.* est 2° *m* *om.* est 3° g_1n_2 8 secula obb_1gpp_1 *om.* de p_1 9 forti *Gm* 10 *om.* idem Gp_1, omne quod *supra lin.* *G*, id est *gmnpt* quod] *pr.* et g_1n_2 *om.* quod bb_1 *om.* diuina p_1 + est p_1 11 est] + et g_1mp, es et *p* 12 naturae *o* (-e *n*) pp_1 queratur og_1npt, neque ratur *g*, quaeratur ur *ras.* *p*, + aliquis *p* genitus sit] genuit filium $bb_1gg_1mnp_1$ angeli] *pr.* et $bb_1gg_1mnn_2p_1t$, *om.* et *oGp* 13 > incognitum est p_1 unde] + et *m*, + de gp_1, + isdem *bnt*, + hisdem $gmpp_1$ eximius *ras.* *g*] magnificus bb_1 Esaias dicit] Isaias ait *n* 14 enarrauit $ofgbmpp_1$ dixisset bb_1gmnpp_1t nemo... 15 nullus] nullus...nemo $bgmpp_1t$, nullus...nullus *g* innarrabilis *ognt*, inestimabilis (-es *o*) *omt*, instimabilis *g*p*, *om.* et inaestimabilis g_1n_2 seruolis *o*, seruis *p* *om.* suis (*eras.*) n_2

1 Cf. Rufinus *in Symb. Apost.* c. 6, Jesus Hebraei uocabuli est nomen, quod apud nos 'Saluator' dicitur. Christus a chrismate, id est ab unctione appellatus
6 Cf. Eucherius *ad Johann.* 2, homo et deus, hoc est Christus, una persona est
15 inaestimabilis: cf. Vigil. Thaps. *c. Pallad.*: Pater deus immensus aeternus incomprehensibilis inaestimabilis est et Filius eius deus et dominus

discutiendus est, sed fideliter credendus, et puriter diligendus. [ET HOMO
EST EX SUBSTANTIA MATRIS IN SAECULO NATUS. dei filius uerbum patris
caro factum. non quod diuinitas mutasset deitatem, sed adsumpsit
S. John i. 14. humanitatem. hoc est *uerbum caro factum est* ex utero uirginali; ueram
humanam carnem traxit, et de utero uirginis uerus homo sicut et uerus
deus est in saeculo natus, quia mater quae genuit uirgo ante partum
et uirgo post partum permansit. IN SAECULO, id est, in isto sexto miliario
in quo nunc sumus. deus et homo Christus Jesus, unus dei filius et ipse
uirginis filius. Quia dum deitas in utero uirginis humanitatem adsumpsit,
et cum ea per portam uirginis integram et inlaesam nascendo mundum
ingressus est uirginis filius; et homo quem adsumpsit idem est dei filius, sicut
iam supradiximus, et deitas et humanitas in Christo, et dei patris pariter et
30 uirginis matris filius. PERFECTUS DEUS PERFECTUS HOMO EX ANIMA
RATIONALI: et non ut Apollinaris haereticus dixit primum quasi deitas
pro anima fuisset in carne Christi. postea cum per euangelicam auctoritatem fuit conuictus, dixit: 'Habuit quidem animam quae uiuificauit
corpus sed non rationalem.' e contrario dicit qui catholice sentit, EX

1 discuciendus *g*, discutiandus *t*   est *supra lin.* n_2 puriter] pariter $g_1mnn_2pp_1t$ homo] hoc *g*   2 *om.* EST *m*   seculo (sec- *semper ogt*)] secula *mt*   filium p_1 uerbo *o*   *om.* patris b_1m 3 factum] + et b_1, + est *n*   4 *om.* est 2° *n*   uirginali] uirginis b_1gnpt 5 uirginis] uirginali b_1mp (-e *gt*)   6 *om.* est b_1gmnt natus] + est b_1mnpp_1, + natus est *g*, + salua uirginitatis gratia bb_1gmnpp_1t quae] qui *g*, que *n*, qua *b*   genuit] + et $bfgmnpp_1t$ 7 permansit (-sisse *g*) in seculo obb_1gnt, secula *p*   *om.* est *b*   *om.* isto p_1 sexto] saeculo *t**   8 Jesus] deus *fg*, + deus bb_1pp_1 ipse] + est *p*   *om.* deus...filius *m*   9 dum] quum *G*, cum *n*   10 ea] eam *Gt*   portam u.] totam uirginitatis *n*   inlesam obb_1gt, illaesam *m*   11 ingresus *n*, ingressa *p*   hominem oGb_1g idem] id obb_1gnpp_1 *om.* est *ft*   filium op_1 12 *om.* iam b_1fpp_1 et 1°] ut obb_1fgt et 2°] ut p_1 *om.* et 3° *f*   13 *om.* matris *f*   filius] + est b_1gnpp_1, + sit *f*   perfectus deus] + perfectus quidem deus in diuinitate n_2 homo] + id est (idem *b*) uerus deus et (*om.* et *bgnt*) uerus homo bb_1gmnpp_1t (Troyes), + in humanitate unus et uerus propriusque dei filius n_2 14 rationale *og* (-bile *n*), -tione *t* (f. 20 *verso*, f. 20 *recto lacuna*)   ut] sicut *n*   apolonaris *p*, paulinaris obp_1, paulo naris *gt*, paulonantes *n*   ereticus *mo* (he- *ngt*)   Primum *m*   15 pro anima] per animas p_1 euangelium *p**, euangelii *p corr.*, euangelica authoritate p_1 16 fuit] fuisset b_1m *om.* dixit p_1 quae] que b_1, qui *o*   uiuificat *g*   17 rationabilem b_1p e contrario] *pr.* et b_1gmpp_1, *om.* e gp_1, contrarie *n*, + iste $gmnpp_1t$ dixit p_1t qui] quia *n*   catholicae *m*

7 uirgo post partum: cf. Caesarius Ps.-Aug. *Serm.* 244   Cf. Greg. Turon. *Hist.* Prol., Credo beatam Mariam ut uirginem ante partum ita uirginem et post partum. 13 S. Gall 27 + Perfectus quidem deus in diuinitate. perfectus homo in humanitate unus et uerus propriusque dei filius   Cf. S. Hil. *De Trin.* III. 11, Hic enim uerus et proprius est filius, origine non adoptione, ueritate non nuncupatione, natiuitate non creatione

ANIMA RATIONALI ET HUMANA CARNE SUBSIStit, id est plenus homo
atque perfectus.] AEQUALIS PATRI SECUNDUM DIUINITATEM MINOR PATRI 31
SECUNDUM HUMANITATEM: id est secundum formam serui quam adsumere
dignatus est. [quia certe] DEUS SIT ET HOMO, NON DUO TAMEN SED UNUS 32
EST CHRISTUS: id est duae substantiae in Christo, deitas et humanitas,
non duae personae sed una. UNUS AUTEM NON CONUERSIONE DIUINITATIS 33
IN CARNE SED ADSUMPTIONE HUMANITATIS IN DEO: id est non quod diuinitas quae inmutabilis et inconuertibilis est caro, sed ideo unus eo quod humanitatem adsumpsit. incipit esse quod non erat, et non amisit quod erat. incipit esse homo quod antea non fuerat, non amisit deitatem
quae inmutabilis in aeternum permansit. VNUS OMNINO, NON CONFUSIONE 34
SUBSTANTIAE, SED UNITATE PERSONAE: [id est, diuinitas inmutabilis cum homine, quem adsumere dignatus est, sicut scriptum est, *Verbum tuum, domine, in aeternum permanet:*] id est diuinitas cum humanitate ut diximus duas substantias unam esse in Christo; ut sicut ante adsumptionem carnis aeterna fuit trinitas ita post adsumptionem humanae naturae uera permaneat trinitas [ne propter adsumptionem humanae carnis dicatur esse quaternitas, quod absit a fidelium cordibus uel sensibus

Ps. cxix. 89.

1 racionali *m*, rationale *ognt* (-abile p_1) subsistens bb_1gmp_1t id est] idem b_1 2 adque *t* equalis *ogm* patri ob_1gnpp_1t] patre *Gm* (cf. Troyes l. 20 minorem patri) 3 est] +usque hic *n* 4 quia] qui $obmnpp_1$ certe] licet *m* tamen] + sunt bb_1 5 duae] due g_1, duo (*bis*) b_1 substantie gg_1n 6 due (duo *t*) persone gg_1nt una] + persona bp_1, + est persona gg_1mn_2pt autem] enim *n* 7 carnem...deum *Gb*, carne *t*, deum m^{corr} id est] idem b_1, *om.* id est g_1 8 que *t* immutabilis (imu- *g*) *ogp*, incommutabilis $bb_1g_1mn_2p_1t$ inconuertibilis] incorruptibilis bb_1G, + facta est *G* *om.* et inconuertibilis *m* caro] sit conuersa in carnem (carne *m*) sed b_1m, neque diuinitas que inmutabilis est in humanitatem conuersa est (Troyes) > unus ideo p_1 9 incipit] coepit *m* (*bis*) 10 *om.* homo *obG* 11 quae] qui *n*, quia mn_2pp_1t imutabilis *g* incommutabilis *m* + deitas *n* eternum *g* *om.* in aeternum *mn* permanet $bb_1fg_1mnn_2t$ *om.* unus...personae *f* 12 persone *n* incommutabilis b_1 13 quem] quae *g*, que *n* adsumere] ad hominem *n* dignata *m* *om.* est 1° *n* 14 *om.* id est g_1 diui/nitas *g*, + enim g_1 15 unam] + personam *m* antea *n* assumptionem *n* 16 trinitas] unitas p_1 humane (*bis*) np_1t 17 *om.* naturae p_1, nature *nt* maneat $bb_1gg_1mnn_2pt$ *om.* ne p_1 propter] post *f* *om.* adsumptionem p_1 humani obb_1gp, > carnis humanae *f* 18 a] ad *t*

1 plenus: cf. Faustus (Eusebius) plenitudo 3 formam serui: "This phrase," says Dr Swainson, "comes of course from S. Augustine, possibly through Alcuin." More likely direct from S. Hilary *De Trin.* x. 19, neque alius in forma dei quam qui in forma serui perfectus homo natus est 10 Eucherius. non amittendo quod erat; sed assumendo quod non erat. Cf. Fides Roman., non amisit quod fuerat sed coepit esse quod non erat. S. Hil. *De Trin.* III. 16, non amiserat quod erat sed coeperat esse quod non erat, non de suo destiterat sed quod nostrum est acceperat 18 Faustus *De S. S.* II. 4, impietatem quaternitatis. Cf. Fortunatus *Ex. in Symb. Apostol.*, Quod uero deus maiestatis de Maria in carne

25 dici aut cogitari, nisi: ITA UT SUPRADICTUM EST ET UNITAS IN TRINITATE
35 ET TRINITAS IN UNITATE UENERANDA SIT. NAM SICUT ANIMA RATIONALIS
ET CARO UNUS EST HOMO ITA DEUS ET HOMO UNUS EST CHRISTUS: et
si deus dei filius nostram luteam et mortalem carnem, nostrae redemp-
tionis conditionem, adsumpsit, se nullatenus inquinauit neque naturam
deitatis mutauit.] quia si sol aut ignis aliquid inmundum tetigerit quod
tangit purgat, et se nullatenus coinquinat. ita deitas sarcinam quoque
nostrae humanitatis adsumpsit, se nequaquam coinquinauit, sed nostram
naturam carnis quam adsumpsit, purgauit [et a maculis et sordibus pec-
Is. liii. 4. catorum ac uitiorum expiauit. sicut Esaias ait: *Ipse infirmitates nostras*
accepit, et aegrotationes portauit. ad hoc secundum humanitatem natus
est, ut infirmitates nostras acciperet et aegrotationes portaret; non quod
ipse infirmitates uel aegrotationes in se haberet quia salus mundi est, sed
ut eas a nobis abstolleret, dum suae sacrae passionis gratia ac sacramento,
Col. ii. 14. *chirographo adempto*, redemptionem pariter et salutem animarum nobis
36 condonaret. QUI PASSUS EST PRO SALUTE NOSTRA, id est secundum id
quod pati potuit, quod est] secundum humanam naturam. nam secundum

1 dici] dicere *G* cogitare $ob_1Gfgmnpp_1t$ ut] sicut b_1 2 rationale *p* (-lés *t*) 3 *om.* deus $fmpp_1t$ 4 *om.* dei *g* nostrae (-e *bn*)] nostri ob_1g, *om.* nostrae *p* *om.* redemptionis *m* 5 conditionis ob_1Gfm, conditioni est *g*, conditione *n* (-icione) *p* et ditionem *b* (-in b_1) adsumpte *n*, sed tamen *m* *om.* se *n* natura *g* 6 quia si] quasi obb_1, quia sicut *G* *om.* aut *t* immundum *m*, in mundum onp_1 7 *om.* et se p_1 eo coinquinat *f*, quoinquinat g^*p_1 sarcina $bgg_1n_2p_1t$ quoque q; *t*, que obb_1gn, quam *p*, quam ex *m* 8 nostram humanitatem *bgn* (-a -e mpp_1) adsumpsit (ass- *b*)] + et *g*, assumpta (ass-) n_2 *om.* se gg_1mn_2t quoinquinat g^* nequaquam coinquinauit se *bp* sed] *om.* p^*, + in p^{corr} nostrae naturae (-e *bnt*) carnem (-is *n*) bb_1gmnpp_1t 9 *om.* carnis quam adsumpsit g_1n_2 quam] quem p_1 *om.* a p_1 purgauit aeternam maculis *p* 10 ac] aut pp_1t 11 f. egrotationes MSS. *omnes* (*tris*) adhuc *n* 12 infirmitas nostra *o* *om.* et *n* aegrotationes] + et *n* portaret] portauit *p*, porta ʳet (*ras.*) *t* 13 uel] ut *n* *om.* in se *n* quia] qui bb_1fmn *om.* est *p* 14 *om.* ut *b*] quod *n* eas] ea bb_1 abstolleret gp_1] abstuleret ob_1G (-it *bn*), abstoleret *p*, tolleret *m* sue *bnt*, *om.* suae *f* sacre *obgnt* gratia a sacramento (sacrem- *t*) *bt* gratiae (-e *bn*) obb_1gn gratiam et *m* sacramenta bb_1mp_1 15 cyrographo ob_1, cẏr- *m* (-fo *b*), ciro grafo *g* redemtionem *g* pariter] *pr.* et *n* salutem] salute *g*, saluti nostrae *n* *om.* animarum...nostra *n* 16 condonauit $oGfpp_1t$, nobis cum donauit *g* qui] quia *t*, *om.* qui pp_1 *om.* secundum p_1, *pr.* id est g_1 17 *om.* est *t* humana natura p_1 nam] non *g*

natus est, non est sordidatus nascendo de uirgine, qui non fuit pollutus hominem condens de puluere. Denique sol aut ignis si lutum inspiciat quod tetigerit purgat et se tamen non inquinat 5 Faustus *Ep.* 5, (E) sola caro per conditionem mortis. *Ep.* 7, per susceptam serui conditionem domini ostendisse pietatem. Vig. Thaps. *De Trin.* XI., nec debes diuinam altitudinem ad humilem deuocare conditionem. Cf. *Gallicanische Messe*, Mone. p. 17, Secundum diuinam potentiam creauit omnia, secundum humanam conditionem liberauit hominem

diuinitatem dei filius impassibilis est. DESCENDIT AD INFERNA, qui protoplaustum Adam et patriarchas et prophetas et omnes iustos, qui pro originali peccato ibidem detinebantur, liberaret, [et de uinculis ipsius peccati absolutos, de eadem captiuitate infernali loco *suo sanguine* Apoc. v. 9.
redemptos ad supernam patriam et ad perpetuae uitae gaudia reuocaret. reliqui qui supra originale peccatum principalia crimina commiserunt, ut adserit scriptura in poenali Tartaro remanserunt. sicut in persona Christi dictum est per prophetam: *Ero mors tua, O Mors:* id est, morte Hos. xiii.
sua Christus humani generis inimicam mortem interfecit, et uitam dedit. 14.

1 diuinitatem] humanitatem *n* inpassibilis *on* discendit *t* ad inferos *mn* qui] quo *G*, ut mnn_2 protoplaustrum *n**, protoplausteo *g* 2 patriarcas *n* 3 originale *gt* detenebantur *ognt*, tenebantur bpp_1 uinculo *m* *om.* ipsius *p* 4 absolutus *g* (-tis b_1pp_1t) eodem *ofgmnp* captiuitatem *gnp** infernale *gt* sanguinem *g* 5 redemptus *gt* perpetuam obb_1gt (-a *n*) uitam gp_1t, uite obb_1 reuocare *g* 6 reliqui] reliquis *gt* + uero *m* supra] super gpp_1 originalem p_1 (-lēs *t*), orientali *n* peccato *ofmnp* crimina] culpa p_1, principalem culpam *p* commiserunt (comi- *o*, conmi- *n*, commiss- *g**)] comiserant p_1 7 asserit *m*, ut serit *p*, penali *om* (-e *gnt*) tartarus *g* 8 tuus *g* O Mors] Christus p_1 9 inimica *p* interficit *obnt*

1 Eucherius *de Genesi* 42 (saluator) quem nos etiam ad inferna descendisse fatemur and *ad Lucam* 7 ante aduentum domini nostri Jesu Christi ad inferna. Cf. Lucidus, *Ep. ad Faustum, Euphronium et alios*, condemning the opinion that patriarchs and prophets before the time of our Redemption had passed into and were living in Paradise. In *Serm.* 2 (Eng.) Faustus instances Joseph's imprisonment as a type of Christ's descent into Hell: qui non solum in potestate habuit in carcere uinctos, sed etiam de ipso inferni carcere praedam, quam diabolus ceperat, fortiter et feliciter reuocauit. *ascendens in altum captiuam duxit captiuitatem*, id est quos diabolus ceperat ad mortem ille recepit ad uitam. Cf. Eucherius, Ascendere dicitur deus cum Filius carnem ex nobis assumptam in coelum ueluti *captiuam duxit captiuitatem*, quia naturam humani generis, quae a diabolo in mundo captiua retinebatur, assumens secum in coelum, ubi nunquam antea fuerat tanquam captiuam deportauit. Cf. Ps.-Gennadius *de Fide* quoted by Caspari from Munich Cod. Lat. 14,468 (see p. xxxii supra) Anima descendit ad inferna et omnes inde iustorum animos liberauit et secum ad regnum caelorum prouexit ac diabolum in Tartarum religauit...Tertia die in eadem carne resurrexit...in eadem uero carne die quadragesimo ascendit in caelum et sedet ad dextram dei patris omnipotentis. Venturus est inde iterum iudicare uiuos et mortuos, uiuos eos qui tunc in carne inueniendi sunt, mortuos qui ante de hoc saeculo exierunt. Gregory of Tours expresses the same thought. § 497 Et quae fuit necessitas Filio Dei de caelo descendere carnem assumere, mortem adire, inferna penetrare, nisi ut hominem quem plasmaverat, non permitteret in morte perpetua derelinqui? Sed et iustorum animae quae usque passionem eius infernali ergastulo tenebantur inclusae eo ueniente laxatae sunt. Nam discendens ad inferos, dum tenebras noua luce perfudit, animas eorum secum, ne hoc exitu amplius cruciarentur, eduxit, iuxta illud, *et in sepulchro eius resurgent mortui* 7 poenali Tartaro: cf. Faustus (Eng.) *Serm.* 14 in profundo Tartari

Ero morsus tuus, inferne: partem morsit inferni pro parte eorum quos
liberauit; partem reliquit pro parte eorum qui pro principalibus criminibus
in tormentis remanserunt.] SURREXIT A MORTUIS, primogenitus mortuorum
Rom. viii. 29. et alibi apostolus dicit: *Ipse primogenitus* ex *multis fratribus.* [id est
S. Matt. primus a mortuis resurrexit. *Et multa sanctorum dormientium corpora*
xxvii. 52. *cum eo surrexerunt.* sicut euangelica auctoritas dicit: Sed *ipse* qui *caput*
37 *est* prius; deinde qui membra sunt continuo. postea ASCENDIT AD CAELOS,
Col. i. 18. sicut] psalmista ait, *Ascendit in altum, captiuam duxit captiuitatem:* id est,
Ps. lxvii. 19 (Vulg.). humanam naturam quae prius fuit *sub peccato uenundata* et captiuata
Rom. vii. 14. eamque redemptam captiuam duxit in caelestem altitudinem; et ad
caelestis patriae regnum sempiternum ubi antea non fuerat eam conlocauit
in gloriam sempiternam. [SEDET AD DEXTRAM PATRIS: id est, prosperitatem paternam et eo honore quod deus est. INDE UENTURUS IUDICARE
UIUOS ET MORTUOS: UIUOS dicit eos quos tunc aduentus dominicus in
corpore uiuentes inuenerit; et mortuos iam ante sepultos. et aliter dicit,
38—40 UIUOS iustos et MORTUOS peccatores. AD CUIUS ADUENTUM OMNES HOMINES

1 infernae *ob* (-nę *t*) (-ni *g*) morsit *m*] *marg.* et Momordit *m* inferni] infernum *ofgmnpt* 2 reliquit] reliquid *ogmt*^{corr} *om.* pro *n* pro criminalibus peccatis p_1, criminis *p* 3 in] *pr.* ibi *n* + tertia die resurrexit *G* surrexit] + Christus *n* primogeniti *p* 4 apostulus *o* primogenitor *p* surrexit ipse qui est primogenitus in multis g_1n_2 id est] idem b_1 5 surrexit p_1 multa] multas p_1 dormientium (dormicium *g*)] + corpora bb_1mpp_1t > corpora dormientium *n* *om.* corpora *oGfg* 6 *om.* cum eo p_1 surrexit *t* in euangelica auctoritate obb_1, in euangelica auctoritas *g*, in euangelio auctoritas *n*, euangelica auctoritas mpp_1 capud obb_1t 7 qui] quae *ofg* membro *g* sunt. Continuo *p* celos *gt* 8 salmista *g* sicut p. ait] et salmista g_1 ascendit] ascendens *bm*, + deus b_1 id est] idem g_1 9 quae] que *nt* *om.* prius *n* *om.* fuit g_1mp uenundata fuerat *p*, uenumdata g_1 captiuata] + erat g_1 *om.* et capt. *nt* captiu.] *hic def.* n_2 10 eaque fp_1, eademque *m* redemtam *m*, redempta *og* (-am pp_1), depraedatam *n*, redemptio *f* celestem *g*, celestes (cael- b_1) altitudines b_1g_1 ad] a *g* 11 celestis *bg*, caelestem p_1, caelestem patriam *ofGn*, patrie *b* *om.* ad caelestis...sempiternam g_1 eam] et *m* collocauit g_1mn 12 sempiternum *g* 13 et] + in $bgmnpp_1t$ honorem *g* quod] quo *Gg* uenturus] + est *Gm* 14 et] ac *n* 15 uiuendos $obgGpp_1$ *om.* iam *t* antea *m*, ante ea *t* sepultus *gn* dicit] + iudicare *g* 16 uiuos] + dicit *n*

9 sub peccato uenundata: cf. Rufinus *in Symb. Apost.* 15, peccatis nostris uenundati sumus 12 S. Gall 27 + in ea scilicet carne in qua natus in qua passus in qua aetiam surrexit. in qua et ad celos ascendit in ipsa uenturus est ad iucandum. Ergo nec hoc credentibus impossibile iudicetur, quia qui potuit hominem de terra componere poterit hunc ex homine in angelis tranformare 16 S. Gall 27 + Reddent autem in die iudicii rationem hi qui offendicula et detractiones et scandala fratribus propter inuidiam et liuorem generant. Apostolus in quid unusquisque propriam mercedem accipet. (39) secundum suam laborem (40) hic sensus in promptum est

RESURGERE HABENT CUM CORPORIBUS SUIS ET REDDITURI SUNT DE FACTIS PROPRIIS RATIONEM. ET QUI BONA EGERUNT IBUNT IN UITAM AETERNAM QUI UERO MALA IN IGNEM AETERNUM. HAEC EST FIDES CATHOLICA QUAM NISI QUISQUE FIDELITER FIRMITERQUE CREDIDERIT SALUUS ESSE NON POTERIT.

2 abent p_1 3 qui] *pr* et *obGg*, et qui male egerunt *n* (cf. et qui mala Paris Com.) catolica p_1 5 poterit] + Explicit expositio fidei catholicae *m* (in red).

ADDITIONAL NOTES ON THE FORTUNATUS COMMENTARY.

1. I may here add a list of the variations which Card. Pitra's collation of the Leyden MS. presents when compared with Goldast's text (G) in the *Manuale Biblicum*. I give the pages and lines of my text.

p. 28 Euphronii] *pr.* Beati p. 29. 2 *om.* et 2° 3 *om.* et 1° 10 *om.* a, spiritu ovis, attendit 13 *om.* aperte qui] quia 14 scilicet] sicut 15 sicut] sic 18 sunt] est p. 30. 1 *om.* eo quod a nullo est genitus 3 alia *pr.* item sancti] sanctus 5 *om.* id est claritas 6 >gloria est potestatis 7 *om.* et 1° 8 increatus] immensus *om.* et 10 *om.* et 12 *om.* et 13 deus] solus 15 *om.* et 16 omnium] omnem p. 31. 2 *om.* et + et tamen non tres dii sed unus est deus 5 *om.* et + et tamen non tres domini sed unus est dominus 6 eo] ex 7 *om.* id est sicut distinctum 8 *om.* et 1° et 2°] ac 10 *om.* similiter 14 ergo] igitur quia] qui (*tris*) 15 nec] non (*tris*) p. 32. 4 sicut] scilicet sed] sic et] id est 10 uocabula] nomine 16 recte] certe p. 33. 3 ipsius] ipsa, Isaias 5 tuus] + tuus 10 omne quod *supra lin.* (GL)] *infra lin.* per omnia quod (L) 14 nemo] + igitur scrutetur *om.* prophetarum nullus 15 *om.* deus *om.* suis p. 34. 1 sed] si credendus] + est, pariter 2 sic filius patris uerbum caro factum 5 >est uerus deus et 7 *om.* isto 10 ea] eam 11 idem est] id est 16 qui] quae uiuificat p. 35. 1 *om.* et humana carne 4 >tamen duo 5 deitas] diuinitas 8 >inmutabilis est et inconuertibilis est caro 10 esse] + homo deitatem] diuinitatem 11 quae] quia 14 *om.* ita post adsumptionem humane naturae uera permaneat trinitas p. 36. 1 *om.* dicere aut cogitare 4 deus] + dicitur nostram assumens luteam et mortalem carnem 6 deitatis] diuinitatis sicut] si ignis] + si tetigit 7 deitas] diuinitas 8 *om.* se nequaquam...adsumpsit 13 uel] et 14 ut] quod p. 37. 4 infernali] *pr.* et 7 persona [Christi] p. 38. 1 partem] partim (*bis*) morsit] momordit 4 ex multis fratribus] ex mortuis 7 continuo postea 8 altum] occasum 10 eamque] eamdem 12 prosperitatem] potestatem (Cod. prosperitatem, mox quod Deus) 14 quod] quo 15 uiuendos] uiuentes dicit] judicare

2. The interpolations in *m* are as follow:

p. 28, l. 2. QUAM NISI QUISQUE INTEGRAM INUIOLATAMQUE SERUAUERIT ABSQUE DUBIO IN AETERNUM PERIBIT.

credentia] + (Alcuin, *De fid. trin.* I. 2) Primo ergo omnium fides necessaria est, sicut apostolica docet auctoritas dicens: *sine fide impossibile est placere deo.* Constat enim neminem ad ueram peruenire posse beatitudinem, nisi deo placeat; et deo neminem placere posse nisi per fidem. Fides namque est bonorum omnium fundamentum, fides humanae salutis initium. Sine hac nemo ad filiorum dei potest consortium peruenire, quia sine ipsa nec in hoc seculo quisquam justificationis consequitur gratiam; nec in futuro uitam possidebit aeternam. Et si quis hic non ambulauerit per fidem, non perueniet ad speciem beatae domini nostri Ihesu Christi.

p. 29, l. 1. populorum] + (Isidori Hispal. *Orig.* VIII. 1) Non enim sicut conuenticula haereticorum, in aliquibus regionum partibus coartatur, sed per totum terrarum orbem dilatata diffunditur.

p. 31, l. 5. Isidori *Orig.* VII. 1. Dominus dicitur eo quod dominetur creaturae cunctae uel quod creatura omnis dominatui eius deseruiat.

p. 34, l. 8. *om.* deus...matris filius *m*, + (Isidori *Orig.* v. 38) secula enim generationibus constat et inde secula, quod sequantur; abeuntibus enim alias alia succedunt.

TESTIMONIES SUPPORTED BY ENTIRE TEXTS.

TESTIMONIES					ENTIRE TEXTS			
Date	Province	Diocese	Testimony	Title	Ref. No.	Text	Title	Date
845—882	Rheims	Rheims	Hincmar					
			848 De u. non t. deitate	Catholica Fides	E	Utrecht Psalter	Fides Catholica	c. 830
			859 De Praedestinatione	Catholica Fides	Q	Psalter (of Fulco)	Fides Catholica	c. 850
			852 Capitula	Sermo Athanasii de Fide	D	Psalter (of Charles the Bald)	F. S. Athanasii	c. 850
			Pastoral	Sermo Cath. Fidei				
870	,,	Morinum	Adalbert	Sermo b. Athanasii				
889	,,	Soissons	Riculfus	Sermo Fidei Cath.				
868	,,	Rheims	Ratramnus (Corbie)	Libellus de Fide b. Ath. Alex. Epi.	C	S. Germain 257 Cod. Corbeiensis	F. S. A. Epi.	790
868	Sens	Paris	Aeneas	F. C. S. Ath. Epi. Alex.	P_1	Paris B. N. 13159	No title	795
					P_3	Paris 1451	F. chat. S. Ath. Epi. Alex.	795
†821	,,	Orleans	Theodulf					
			Synod	Cath. F. = credo and Q. u. s. e.				
			Address to clergy	Cath. Fides				
			810 De Spiritu Sco	Symbolum Athanasii				
821	,,	,,	Benedict d'Aniane	Fides Catholica				
†840	Lyons	Lyons	820 Agobard, adv. dogma Felicis	F. C. (b. Ath. ait)				
834	,,	,,	Florus Diaconus	Fides Catholica				
892	Cologne	Liège	Regino, Abbot of Prum	Sermo Athanasii de Fide S. Trinitatis				
						Psalter (Lothaire)	F. C. tradita a s. Ath. Epo. Alex.	833
840—5	,,	?	Synod	Fides S. Ath. Epi.				
865	Hamburg Bremen	Hamburg Bremen	Anskar	F. C. a. b. Athanasio	Y	Golden Psalter (Vienna)	F. S. Ath. Epi. Alex.	867
836	Mainz (Moguntia)	?	Haito of Reichenau	F. S. Athanasii	G_3	S. Gall 27. Psalter (Junius 25)	F. S. A. Epi.	c. 850 c. 820
					G_1	S. Gall 20. Psalter	F. cath. S. A. Epi.	c. 820
750	,,	Mainz	(Boniface)	F. Catholica				
800	Milan	Bobbio	Bobbio. Libellus de Trinitate	——	B	Milan O. 212	No title	780

B. Quotations of Quicunque in early Authors and Commentaries.

Clause	Hincmar, c. 850	Ratramn., 868	Aeneas, 868	Agobard, 820	Theodulf, 800	Benedict, 800	Alcuin, 800	Denebert, 798	Vienna, 1261, and Trèves frag.	Conc. Tol. VI, 633	Commentaries Troyes saec. VIII	Commentaries Fort. saec. V	Clause
1	x				x			x	Vienna saec. XII x		x	x	1
2				x					x				2
3	x					x		x	x		x	x	3
4	x					x		x	x	x	x	x	4
5	x					x		x	x		x	x	5
6	x					x		x	x		x	x	6
7							x				x	x	7
8											x	x	8
9											x	x	9
10											x	x	10
11											x	x	11
12													12
13											x	x	13
14											x		14
15	x										x	x	15
16	x										x	x	16
17											x	x	17
18											x	x	18
19	x										x	x	19
20	x	x	x		x		x	x		x			20
21	x	x	x		x		x	x		x			21
22		x	x		x		x	x		x			22
23			x		x						x	x	23
24	x		x		x		x	x	x		x		24
25	x		x		x		x	x				x	25
26	x		x		x		x	x	x				26
27									Trèves frag. saec. VIII x				27
28									x	x	x	x	28
29									x	x	x	x	29
30									x		x	x	30
31									x	x	x	x	31
32									x		x	x	32
33									x		x	x	33
34									x	x	x	x	34
35										x	x	x	35
36									x	x	x	x	36
37									x	x	x	x	37
38	x								x		x	x	38
39									x	x	x	x	39
40									x			x	40

C. List of Commentaries.

No.	Name	MSS.	Date	First Words	Last Words	Sw. Om. (E. H.)
1	Fortunatus	1. Junius 25	IX	Fides dicitur credulitas	...saluus esse non poterit	
2	Troyes	Troyes 804	X	Fides dicitur credulitas	...ut haereticus deputabitur	Om. 2
3	Stavelot	1. B. M. Add. MSS. 18,043	X	Hic b. Ath. liberum arbitrium	...saluus esse non poterit	Om. 63
4	Orleans	Orleans 94	IX	Qualiscumque homo...	...ut haereticus reputabitur	Om. 4
5	Oratorian	1. Vat. Reg. 231	X	Quod dicitur in capite	...regnat per infinita semper saec. saeculorum	Om. 11
6	Bouhier	1. Troyes 1979	X	Fides quae credentem saluat	...de illius laude et nos gloriemur	Om. 23
7	Paris	1. Paris B. N. 1012	X	Chatolica dicitur uniuersalis	...saluus esse non poterit	Om. 26
8	Cologne	1. Cologne XLV. (Darmstad. 2040)	X	Quicunque dicitur quia non est Deus personarum acceptor		
		2. Munich 17,181	XI			Sw. 454
		3. „ 14,617	XV		... ...	
9	Milan (1)	1. Milan T. 103	X	Fides est credulitas illarum rerum quae non uidentur	1. ad quaerendam rectae fidei semitam prouocet	
		2. „ M. 79	XI/XII	Nos. 1—5 on cl. 1. Hic b. Ath. liberum arbitrium	4, 5, 6, 7, 8. end with saluus esse non poterit	
		3. Laud. Lat. 105				
		4. Trèves 222	XIII/XIV			
		5. Trèves 531	XIV			
		6. B. M. Reg. 8. B. XIV	XII			
		7. Vienna 701	XII	Nos. 6, 7, 8 on cl. 1. Quicunque id est unusquisque		
		8. Printed in B. M. 3505. e. 58. Cologne 4^0				
10	Munich (1)	1. Munich 14,610, f. 61 2. „ „ f. 114	X	Quicunque u. s. e. ad heb. 9. impossible est sine fide	... ...	
11	Hampole	1. Dresden A. 60	XII			Om. 62
12	Milan (2)	Milan L. 81	XII	Fides est trinitatis confessio		
13	York	York Chapter Lib. XVI. 7.7.	XII	Generauit equalis pater cl. 1—25		

C. List of Commentaries.

No.	Name	MSS.	Date	First Words	Last Words	Sw. Om. (E. H.)
14	Abelard	Printed Mg. 178	XII	Voluntate quippe propria		
15	Hildegarde	Printed Mg. 97	XII	O Filiae quae vestigia Christi		
16	S. Bernard	Vienna 777	XIII		... ...	Sw. 455
	Munich (2)	Munich 12,715	XIII	Fides est uoluntaria certitudo		Sw. 457
17	Cambrai	Cambrai 152	XIII			
18	Simon of Tournay	1. Paris B. N. 18,068	XIII	Apud Aristotelem argumentum est	... ...	Om. 80
19	Alexander Nequam	Oxf. Bodl. Rawlinson MSS. C. 67	XIII	Dicit Apostolus fides est fundamentum		
20	Alexander Neckham	1. Oxf. Bod. Cat. 2339	XIII	Haec est enim uictoria quae uincit mundum (1–4)	[Preface Caput aquile uisus ab Ezechiele	
		2. " " 2330	XIII ex.			
		3. B. M. Harleian 3133	XIII		Part of it is found in an incomplete commentary in Oxf. Bodl. Cat. 2339: note on 1st clause, Quicunque adultus]	Om. 81
		4. Cambrai 977	XIII			
21	Turin	Turin XVIII	XIV			Sw. 459
22	Alexander de Ales	1. Bodl. Laud. Lat. 493	XIV	Hic tractatus de symbolo Sancti Anastasii. Expositio diuisa est in tres partes prohemium tractatum epylogum (1–4)		Om. 82
		2. Munich 56,668	XIV			
		3. Camb. U. Lib. KK. W. 4	XV			Sw. 459
		4. Printed Summa III. 69				
23	Albertus (Canon reg. Dyessensis)	Munich 5668	XIV			
24	Mainz	Mainz 266	XV	Primo ergo omnium		
25	Petrus de Osoma	Printed at Paris	1478			
26	Fr. Pelbartus (Ord. Min.)	" Hagenau	1531			
27	Dionysius Carthusianus	" Cologne	1538			Om. 84

Dom Morin has kindly sent me the following reference to be added to this list. In the library of Valenciennes MS. 202 (194), saec. XIII, from the Abbey of S. Amand, ch. v. fol. 7 *De tercio simbolo Anastasii pape.* Circa tercium simbolum quaeritur primo de hoc quod ibi dicitur Alia est enim persona Patris. The author quotes Anselm *De Incarnatione.*

D. VICTRICIUS OF ROUEN.

Victricius, Bp of Rouen (†407)[1], was a friend of Martin of Tours and of Paulinus of Nola. Possibly by birth a Briton, he had been a soldier and suffered for the Christian faith. In 393 he went to Britain to aid in the struggle against heresy. His own words are worth quoting: Hoc ego Domini Jesu et vestrum salutare praeceptum intra Britanniis exercui, si non ut debui, tamen ut potui. Sapientibus amorem pacis infudi, docilibus legi, nescientibus inculcavi, ingessi nolentibus.

But he fell under the reproach of heresy, and had to go to Rome in 403 to clear himself before Innocent I. From a letter of Paulinus we gather that he composed some sort of confession of faith in his own defence. From certain similarities of expression Mr Harvey[2] conjectured that this might have been the Quicunque; e.g.:—

Ep. XXXVII. 5. Cum ergo fides et confessio tua, ut credimus atque confidimus coaeternam trinitatem unius diuinitatis et substantiae...cumque patrem deum et filium deum et spiritum sanctum deum...doces, unitatem trinitatis sine confusione iungens et trinitatem ipsius unitatis sine separatione distinguens, ita ut nulla alteri persona conueniat, et in omni persona trium deus unus eluceat, tantus quidem filius quantus et pater, quantus et spiritus sanctus.

6. Et filium dei ita praedicas ut eumdem et filium hominis consistere non erubescas...homo totus et corporis nostri et animae assumtione: animae autem rationalis.

There is nothing closer in Victricius' confession in the fourth Book of his 'De Laude Sanctorum,' and the suggestion that he was the author of the Quicunque is quite unconvincing, but the quotations at all events show the direction of thought in his time.

[1] The author of a treatise 'De Laude Sanctorum,' printed in Galland, *B. Pat.* VIII. 228, from a MS. of S. Gall, of 8th century with notes by a Notker of 9th or 10th century (=Notker Balbulus?).

[2] *Hist. Three Creeds.* London, Parker, 1854.

E. Fulgentius of Ruspe.

The writings of Fulgentius (†533), Bishop of Ruspe in North Africa, contain parallels to the Quicunque.

There is no evidence of quotation, and there is unmistakeable weakening of phrases which were derived by the Quicunque from Augustine:

Ad Ferr. Ep. XIV. Cum una sit naturaliter sempiterna uirtus ac diuinitas patris et filii et spiritus sancti.......Nec tamen tres dii sed unus naturaliter deus est pater et filius et spiritus sanctus. Omnipotens est pater sed omnipotens est filius omnipotens est spiritus sanctus; nec tamen tres dii omnipotentes sed unus deus omnipotens est pater et filius et spiritus sanctus. Aeternus est sine initio pater, aeternus est sine initio filius, aeternus est sine initio spiritus sanctus; nec tamen tres dii aeterni sed unus deus aeternus est pater et filius et spiritus sanctus. Immensus est pater, sed immensus est filius et immensus est spiritus sanctus: nec tamen tres dii immensi sed unus deus immensus est pater et filius et spiritus sanctus.

Again we may note the prolixity of the following sentence: Principaliter atque indubitanter toto corde retine patrem deum et filium deum, et spiritum sanctum deum, id est sanctam atque ineffabilem trinitatem unum esse naturaliter deum.

De Fide Orth. In quo, sicut est plenitudo diuinae naturae, ita est et plenitudo humanae substantiae. Inest enim illi naturalis ueritas diuinitatis, naturalis ueritas animae rationalis, et naturalis ueritas carnis...unam naturam tres personas in trinitate deo et unam personam duasque naturas in unigenito dei filio.

Obj. Arr. Nec personas confundere, nec substantiam separare.

Ad Tras. III. (Christi) in quo perfectus homo plenus est gratiae, et in quo perfectus deus plenus est ueritatis.

Ad Col. IV. Personarum uero proprietas demonstret alium esse patrem alium filium alium spiritum sanctum.

Ex. Ep. ad Cor. I. XII. Quia deo competit naturaliter dominum esse omnium rerum.

id. XVI. Vna est naturaliter aeterna diuinitas.

Sed homo Christus Jesus totius est trinitatis operatione plasmatus.

id. XVI. Spiritus sanctus qui naturaliter a patre filioque procedit.

F. L'ORIGINE DU MANUSCRIT CÉLÈBRE DIT LE PSAUTIER D'UTRECHT PAR PAUL DURRIEU. Paris, Leroux, 1895.

Count Durrieu has made a very careful study of the characteristic features of MSS. executed in the schools of Metz and Rheims in the first half of the 9th century. He compares the Utrecht Psalter with MSS. now in the Library at Rheims which are connected with Hincmar. Narrowing still further the circle of his enquiry he finds and illustrates the close resemblances between the Utrecht Psalter and the Gospels of Ebbo, Hincmar's predecessor, now in the library of Épernay. This MS. was executed under the direction of the Abbot of the Monastery of Hautvilliers in the diocese of Rheims A.D. 816—845. He would therefore assign the same date and origin to the Utrecht Psalter. This theory would apply only to its present form and would leave Sir E. M. Thompson's theory of an earlier archetype untouched.

G. Table of parallels in Augustine, Vincentius, Faustus and others.

Quicunque.	S. Augustine.
1. Quicunque uult saluus esse, ante omnia opus est ut teneat catholicam fidem.	De Utilit. Cred. 29. *Catholicae* disciplinae maiestate institutum est, ut accedentibus ad religionem *fides* persuadeatur *ante omnia*. c. Max. II. 23. Haec est fides nostra, quoniam haec fides est recta, quae fides etiam Catholica nuncupatur. Enarr. in Ps. X. c. 3. Haeretici... simplici fide catholica contenti esse nolunt; quae una paruulis salus est.
2. Quam nisi quisque integram inuiolatamque seruauerit, absque dubio in aeternum peribit.	
3. Fides autem catholica haec est, ut unum deum in trinitate, et trinitatem in unitate ueneremur.	
4. Neque confundentes personas, neque substantiam separantes.	S. Augustine objected to this use of substantia, cf. De Trin. v. 10, 'In Deo substantia proprie non dicitur.' He (in v. 11) used the phrase tres substantiae = hypostases = personae. But Faustus De Spu. Sco. I. 11, unitas substantiae, explaining ad substantiam pertinet quod subsistit, ad personas pertinet, quod proprie sibi unaquaeque subsistit.

Vincentius.	Faustus, Eucherius.
1. c. 36. Catholica fides. c. 4. Inter sacraria catholicae fidei salui esse potuerunt.	
2. c. 7. Qui uiolauerunt fidem tutos esse non posse. inuiolatam illibatamque conserua. c. 34. Catholicorum hoc fere proprium,...damnare profanas nouitates: et sicut dixit, atque iterum dixit apostolus: si quis annunciauerit, praeterquam quod acceptum est, anathemate.	
3. c. 22. 18. Catholica ecclesia unum deum in trinitatis plenitudine, et item trinitatis aequalitatem in una diuinitate ueneratur.	3. Faustus (Eng.) serm. 9. Trinitas sine separatione distincta. Pater et filius et spiritus sanctus unus deus credantur tres personae et non tres substantiae.
4. c. 22. Ut neque singularitas substantiae personarum confundat proprietatem, neque item trinitatis distinctio unitatem separet deitatis.	4. Faustus (Eng.) serm. 9. Credatur a nobis unitas sine confusione coniuncta, trinitas sine separatione distincta. Cf. De Spu. Sco. (Eng.) II. i. 12. Inseparabilem in personis trinitatem.

Quicunque.	S. Augustine.
5. Alia est enim persona patris, alia filii, alia spiritus sancti.	
6. Sed patris, et filii, et spiritus sancti, una est diuinitas, aequalis gloria, coaeterna maiestas.	
7. Qualis pater, talis filius, talis et spiritus sanctus.	
8. Increatus pater, increatus filius, increatus et spiritus sanctus.	
9. Immensus pater, immensus filius, immensus et spiritus sanctus.	
10. Aeternus pater, aeternus filius, aeternus et spiritus sanctus.	10. Serm. 105. Aeternus pater, coaeternus filius, coaeternus spiritus sanctus.
11. Et tamen non tres aeterni, sed unus aeternus.	
12. Sicut non tres increati, nec tres immensi, sed unus increatus et unus immensus.	
13. Similiter, omnipotens pater, omnipotens filius, omnipotens et spiritus sanctus.	13. De Trin. v. 8. Itaque omnipotens pater, omnipotens filius, omnipotens spiritus sanctus.
14. Et tamen non tres omnipotentes, sed unus omnipotens.	14. ib. Nec tamen tres omnipotentes, sed unus omnipotens.
15. Ita deus pater, deus filius, deus et spiritus sanctus.	15. De Trin. I. 5. Haec est catholica fides...sed in ea nonnulli perturbantur cum audiunt deum patrem et deum filium et deum spiritum sanctum.

Vincentius.	Faustus, Eucherius.
5. c. 19. Quia scilicet alia est persona patris alia filii alia spiritus sancti.	5. Faustus (Euseb.) De Trin. Est pater, alter est filius, alter est spiritus sanctus. Cf. Pelag. Symbol. in Lambec. II. 274. Impietatem Sabellii declinantes, tres personas expressas sub proprietate distinguimus—Aliam patris, aliam filii, aliam spiritus sancti esse personam.
6. ib. Sed tamen patris et filii, et spiritus sancti non alia et alia, sed una eademque natura.	6. ib. Confutantes Arium, unam eandemque dicimus trinitatis esse substantiam. Faustus (Eng.) serm. 30. *Coaeternitatem...maiestatis.*
7.	7. Philastr. Haer. 45. Qualis immensa est patris persona talis est et filii, talis est sancti spiritus.
8.	
9.	9. (13) Eucherius, Lib. sp. intell. Immensus est, quia quantitas eius uel qualitas a nullo ex creaturis metiri possit.
10.	
11.	
12.	
13.	13. Eucherius, ib. Omnipotens deus pater et filius et spiritus sanctus unus et trinus...Solus inuisibilis immensus atque incomprehensibilis.
14.	
15.	15. (16) Faustus (Eng.) serm. 31. Pater itaque deus, filius deus, spiritus sanctus deus, non tres dii, sed unus deus est.

Quicunque.	S. Augustine.
16. Et tamen non tres dii sed unus est deus.	16. Et tamen hanc trinitatem non tres deos sed unum deum. Cf. VIII. 1. Deus pater deus filius deus spiritus sanctus, nec tamen tres dii.
17. Ita dominus pater, dominus filius, dominus et spiritus sanctus.	17. c. Maxim. II. 23. Sic et dominum si quaeras, singulum quemque respondeo.
18. Et tamen non tres domini, sed unus est dominus.	18. ib. Sed simul omnes non tres dominos deos, sed unum dominum deum.
19. Quia sicut singillatim unamquamque personam et deum et dominum confiteri christiana ueritate compellimur; ita tres deos aut dominos dicere catholica religione prohibemur.	19. De Civit. Dei XI. 24. Cum de singulis quaeritur, unusquisque eorum et Deus et omnipotens esse respondeatur; cum uero de omnibus simul, non tres Dii, uel tres omnipotentes, sed unus Deus omnipotens. De Trin. v. 14: singillatim.
20. Pater a nullo est factus, nec creatus, nec genitus.	20. Serm. 140. Dicimus patrem Deum de nullo.
21. Filius a patre solo est, non factus, nec creatus, sed genitus.	21. Ep. 170. Filius patris solius—Hunc quippe de sua substantia genuit, non ex nihilo fecit.
22. Spiritus sanctus a patre et filio, non factus, nec creatus, nec genitus est, sed procedens.	22. De Trin. XV. 11. De filio spiritus sanctus procedere reperitur. ib. v. 14. Neque natus est sicut unigenitus, neque factus.
23. Unus ergo pater non tres patres; unus filius non tres filii; unus spiritus sanctus non tres spiritus sancti.	23. c. Maxim. II. 23. Unus est pater, non duo uel tres; et unus filius, non duo uel tres; et unus amborum spiritus, non duo uel tres.
24. Et in hac trinitate nihil prius aut posterius, nihil maius aut minus, sed totae tres personae coaeternae sibi sunt, et coaequales.	24. Serm. 214 (Maclear says 215). In hac trinitate non est aliud alio maius, aut minus.

	Vincentius.	Faustus, Eucherius.
16.		
17.		
18.		
19.		
20.		
21.		
22.		22. Faustus (Eng.) III. Ep. 3. Genitus ergo ingenitus et ex utroque procedens personas indigitat. Cf. De Spu. Sco. I. 13. Mitti a patre et filio dicitur et de ipsorum substantia procedere.
23.		
	24. Cf. Origen De Prin. I. 7. Nihil in trinitate maius minusue dicendum est. Claud. Mam. De statu animae I. c. 15. Nec in illa ex eadem trinitate persona minor est quam in tribus, nec in tribus major est quam in singulis.	24. Faustus (Eng.) III. serm. 31. Maius autem aut minus ignorat trinitas...Nam etsi distinctionem recipit trinitas gradum tamen nescit aequalitas.

Quicunque.	S. Augustine.
25. Ita ut per omnia, sicut iam supradictum est, et trinitas in unitate, et unitas in trinitate ueneranda sit.	25. De Trin. VII. 4. Unitas trinitatis.
26. Qui uult ergo saluus esse, ita de trinitate sentiat.	
27. Sed necessarium ad aeternam salutem, ut incarnationem quoque domini nostri Iesu Christi fideliter credat.	27. Serm. 264. Necessariam fidem incarnationis Christi.
28. Est ergo fides recta, ut credamus et confiteamur, quia dominus noster Iesus Christus, dei filius, deus pariter et homo est	28. Enchiridion, 35. Proinde Christus Iesus, dei filius, est et deus et homo.
29. Deus est ex substantia patris ante saecula genitus: homo ex substantia matris in saeculo natus.	29. ib. Deus ante omnia saecula: homo in nostro saeculo—unus dei filius, idemque hominis filius.
30. Perfectus deus, perfectus homo, ex anima rationali et humana carne subsistens.	30. Serm. 238. Aduersus Arium, ueram et perfectam uerbi diuinitatem; aduersus Apollinarem, perfectam hominis in Christo defendimus ueritatem.
31. Aequalis patri secundum diuinitatem; minor patri secundum humanitatem.	31. Ep. 137. Aequalem patri secundum diuinitatem, minorem autem patri secundum carnem, hoc est secundum hominem.

Vincentius.	Faustus, Eucherius.
25. c. 22. Neque item trinitatis distinctio unitatem separet deitatis. c. 34. Trinitatis unitatem descindere...unitatis trinitatem confundere.	25. Faustus (Eng.) p. 107. Trinitatem in unitate subsistere.
26. c. 18. Recta sentiens nec in trinitatis mysterio, nec in Christi incarnatione blasphemat.	
	27. Faustus, De Spu. Sco. II. 25. Hoc loco necessarium (uidetur ut in Christo deo pariter et homine unam personam et duas substantias testimoniis adseramus). cf. infra cl. 28.
28. c. 19. Unus idemque Christus, unus idemque filius dei,...unus idemque Christus deus et homo. Cf. infra on cl. 32. Ecclesia unum Christum...deum pariter atque hominem confitetur.	28. Eucherius, ad Joann. 2. Quia licet assumpserit hominem, tamen homo et deus, hoc est Christus, una persona est. Faustus (Eng.) II. De Spu. Sco. II. 4. (p. 139). Si in Christo deo pariter et homine duas substantias dicimus.
29. c. 19. Idem ex patre ante saecula genitus; idem in saeculo ex matre generatus. c. 21. Natus ex uirgine. Cf. Nicetus Expl. Symb. Quia plus homo innocens et purus redditur quam cum de matris suae utero *generatur*.	29. Faustus (Euseb.) Hom. I. de Ascensione. Geminae substantiae redemptor noster. S. Hil. Comm. in Matt. IV. 14. *Filium ex patris substantia* atque intra patris substantiam consistentem, primum in hominem corporatum dehinc morti hominis *conditione* subjectum...
30. c. 20. Perfectus deus, perfectus homo; in deo summa diuinitas, in homine plena humanitas,...quippe quae animam simul habeat et carnem. ib. supra uses term subsistere.	30. (35. 33) Faustus (Euseb.) De Nat. Dom. II. Perfectus deus et uerus homo, unus Christus:...sed tamen dei et hominis una persona: ita coniunctus deus homini sicut anima corpori. Ita est pro nostra salute misericors humiliata maiestas, ut tunc non adimeret dignatio dignitatem; *assumpta* est enim *humanitas:* non absumpta diuinitas.
31. c. 19. Duae substantiae sunt,... una ex patre deo, altera ex matre uirgine; una coaeterna, et aequalis patri, altera ex tempore et minor patre. Idem patri et aequalis et minor.	31. Faustus (Eng.) serm. 2. Secundum diuinitatem aequalis patri, secundum humanitatem minor etiam angelis.

Quicunque.	S. Augustine.
32. Qui licet deus sit et homo, non duo tamen, sed unus est Christus.	32. In Johan. Tract. 78. Agnoscamus geminam substantiam Christi; diuinam scilicet qua aequalis est patri, humanam qua major est patri ...utrumque autem simul non duo, sed unus est Christus.
33. Unus autem, non conuersione diuinitatis in carne, sed adsumptione humanitatis in deo.	33. Enchir. 34. Verbum caro factum est, a diuinitate carne suscepta, non in carnem diuinitate mutata. Serm. 187. Assumpta humana substantia.
34. Unus omnino, non confusione substantiae, sed unitate personae.	34. Serm. 186. Idem Deus qui homo, et qui deus idem homo: non confusione naturae, sed unitate personae.
35. Nam sicut anima rationalis et caro unus est homo; ita deus et homo unus est Christus.	35. In Joh. Tract. 78. Sicut enim unus est homo anima rationalis et caro; sic unus est Christus deus et homo.
36. Qui passus est pro salute nostra, descendit ad inferna, tertia die resurrexit a mortuis.	36. Ep. 164. Quis ergo, nisi infidelis, negauerit fuisse apud inferos Christum?...antequam dominus in inferna descenderet.
37. Adscendit ad caelos, sedet ad dexteram patris; inde uenturus iudicare uiuos et mortuos.	

Vincentius.	Faustus, Eucherius.
	Eucher. ad Joann. 10. Iuxta quam rationem diuinitatis atque humanitatis, etiam in reliquis quae aut aequalitatem cum patre, aut humilitatem eius sonant, facile intellectus patebit.
32. c. 18. Unum Christum Iesum, non duos, eundemque deum pariter atque hominem... et hoc totum unus est Christus.	32. Eucherius ad Joann. 2. Quia licet assumpserit hominem, tamen homo et deus, hoc est Christus, una persona est.
33. c. 19. Unus autem non... diuinitatis et humanitatis confusione sed unitate personae. Cf. whole argument c. 19 ad fin. c. 20. Deus Verbum assumendo et habendo carnem. 34. c. 19. Unitate personae. (Cf. utriusque substantiae...proprietas...salua personae unitate.)	33. Faustus (Euseb.) Hom. de Latrone beato. In una eademque persona quam bene manifestantur humana pariter et diuina?
35. c. 20. (Igitur) sicut anima connexa carni nec in carnem uersa, non imitatur hominem, sed est homo,...ita etiam Verbum deus,...uniendo se homini...factus est homo,... et ex duabus substantiis unus est Christus. Claudianus Mamercus, presb. Viennensis, De statu animae i. 3. Quia sicut anima et corpus in diuersa substantia unus est homo ita deus et homo ex diuersa substantia unus est Christus.	35. Faustus (Eng.) III. Ep. 7. Nos uero...in Christum ita perfecta et inseparabili distinctione credamus ut dei et hominis simplicem personam et duplicem nouerimus esse substantiam. sicut anima et corpus hominem facit, ita diuinitas et humanitas unus est Christus.
	37. Eucherius, Lib. Formularum. Secundum corpus sepultus est, sec. uero animam in inferna descendit.

Quicunque.	S. Augustine.
38. Ad cuius aduentum omnes homines resurgere habent cum corporibus suis, et reddituri sunt de factis propriis rationem.	
39. Et qui bona egerunt ibunt in uitam aeternam, qui uero mala, in ignem aeternam.	
40. Haec est fides catholica, quam nisi quisque fideliter firmiterque crediderit, saluus esse non poterit.	Serm. 205. Cauete, dilectissimi, ne quis uos ab ecclesiae catholicae fide ac unitate seducat. Qui enim uobis aliter euangelizauerit praeterquam quod accepistis, anathema sit.

	Vincentius.	Faustus, Eucherius.
38.		38. Faustus (Euseb.) Hom. I. de Ascensione. (Anima) resumere proprii corporis desideret indumentum.
39		
40		

H. Lerins in the Vth Century.

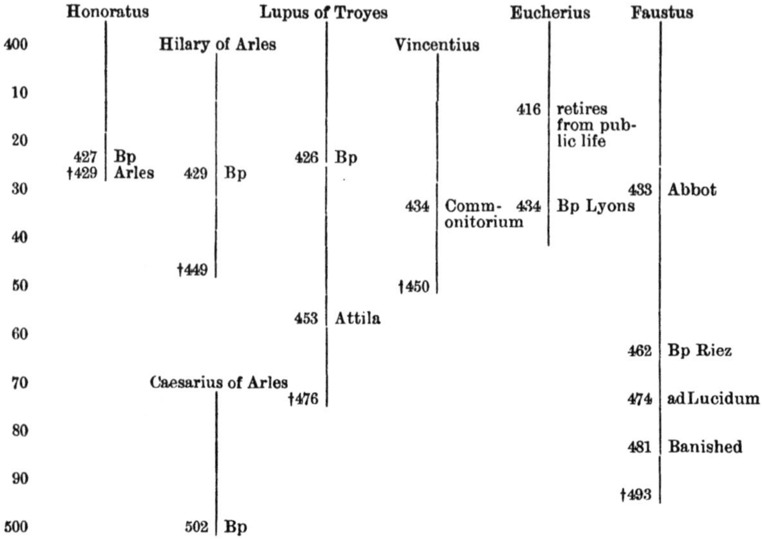

I. The Fides Romanorum and the Creed of Damasus.

These professions of faith are printed by Dr G. L. Hahn in the 2nd edition of the *Bibliothek der Symbole* (p. 204) as the 1st and 2nd of the Creeds falsely ascribed to Damasus. I have employed Mr Ommanney's titles in speaking of them.

The popularity of the *Fides Romanorum* as a confession of faith is shown by the fact that Prof. Maassen (p. 395) has found it in eight collections of canons, and accordingly in a large number of MSS.

In three of these collections, viz. those contained in the MS. of S. Blasien, in Colbert's MS., and in the MS. of Diessen, it is divided into two portions. The first has only the title *Expositio Fidei;* the second, beginning with the words 'Credimus Ihesum Christum,' is called *Eiusdem Sermo.*

In the other five collections it is found in a single form. The collections of the Vatican MS. and the 'enlarged Hadriana' call it *Fides catholicae ecclesiae Romanae.* The collections in Pithou's MS. and the MS. of S. Maur have the title *Fides Romanorum.* In Quesnel's collection it is called simply *Alter libellus fidei.*

Its history is most obscure. The Ballerini attributed it to Gregory Nazianzen. Dr Kattenbusch[1], following the Benedictine authors of the *Hist. lit. de France* (I. 2), with more reason has attributed it to Phoebadius, Bishop of Agen († c. 392).

It was quoted in the 5th century by Vigilius of Thapsus in his *De Trinitate*, ix.; in the 9th century by Hincmar *De Praedestinatione*, and by Ratramn *C. Graec. Opposita*. Vigilius wrote under the name Athanasius, to whom both Hincmar and Ratramn (most probably following Vigilius) ascribe this profession of faith.

Without collations of the earliest MSS. (e.g. Cod. Sanblasianus of the 6th century) I am not able to discuss its relation to the Creed of Damasus.

Dr Kattenbusch[2] kindly sent me a collation of a late form, in which it is combined with the Creed of Damasus, from Codex Cusanus C. 14 (Misc., saec. XII). He cannot discover the history of the Creed of Damasus.

The personal appeal, 'Haec lege, haec retine,' and the fact that it was used with the Quicunque in the canon of the IVth Council of Toledo, have led me to wonder whether it could be the reply of Bishop Damasus to the treatise addressed to him by Priscillian. This suggestion would account for its use in Spain.

For purposes of reference I have reprinted Mr Ommanney's transcriptions of the 'Fides Romanorum' from two Paris MSS. B. N. 3836 and 1451, and of the Creed of Damasus from Paris B. N. 1684.

Fides Romanorum (I).

Transcribed by Mr Ommanney (*E. H.* p. 399) from Paris B. N. 3836, saec. VIII. [N.B. This MS. contains the Trèves fragment and belongs to the Collection of Canons found in the MS. of S. Blasien.]

Incipit Expositio Fidei.

Credimus unum deum patrem omnipotentem et filium eius unicum dominum nostrum conceptum de spiritu sancto Ihesum Christum deum et dominum nostrum et spiritum sanctum deum. Non tres deos, sed patrem et filium et spiritum sanctum unum deum esse confitemur: non sic unum deum solitarium, nec eundem qui ipse sibi pater sit, ipse et filius; sed patrem uerum, qui genuit filium uerum, ut est, deus de deo, lumen de lumine, uita ex uita, perfectum de perfecto, totum a toto, plenum a pleno, non creatum sed genitum, non ex nihilo sed ex patre, unius substantiae cum patre; spiritum uero sanctum deum, non ingenitum neque genitum, non creatum nec factum, sed patris et filii, semper in patrem et filium coaeternum ueneramur: unum tamen deum, quia ex uno patre totum, quod patris est, deus natus est filius. Pater filium generans nec minuit

[1] *Das apostolische Symbol*, p. 171.

[2] Letter of April 8, 1895.

nec amisit plenitudinis suae deitatem. Totum autem quod deus pater est, id esse et filium ab eo natum certissime tenentis cum spiritu sancto unum deum piissime confitemur. Explicit.

INCIPIT EIUSDEM SERMO.

Credimus Ihesum Christum dominum nostrum dei filium, per quem omnia facta sunt que in caelis et quae in terra uisibilia et inuisibilia, propter nostram salutem discendisse de caelo, qui nunquam desierit esse in caelo, natum de spiritu sancto et uirgine Maria. Verbum caro factum non amisit quod fuerat, sed coepit esse quod non erat; non demutatum, sed deum permanentem, etiam hominem natum, non putatiue sed uere, non aereum sed corporeum, non fantaseum sed carneum, ossa sanguinem sensum animam habentem. Ita uerum hominem et uerum deum intelligimus et uerum deum uerum hominem fuisse nullo modo ambigamus confitendum. Hunc eundem dominum Ihesum Christum adimplisse legem et prophetas, passum sub Pontio Pilato, crucifixum secundum scripturas, tertia die a mortuis resurrexisse, adsumptum in caelis sedere ad dexteram patris, inde uenturum iudicare uiuos et mortuos. Expectamus in huius mortem et sanguinem mundatos remissionem peccatorum consecutos resuscitandos nos ab eo in his corporibus in eadem carnem qua natus et passus et mortuos et resurrexit et animas cum hac carne uel corpora nostra accepturos ab eo ad uitam aeternam premium bonum meriti aut sententiam pro peccatis aeterni supplicii.

FIDES ROMANORUM (II).

Transcribed by Mr Ommanney (*E. H.* p. 398) from Paris B. N. 1451, saec. VIII *ex.*

INCIPIT FIDES ROMANORUM.

Credimus in unum deum omnipotentem et unigenitum filium ejus Ihesum Christum deum et saluatorem nostrum et spiritum sanctum deum. Non tres deos, sed patrem et filium et spiritum sanctum unum esse confitemur: non sic[1] unum deum solitarium, nec eundem qui ipse sibi pater sit, ipse filius, sed patrem uerum, qui genuit filium uerum, id est, deus de deo, lumen de lumine, uita ex uita, perfectum ex perfecto, totum a toto, plenum a pleno, non creatum sed genitum, non ex nihilo, sed ex patre, unius substantiae cum patre; spiritum uero sanctum deum, non ingenitum neque genitum, non creatum nec factum, sed patris et filii, semper in patre et filio coaeternum ueneramur: unum tamen deum, quia ex uno patre totum quod patris est, deus natus est filius, in patre totum, quod deus est, totum genuit filium. Pater filium generans non minuit nec amisit plenitudinis suae deitatem. Totum autem quod est deus pater id esse et filium a deo natum certissime tenentis cum spiritu sancto unum deum piissime

[1] Cod. *si*.

confitemur. Credimus Ihesum Christum dominum nostrum dei filium, per quem omnia facta sunt, quae in caelis et quae in terra, uisibilia et inuisibilia, propter nostram salutem discendisse de caelo, qui nunquam desierit esse in caelo, et natum de spiritu sancto ex uirgine Maria. Verbum caro factum non amisit, quod erat, sed coepit esse quod non erat, non demutatum, sed deum permanentem etiam hominem natum, non putatiue sed uere, non aerium sed corporeum, non fatasiam sed carneum, ossa sanguinem sensum et animam habentem. Ita uerum hominem ut uerum deum, unum eundemque uero hominem et uerum deum, intelligimus, ita ut uerum deum uerum hominem fuisse nullo modo[1] ambigamus confitendum. Hunc eundemque Ihesum Christum adimplisse legem et prophetas, passum sub Pontio Pilato, crucifixum secundum scripturas, mortuum esse et sepultum secundum scripturas, tertia die a mortuis resurrexisse, adsumptum in caelis sedere ad dexteram patris, inde uenturum iudicare uiuos et mortuos. Expectamus in huius morte et sanguine mundatos remissionem peccatorum consecutos resuscitandos nos in his corporibus et in eadem carne, qua nunc sumus, sicut et ipse in eadem carne, qua natus passus et mortuus[2] est et resurrexit, et animas cum hac carne uel corpora nostra accepturas ab eo ad uitam aeternam praemium boni meriti, aut sententiam pro peccatis aeterni supplicii.

THE CREED OF DAMASUS.

Transcribed by Mr Ommanney (*E. H.* p. 401) from Paris B. N. 1684, saec. XI *ex.*

[The words printed in small capitals represent the common matter found also in the Fides Romanorum II.]

ITEM EIVSDEM (i.e. Hieronymi) DE FIDE APVD BETHLEEM.

CREDIMUS IN UNUM DEUM patrem OMNIPOTENTEM ET in unum dominum IHESUM CHRISTUM FILIUM dei ET in SPIRITUM SANCTUM DEUM. NON TRES DEOS SED PATREM ET FILIUM ET SPIRITUM SANCTUM UNUM deum colimus et CONFITEMUR: NON SIC UNUM quasi SOLITARIUM, NEC EUNDEM, QUI IPSE SIBI PATER SIT, IPSE et FILIUS, SED PATREM esse QUI GENUIT, FILIUM esse qui genitus sit, SPIRITUM UERO SANCTUM, NON GENITUM NEQUE INGENITUM, NON CREATUM NEQUE FACTUM, SED de patre procedentem, patri et filio COAETERNUM et coaequalem et cooperatorem, quia scriptum est: *verbo domini caeli firmati sunt*, id est, a filio dei, et *spiritu oris eius omnis uirtus eorum*, et alibi: *Emitte spiritum tuum et creabuntur et renouabis faciem terre.* Ideoque in nomine patris et filii et spiritus sancti unum confitemur deum, quia deus nomen est potestatis non proprietatis. Proprium nomen est patri pater, et proprium nomen est filio filius, et

[1] Om. reads (by misprint?) *nodo.*

[2] Cod. *mortuos.*

proprium nomen est spiritu sancto spiritus sanctus. In hac trinitate unum deum credimus, quia ex uno patre, quod est unius cum patre naturae uniusque substantiae et unius potestatis. Pater filium genuit, non uoluptate, nec necessitate, sed natura. Filius ultimo tempore ad nos saluandos et ad implendas scripturas descendit a patre, QUI NUNQUAM DESIIT esse cum patre, et conceptus est de spiritu sancto, et NATUS EX UIRGINE, carnem ANIMAM ET SENSUM, hoc est perfectum suscepit hominem, nec amisit quod erat, sed coepit esse quod non erat; ita tamen ut perfectus in suis sit et uerus in nostris. Nam qui deus erat homo natus est, et qui homo natus est operatur ut deus; et qui operatur ut deus ut homo moritur; et qui ut homo moritur ut deus surgit. Qui deuicto mortis imperio cum ea carne qua natus et passus et mortuus fuerat, resurrexit, ascendit ad patrem, sedetque ad dexteram eius in gloriam, quam semper habuit habetque. IN HUIUS MORTE ET SANGUINE credimus EMUNDATOS NOS ab eo RESUSCITANDOS die nouissima IN QUA NUNC uiuimus CARNE et habemus, consecuturos ab ipso aut UITAM AETERNAM PRAEMIUM BONI MERITI aut poenam PRO PECCATIS AETERNI SUPPLICII. Haec lege, haec retine, huic fidei animam tuam subiuga, a Christo domino et uitam consequeris praemia.

J. Ps.-Gennadius de Fide.

Gennadius, Massiliensis episcopus, de fide disputans, inter caetera dixit[1]:

Credimus, unum esse deum patrem et filium et spiritum sanctum, sine initio existentem ac sine fine, ante omnia tempora, aeternum, inuisibilem, incommutabilem et incircumscriptum, cuius origo incomprehensibilis est, quia nec cogitatione, neque ullo modo humana fragilitas debet, nec ualet eius originem perscrutari. Patrem ideo dicimus, quia habet filium sibi per omnia coaequalem, coaeternum et coomnipotentem. Filium dicimus eo, quod habet patrem, a quo est ipse aeternus et sine initio genitus. Spiritum sanctum dicimus et credimus eo, quod est ex patre et filio aequaliter procedens, non factus, nec creatus nec genitus, sed coaeternus et coaequalis per omnia patri et filio. Hanc uero trinitatem, id est patrem et filium et spiritum sanctum, non tres deos, sed unum esse deum certissime confitemur. Et credimus, deum patrem omnipotentem per coomnipotentem filium suum condidisse omnia, quae sunt in caelo et in terra et in mare, uisibilia et inuisibilia, caelestia atque terrena, ut psalmista ait: *Verbo domini coeli firmati sunt, et spiritu oris eius omnis uirtus eorum.* Pater ergo principium est deitatis, quia sine patris nomine nomen filii non est; neque sine filio nec pater dici potest;

[1] p. xxxii *supra*: from Caspari, *Kirchenhistorische Anecdota*, I. p. 301.

non enim confusa, id est in unam personam commixta, est sancta haec trinitas, neque separata, aut diuisa natura diuinitatis, sed pater in persona semper dicitur et est pater, filius in persona semper dicitur et est filius, spiritus sanctus semper dicitur et est in sancta trinitate tertia persona; non tamen tres dii, sed unus deus, qui fecit et continet in potestate sua omne, quod est, ipse uero solus incomprehensibilis permanet.

Filius ergo dei, qui dicitur uerbum dei et sapientia dei, carnem adsumpsit ex uirgine Maria, ut sicut ex deo patre est genitus uerus deus, ita fieret ex homine uerus homo; non tamen in his duabus naturis duas habens personas, sed una persona deus et homo, non adoptiuus, neque putatiuus, sed uerus et proprius filius dei. Natus est ergo dei filius ex uirgine Maria, non per hominem, id est ex uiri coitu, sed per uirtutem spiritus sancti conceptus ex uirgine, ut ait ei angelus dei: *Aue Maria, gratia plena! dominus tecum* et caetera. *Concipies et paries filium, et uocabis nomen eius Iesum.* Ait autem Maria ad angelum: *Quomodo fiet istud, quoniam uirum non cognosco?* Et dixit ei angelus: *Spiritus sanctus superueniet in te, et uirtus altissimi obumbrabit tibi, et quod nascetur ex te sanctum uocabitur et est filius dei.* Et ita natus est ex uirgine Maria uerus homo cum anima rationali et carne cum sensibus suis; per quos sensus ueros in passione et ante passionem carnis dolores sustinuit, et in eadem carne mori dignatus est pro redemptione mundi, permanens in diuinitate impassibilis. Mortuus est autem pro nobis idem dei filius in carne, quam suscepit pro nobis, et mortuus iacuit in sepulchro. Anima uero sua cum diuinitatis eius potentia descendit ad inferna et omnes inde iustorum animas liberauit et secum ad regnum caelorum prouexit ac diabolum in tartarum religauit. Tertia uero die, anima remeante, in eadem carne resurrexit et omnibus in se credentibus portas regni caelestis aperuit. In eadem uero carne die quadragesimo ascendit in caelum et sedet ad dexteram dei patris omnipotentis. Venturus est inde iterum iudicare uiuos et mortuos, uiuos eos, qui tunc in carne inueniendi sunt, mortuos qui ante de hoc saeculo exierunt. Sicut enim Christus in eadem carne, qua mortuus iacuit in sepulchro, tertia die resurrexit, ita et nos in futuro iudicio id est in aduentu Christi, in eadem carne, in qua nunc uiuimus, omnes resurrecturi sumus, et recepturus erit tunc unusquisque praemium meritorum suorum, siue bonum, siue malum; ideoque praeueniamus nunc, usquedum possimus, faciem domini pura confessione et poenitentia digna malorum, quae fecimus, ut in illo tremendo iudicio dei non cum impiis et peccatoribus in poenas retrudamur aeternas, sed dei misericordia largiente atque auxiliante, cum sanctis et iustis aeterna gaudia mereamur.

INDEX.

Adalbert xxvi, l
Adoptianism xlii ff., lii, lv ff., lx, lxiv
Aeneas xxvii
Agobard xxix, xlii
Alcuin xxii, xxxviii ff., xlii f.
Anskar xxvii, xxx
Apollinarianism lx f., lxxiv
Atto xxxiii
Augustine lxxii ff.
Autun, Canon of lxxvii f.
Avitus xiii, xviii, lxxxv f., xcviii f.

Bacchiarius xxi, lxxv
Benedict d'Aniane xxviii, xxxv
Boniface xxxi f.
Bruno xlviii f.

Caesarius xiii, xvii f., xxiii, lxxxi—lxxxv, lxxxix, xcviii
Columban lxxxiv n., xcix

Damasus, Second Creed of xxi, lxviii, lxxix f.
Denebert xiv f., xx, xxxiii ff., xcvii

Eucherius lxvi, lxix, lxxxix, xciv
Euphronius of Autun xviii, lxiv f., lxix f., lxxviii, xcviii f.
Eusebius of Emesa xci
Eutychianism xxxvii, lxi, lxxiv f., lxxxvii, xciii f.

Faustus xviii, xxii, lxv f., lxix, lxxiii, lxxxix ff., xciv ff.
Felix of Urgel xxix, xlii, lv

Florus xxix
Fortunatus, Venantius xxiv, xxxviii, lxiv f.
Fulco xxv
Fulgentius xxxii, liii

Gennadius xx
Goldast, Melchior lviii, lxiv, lxix ff.

Haito xxxi, xxxix
Hilary of Arles xiii, xviii, xxxv, xxxviii, lxxxix, xci, xcv ff.
Hincmar xxiv—xxvii
Honoratus lxxxix, xcv f.

Isidore lxxx

Jesse, Letter of xxix

Leporius lxxiii
Lucidus lxv
Lupus xxxviii, lxv, lxxxix f.

Milliary, sixth lxi ff.
Monks of Mt Olivet xxvii
Monothelitism lii, lv, lxi

Nestorianism lii, lvi, lxi, lxxiv f., xciii, xcviii
Nicetus of Trèves xxxviii
Notker Labbeo xlviii f.
Notker of Stavelot xlviii f.

Paulinus xv, xxxviii, xl, xliii f.
Pelagius, Creed of lxxiv

Pirminius xxiv, xlvii, lxv f.
Priscillian xviii, lxxv ff., xcvii.
Procession Controversy, The lxi

Rabanus Maurus xxxix
Ratramn xxvii, lxxviii, lxxxviii
Regino xxx
Riculfus xxvii
Rolle of Hampole l, liv

Salvian xc f.
Sidonius Apollinaris lxv, xc
Stavelot Abbey xlviii

Theodulf xxviii, li ff., lix, lxix, lxxxviii. His Commentary xlvi f.
Toledo, Councils of xviii, lxvii f., lxxix, xcviii
Trèves fragment, The xiv f., xxi, xxxii f., xxxv—xxxviii, xliv, xcii

Utrecht Psalter, The xxii f.

Vigilius of Thapsus xxiv, liii, lxxxvi—lxxxix
Vincentius xiii, xv, xviii, lxxxix, xci—xcv

Walafrid Strabo xxxix